Fight Against Fears

Fight

Against

Fears

by
LUCY FREEMAN

CROWN PUBLISHERS INC. - NEW YORK

Copyright, 1951, by Lucy Freeman
Sixth Printing, October, 1952

Manufactured in the United States of America

To Mother and Father

"Thou shalt lie down and
none shall make thee afraid."
—The Book of Job

CONTENTS

INTRODUCTION

I first read Lucy's story as I flew four miles above the Atlantic on my way to Dublin to attend a meeting of the World Federation for Mental Health. It was a fortunate circumstance that I could reflect on her effort with a detachment impossible had I been closer to the scene and the cast of her drama.

It goes without saying that "the evil that men do" lives long after its first occurrence. The psychiatrist can guess at the meaning of such experiences and the ways in which they survive. But only the individual concerned can tell for certain what really happened. In the course of living and growing, one's life story becomes very confused. Sequences are reversed, relationships are distorted, memories fade and, as a result, one's past normally becomes a jumble that defies easy reconstruction. The analyst must know the resources of the human species for avoiding the discomfort of unpleasant thoughts and the concealments, disguises and obliterations that are used to that end.

Most people live what more or less might be called refracted lives. This is true in the sense that they can see some of their experiences quite clearly, whereas others have been twisted out of line so that either they are not seen at all or they take on a very blurred appearance. We are born with marvelous capacities for sensing the world about us. This means not only good eyes, ears and other sensory organs, but the physiological mechanisms for processing these sensations into clear memory and good rational sequences.

But things happen to us to dull that heritage. Life for the child is no mere bed of roses. It is a mixture of roses and thorns, sometimes more of one than the other. The things the child senses under certain conditions prove to be painful and make him unhappy. These conditions recur again and again because we live as families, and the people in families have consistent ways of doing things so often painful to the child. These painful experiences are counteracted by devious means. We allow only the more pleasant things to preoccupy us, while the unpleasant are hidden or disguised in fantasy. They are not allowed to come close enough to our conscious living to make us aware and unhappy, nor yet can they be hidden deeply enough to be completely without influence. Thus we begin to live two lives. Some of the influences follow the clear channel, while others are refracted. Only the former stay well in focus unless we become mentally ill, when we may live as in a dream. We try to follow the path pointed out by the happier aspects of our lives, but the unhappy ones constantly get in our way. We cannot contend with both at the same time because it is too painful. Meanwhile the more hidden things create sensitive spots in our souls that we are not very well aware of and that make us behave in strange ways.

If our defenses were restricted sharply to the offending conditions, the result might be truly defensive and in keeping with a sound economy of living. But man has become civilized too fast and his ways are still tuned to the jungle. We must overdo our defenses, just as the hound attacking the fox cannot be satisfied with killing the animal; he must shake it into a rag; he must kill and kill and kill, for jungle experience has told him that if a bit of life remains, danger persists. And so man encountering threats must continue to fear and fear and hate and hate. Opportunities to give vent to both are severely restricted in our civilized lives, and so fear and hate are turned against things other than those for which they were originally intended.

These defensive processes, evolved to be our servants, become our masters. They dominate us. Psychiatric treatment tries to bring under control and neutralize excessive and wrongly directed feelings. It is no new psychological concept that defenses, developed to protect us, have themselves become our illnesses, but recent physiological advances show also that many of our bodily diseases, such as allergies, joint changes in arthritis, pneumonia and endocrine disorders, are also derived largely from overemphasis of defense. The "cure" is literally worse than the disease. In this sense psychiatry has foreseen a principle that is only now emerging in the whole of medicine.

Man, however, is remarkably adjustable. He has a great capacity and is constantly trying new ways to repair his hurts. When successful, he often finds that his devices to escape and heal a psychological wound may have some really positive values in their own right. Examples of this are Lucy Freeman's friendliness, her skill at writing and her very productive energy. As is indicated in her study of herself, these all grew out of her attempts to escape pain. Fortunately her forms of escape have social value in their own right. The sensitivity of one who has endured psychological turmoil leads him to appreciations that escape the normal, healthy person, and so his skills are often superior. At the same time such a person is not always happy with his achievement because he has mixed feelings about it. His sensitivity may torment him under some conditions and serve him well under others. Sometimes his fears and anger are so great that his self-reparative efforts fail entirely.

In the latter instance he must lead two or more lives at the same time, reaping only unhappiness for his effort. In order to bring them into single focus he needs new spectacles for his mind and spirit. It is not easy for him to accept reconciliation, for it runs counter to all of his past wishes to divorce the unhappy associations—wishes designed to save him from discomfort. It takes a skilled person to help preserve what is good and reshape that which is destructive, to know enough to help the patient to understand and to *be* enough to capture his affection. This is the task of the psychoanalyst. He helps the patient to see with the right eye, then with the left, then to pull the blurred and the clear pictures into focus together.

But even beyond understanding and feeling why he behaves as he does, the patient has years of habit to contend with. He has not stored away alternate and better methods of action to replace those that he is trying to shed. He must figuratively learn to walk again. Only then against a better background can he really grow. The repetition of the problems of understanding and feeling in Lucy's story shows how much effort is required to establish new habits and how much the fears that establish the old habits continue to interfere.

This question has often been raised: If our talents derive in part from the same source as our failures, will not analysis level us to mediocrity by removing the evil which inspired the talents? The fact is that analysis levels nothing. It provides the appreciations that allow the discordant aspects of life to be drawn into more happy relation with the whole. If through good fortune talents have developed, these have already moved into the plus side of the individual's make-up and the analysis provides the possibility of building them to even greater heights by revealing and removing interferences. It can help release spiritual qualities which previously had found only more limited expression.

GEORGE S. STEVENSON, M.D.
Medical Director, The National Association for Mental Health, Inc.

New York, N. Y.
April 9, 1951

Fight Against Fears

PREFACE

Pain forced the decision.

Standard routine reeled off by doctor after doctor had not eased agony.

"Get plenty of sleep and eat regular meals."

Trouble is, I can't sleep.

"Here are some pills, then."

How can I eat when everything upsets my stomach?

"Take these pills."

What about the splitting headaches?

"More pills."

Or: "It's the war, this dreadful war. Get away from your work for a few weeks. Relax."

One day war ended, World War II, that is. Another illness struck and again doctors could not help.

Then came a point in pain where I either had to accept suffering and give up all else or try to find a different way to stop torment.

Psychoanalysis was my way.

————

The following description applies just to my own analysis. I can write only of what I know.

This is not a photograph of my life. It is but parts of my life as they unreeled before me. Not all that I felt or thought lies in this book. Many things I cannot write and never intend to write, but the reader who knows his own heart will know them. I have chosen certain ideas, abandoned others, sometimes deliberately, sometimes unconsciously.

Some know what they feel. I did not dare know. Analysis for me was continuous discovery, sometimes shocking discovery. I felt like the intended victim in a murder, with the analyst as hero-detective trying to rescue me from a life of inner terror.

It is dangerous, in a way, to quote the analyst so extensively. The inaccuracy of one word could change the meaning of his thought. It is difficult, too, without appearing dramatic or didactic, to compress five years of analysis into numbered pages.

But this is risk I must take. I have relied on training as reporter and the copious notes I scribbled after each session, part of my fight against fear. If at times the analyst seems abrupt, challenging or like a lecturer, it is because I have quoted in one place what he may have said different times in different ways.

No book can catch the sound of a voice. It was not what he said so much as how he said it. His voice was always even, compassionate, rich with wisdom—truly an invitation to trust.

LUCY FREEMAN.

Chapter I

A Door Opens

I<small>T WAS ONE</small> of those exciting April days that stir the city into warm life. A soft spring breeze touched parks to green awakening. Traffic rumble turned mute in tribute to the songs of birds.

Shivering with inner chill I stood in front of a brownstone house, staring up its wide steps. I died the coward's thousand deaths.

I cannot go through with this, I thought.

But something stronger than the fear of the moment pushed me up the steps, forced my fingers to assault the doorbell. I waited out the terror.

The door opened. He stood smiling quiet welcome.

"Come in," he invited.

The die is cast, no turning back, this is it. Clichés burst forth to dam up rising fear as I followed him down a hallway. Sheep to slaughter, I thought. Then, nonsensically, sheep to sleep to slaughter.

He ushered me into a living room. A piano straddled one corner. Reproductions of two Tahitian scenes by Gauguin splashed color on gray walls. Flowering plants on tables and window-sill gave off greenness, grace, the feel of growth.

"Where's your nurse?" I asked nervously.

"I don't have one," he said. "I leave the door unlocked and my patients ring the bell and walk in."

I was amazed but relieved. The starched, sterile whiteness of nurses only added to the feeling of impending execution in

15

doctors' offices. No nurse, consultation in his parlor—this is like visiting someone at home, I thought.

He started to sit in a comfortable red leather chair next to the fireplace. To his left stretched a brown couch with a small dark green pillow at one end.

I looked at the couch as though corpses had lain on it. "Do I—have to lie down?" I whispered.

"No," he said. "Do what is comfortable."

I jumped at the word "comfortable." I felt uncomfortable when asked to feel comfortable.

I perched stiffly on the couch, edging away from the pillow. Hands trembling, I pulled out a cigarette. He reached over to offer a light.

"Oh, no," I said hastily, fished in my purse for a package of battered matches. I always lit my cigarette even if men were present. Don't let them near you, dear, echoed some lost voice of the past.

Silence surrounded us, threatening and unbearable. I did not know what to say, only that I must say something, say it quickly.

"Where's your notebook?" Nothing like a question to slay a silence.

"I never take notes," he replied, blowing out a lazy, floating puff of smoke.

"Your files must be pretty sparse," I said in wonder.

"I don't keep files."

"You don't?" I thought all analysts kept files.

"I try to make people feel better," he said. "Files don't help my patients."

I sensed a deep calm in this man. He knows what he believes and holds fast to it, I thought.

What did he believe? That was the question. I had to find out what he thought about everything, just as in my job, I asked important people about important matters. (Mrs. Roosevelt, what hope do you hold for the United Nations? Governor Dewey, do you think you will run again for President? Mrs. Truman, how does it feel to live in the White House?)

"What school of psychoanalysis do you represent?" I asked.

"I don't belong to any one school," he replied.

16

"I thought you were Freudian." The Freudian analysts possessed the most prestige in my scanty knowledge.

"Many analysts use Freud but add to his findings from their own experience," he said.

"Oh." I puffed weakly at the cigarette. I had never learned to inhale, felt ashamed at half-smoking. I hoped he would not notice.

I quizzed him unmercifully about his opinion of everyone from Plato to Picasso. An onlooker would have thought our roles reversed. He answered without resentment.

I asked about hobbies, a "must" for reportorial interviews. To my delight he turned out to be a baseball fan. He also liked music. He had earned his way through college playing piano in a jazz band.

"Which do you like better—jazz or classical?" I asked anxiously. I spent hours listening to swing bands beating out the pleading, seductive, low-riding rhythm of the blues.

"I like both," he said quietly. "There's room for everything in this world." (How many times in the next five years I was to hear him say that!)

Maybe in your world, I thought bitterly.

Encouraged by his friendliness I asked a daring question.

"Can I call you John instead of doctor?"

Without waiting for his answer I added facetiously, "After all, I was introduced to you in a bowling alley." I was saying, That gives me the right to think of you not as a doctor but social acquaintance.

He looked amused. He replied, "If you want to." He was quick to know the depth of my fear.

Fifty minutes had elapsed. I stood up hurriedly, not wanting to remain one second over the allotted time. He accompanied me down the hall as though I were a guest.

"I'll be back the day after tomorrow," I said grimly. If he could stand it, I could.

"See you then," he said cheerfully.

I walked down the brownstone steps slowly, feeling foolish at the way I had charged up them. John (now I could call him that) seemed more friend than foe.

Chapter II

MY LIFE WITH DOCTORS

JOHN APPEARED DIFFERENT from other doctors in my tempestuous life with doctors. I confessed this the second session.

"Have you seen many doctors?" he asked.

"Practically never been out of their sight since the day I was born," I wisecracked.

I told him for months I had felt like a caged animal snarling at the world. Even a stroll along the street held torture. It seemed people deliberately pushed and jostled me, and when I turned in anger, laughed at my discomfort.

The sky was my solace. When it shone clear with sun or stars I could accept misery. But when rain cut off the cheer I holed up in my one room whose only window exposed a nearby brick wall against which I often felt like crashing my head.

My desperation made no sense. Ostensibly I possessed all a girl needed for happiness. I worked on what I believed the world's finest newspaper, rubbed shoulders reporter-fashion with great and near-great.

By society's standards I was successful—but I felt miserable. I had never known more people—nor been lonelier. Underneath my reportorial race around the states pulsed an undercurrent of futility. I felt as though unseen enemies forced me daily to walk the psychological plank.

Physical illness in some form had taunted me regularly since childhood. I started off by catching scarlet fever, chicken pox, whooping cough, jaundice, measles (three times) and all the minor ailments such as grippe (hundreds of times), intestinal flu (dozens of times), athlete's foot (once but good). Teeth grew crooked, shoulders slouched and arches fell.

Everything but smallpox sought me. To make up for that neglect, my face broke out with a rash known as acne. Doctors' bills mounted to a substantial sum as Mother and I whirled from one skin specialist to another.

The first wrote out a prescription for tonic, intoned, "Return in a month."

One month later, hand roving over still-raised lumps, he scowled, "Stubborn condition. Needs more time."

We gave him half a year, fled to another. This one decided food caused the outbreak.

"What do you eat, dear?" he asked.

I feared my diet constituted a frontal attack on caloric convention. I omitted breakfast except for coffee. I cut midmorning rest period to race with classmates to the corner drug store for apple pie à la mode. For lunch we devoured peanut butter and grape jelly sandwich on raisin nut bread, followed by chocolate fudge sundae, ice cream and fudge buried beneath mounds of whipped cream, marshmallow and nuts.

Hunger striking in mid-afternoon, we dashed again to the drug store for butterscotch sundae with chocolate ice cream. We demanded that every concoction worthy of the name sundae possess some form of chocolate.

Regretfully we ate supper at home. There we were dished out such uninteresting, unpalatable stuff as green vegetables, meat, fruit.

I admitted to the doctor only, "Maybe I eat too many sweets."

"Give them up unless you want me to take drastic action," he warned.

What action he could threaten more drastic than another pimple, I could not visualize. If it would quiet my erupting face I would give up eating entirely.

As intake of sweets decreased, the acne increased.

"Maybe it's fried foods," grumbled the doctor.

I surrendered fried foods. Nothing happened.

"Maybe it's foods with roughage value," he said irritably.

I gave them up. Nothing happened.

"Foods without roughage value," he spouted angrily.

Nothing happened.

"Foods without———."

Mother and I headed for another before we drove this doctor daft.

Doctors and I drifted apart as failure dogged our efforts. I treasure the mementos, though—graceful bottles once gay with colorful lotions, picturesque wrappers torn off strong soaps for face and hair. One doctor cost me my favorite hairdresser. She refused to use his "special" shampoo because it shredded the skin off her hands. What it did to my scalp I prefer never knowing.

When I went off to college my grandmother took over, commanding me to consume sulphur and molasses. She shipped me a gallon of each. I gagged each morning after dosing with stuff that was good enough for grandmother. I gave it up the day I literally gave it up, scattering breakfast over the classroom of my favorite professor as he embarked on a passionate discussion of the advantages of Great Britain's parliamentary government.

Following the suggestion of the college doctor I hied me to the town's hilltop hospital for ultra-violet ray, then one of the latest treatments for skin disease. It proved similar in spirit to a medieval inquisition as inflicted by the hospital technician, a lady whose sturdy bones seemed made of Vermont granite.

"Hello." She greeted me with a pleasant smile.

"Isn't it nice she's so glad to see me?" I thought. That was my last coherent one.

She hurled me on a hard cot, ordered me to lie motionless. She tossed alcohol in my face to sting the blood into circulation. Seizing a long needle, she probed open sores, announced grimly, "This'll get the pus out."

"All my blood, too," I objected feebly.

She gave no sign of hearing. She was too busy searching for further medical weapons.

As she threw more alcohol at my wounds, to disinfect them with force, I gathered, she allowed hot water to stream from the tap. When she thought it molten enough, she tossed a towel in it. Then she raced from the basin to my side, shrieking in agony because the towel seared her hands. She slapped the steaming towel across my face where it muffled my moans.

"Opens the pores," she claimed in defense.

"Don't let me die with my pores open," I gurgled.

After three or four of these torturing towels, she deigned to turn on the soothing ultra-violet light. It beamed on my battered face, except for my eyes, protected by cotton pads plastered with cold cream. It felt like being caressed with mud.

"Mustn't expose eyes to this light," she warned. "You'll go blind."

"I should live so long," I muttered.

I tottered back to college after the first treatment. Within two hours the skin on my face stretched drum-tight. I felt certain every poison in me had been squeezed out. Within several days the skin peeled off. I cringed around campus hoping no one would think me decaying. When I regained strength I returned to the hospital for several more encounters with the female Frankenstein. Layers of skin left me but the acne did not.

I decided to forsake scientist for mystic. A local fortune teller had gained a reputation for locating lost articles. Maybe she might serve me in reverse and predict how I might lose the acne.

The lady who forecast the Future gazed at the palm of my hand, prophesied a blond young man would flash into my life. (He never appeared.)

"Do you think you could tell me what to do about my unfortunate face?" I asked timidly.

"Ah!" she exclaimed. "It is very important that you get much sleep each night."

"Ah!" I thought. "This is it."

I returned to college to sleep. For months I tumbled to bed early, sacrificing dates, movies and study (in that order of importance). The only result was that I formed such a strong habit that for months if I stayed up past nine, I yawned until I staggered to the sheets.

Long hikes marked my senior year after one professor advised walking as the means to clear complexion. I hated to walk unless over a golf course but I roamed miles through the Green Mountains, cursing each step. Walking brought only more skin abrasions—big blisters on my feet.

That summer my sister-in-law found a doctor she praised as a wizard. She was consulting him for pregnancy but insisted he could cure as well as help create. After subjecting me to a thorough examination, from cardiograph to Wassermann, he

21

reported gas in the stomach from auto-intoxication or self-poisoning. A friend of mine, unfamiliar with medical terms, said she suspected this as I spent too much time in my convertible Oldsmobile. (From what I have learned about myself she was right. The automobile was a kind of intoxication.)

At this point a young doctor strode on the scene, not as scientist but suitor. He looked at my face critically, said, "I had the same thing at your age. You'll grow out of it." He prescribed dancing.

In time the acne did disappear. Lumps became less frequent, less noticeable. I could run my hand over my cheeks without shuddering. But slits of scars still shadow my face.

The acne gave way to other ills. Although exhausted each night, I found it difficult to sleep. Stomach aches assailed, sometimes with revolting results after hamburgers or hot dogs which I ate when other reporters ordered them. I wanted to be one of the gang even at the cost of calamity.

During an annual convention held by the Daughters of the American Revolution in Atlantic City, another reporter and I rushed into a boardwalk restaurant for quick lunch.

"Hamburger and coffee for me," she announced. "Same for you?"

"I guess so," I said. How long could I be slave to a stomach?

We scurried to the Western Union office to file stories, then boarded the New York train. I reached my apartment just in time to throw up for five hours, chiefly hamburger.

The decision of the Daughters, after a violent internal fight, to continue their policy of excluding colored artists from Constitution Hall in Washington, may have helped turn my stomach.

When I felt like living I called up the other reporter to learn how she fared.

"I feel fine," she boomed.

"Didn't that hamburger upset you?"

"Hasn't so far," she said. "I've eaten two more since."

It did not occur to me that my shaky stomach might be more allergic to hamburgers than calmer ones.

A more devastating illness next attacked. My nose tightened up as though tied by a noose. I was forced to breathe through my mouth. Each morning I woke feeling as if someone had slugged me over the head the night before.

The icebox must be leaking gas, slowly asphyxiating me, I thought. I called the superintendent who reported, after a check-up, "She's a little old, maybe, but she works good." I did not believe him but could not question, since he stood as expert on icebox.

"Something's wrong again inside me," I groaned.

Reluctantly I renewed the trek to doctors' offices, following what I had hoped was a forgotten trail. For months, while pain slashed a path of steady agony across my forehead, New York's leading nose and throat specialists peered up clogged nose and down reddened throat. The verdict—sinus.

"That's what my father has been complaining of all these years," I thought in amazement.

Some of our most violent arguments centered on his sinus versus my cigarettes. He insisted that cigarettes hurt his nose, all the while dragging on a huge cigar. We finally compromised. He promised he would not chew gum in my presence, a noise that made me want to rip out my hair, if I would not smoke cigarettes in his.

I called Dad to tell of my latest affliction. He commiserated as did his second wife and their eight-year-old daughter, Alice, both of whom also suffered from sinus. In mutual misery we decided to visit a doctor who, we were informed, possessed no peers in nasal knowledge.

We four ate a hearty lunch, then, silently and stealthily, as though preparing for an illegal operation, crawled to the doctor's office. A nurse instructed us to sit and wait. Soon the door to the inner sinus sanctum opened and out plodded a famous Hollywood comedian, then starring in a Broadway play. His patrician nose shone rose-red. He looked sadder off stage than he had ever looked on screen where a sorrowful look served as his trademark.

"He has terrible sinus," the nurse whispered to us. "The doctor fixes him up every day so he can go on with his performance."

We were admitted to the doctor's den, one by one. I waited to the last, not in gallantry, but because I held the wild hope that the building would blow up and I would be spared. But the earth remained firm and in I stumbled.

A short man, the doctor made up in eagerness what he lacked in stature. Briskly he went to work as though I were a ditch to be dug. He placed before me a machine of fire-fighting proportions.

"What is that?" I pictured my electrocution.

"Just a gadget to drain out your nose," he answered as if he could not imagine why I would be interested.

He proceeded to "drain"—a synonym for pull-the-nose-off-a-stubborn-face.

He then inserted up my nose a piercing instrument, the size of tongs. He twisted it from east to west, north to south. He peered in after it.

"Oh, oh!" he exclaimed in shocked alarm, as if witnessing the birth of an atrocity.

Withdrawing the tongs and returning my nose to me he said emphatically, "You have one of the worst cases of sinus I've ever seen. It's a mystery to me how you breathe."

"I don't really," I said sarcastically. "This is just an imitation."

But my heart raced derby-speed. My hands clenched in despair. What would he say next?

"We must operate!" he announced. "The bone of the left side of your nose is blocking the passageway. At one time or another you must have injured your nose. Do you remember when?"

"I played baseball in grammar school," I said dully. "I often hurt fingers and knees but I don't remember getting hit in the nose."

"Well, you now have a deviated septum," he reported as though I had added a head.

Rushing to the door, he called in the family to behold my useless nose. He told them proudly I suffered one of the most serious cases of sinus it had been his pleasure to discover.

"She must have an operation," he said to my father. "Until we can make hospital arrangements, she should let me relieve the congestion regularly by draining."

I staggered out of his office, numb with misery. My father

reassured me, "You don't have to undergo the operation right away. But keep going to him for treatment. It may make you feel better. Now, let's have a chocolate soda." Dad's unfailing formula for coping with unhappiness was chocolate ice cream.

Three times I returned to that doctor for drainings before I gained courage to break away. One morning as I scanned the obituary page his picture flashed before my startled eyes. He had died of leukemia.

The sinus now caused such headaches and eye strain that I bought glasses. They helped little, only made me feel more conspicuous. I went in search of another doctor.

This one urged me to flee Manhattan's moist climate for the dry warmth of the West. I studied the want ads in out-of-town newspapers, decided to emigrate to New Mexican mesas.

But before forsaking the city I thought I would try a final doctor. Luckily in New York there is always just one more doctor.

A fellow reporter gave me the name of a specialist recommended by our science writer.

"This doc helped me," the reporter said. "Maybe he'll help you. Anyhow, he's a nice guy."

He turned out to be a tall, serious young man who approached my misery methodically. He made me feel he was concerned about my pain, would spare no effort in trying to find its cause.

"We'll try a process of elimination," he said. He sent me to a hospital for x-rays. When he received the photographs, he diagnosed, "Nothing wrong that I can see."

He took specimens of substances in my nose, studied them carefully. They, too, proved normal.

He injected vile-smelling medicines into what felt like the tip of my skull, thrusting a long needle up the nasal interior.

"I'm trying to shrink the membrane in your nose which seems to stay swollen all the time," he said. I liked the way he took the trouble to explain the various processes. It made me feel less like a distressed dunce.

But nothing helped the unyielding nose. Finally, even this determined doctor gave up.

"Did you try anything else before coming here?" he asked.

"Everything," I groaned. "Even a chiropractor, but he only increased my capacity to curse."

Then I asked tremulously, "Do you think an operation would help?"

Perhaps if he advised one I might find the courage to undergo it.

"An operation would make it easier for you to breathe, but there's no guarantee it would clear up your condition," he said. "The obstruction is only on one side of your nose, whereas both sides seem to be affected by the swelling." (How the experts disagree, or may it be some know more than others?)

He confessed, "Nothing medically possible seems to help you. I've done all I can. When the nose bothers you, come back, I'll drain it again."

"It always bothers me," I wailed. "I'd be living here."

He seemed upset at not finding the answer. He walked to the window, stared out at city skyscrapers. He admitted, "We doctors don't know too much about this sort of sinus."

"Just how much do you doctors know?" I asked bitterly.

He went on, thinking aloud, "It may be that the circulatory system, which controls the swelling, is affected by things other than cold weather. Say, by emotional disturbances."

An expression of excitement lit up his pleasant face. The reporter's description of him as "a nice guy" was accurate indeed, I thought.

"Would you like to be a guinea pig?" he asked.

"I'll be any kind of pig if it means a different nose," I retorted. "I'm not proud. Just in pain." The nose throbbed as if a gremlin were using it for a punching bag.

"It's a novel idea," he said, still thinking to himself.

"Whom do I murder?" I asked suspiciously.

"Your own psyche."

"Just what are you suggesting?" I was alarmed.

"Psychoanalysis," he announced, tone triumphant.

"For me?" I gasped.

I had never dreamed of it as a way of easing physical pain. Or, as part of my life.

"Why not?" he asked.

"It costs so much!" That was all I could think of to say.

"Much less expensive in the long run than giving up your job and moving to New Mexico," he commented. "Reporters earn fairly good salaries these days. Scrub floors on the side if you have to."

"Would it be cheaper than leaving the city?" I was stalling for time to think. I felt slightly shaken.

That reminded him he must earn a living.

"Good-bye," he said, politely but firmly. "I hope I've been able to help you." He helped more than either he or I then realized.

I thanked him and walked slowly out of his office.

For weeks I debated whether to undergo an operation or head West or try psychoanalysis. One does not decide to call up a psychoanalyst as readily as another nose and throat specialist.

I put off the decision until the final emotional straw fell, breaking my psychic back.

The city editor generously gave me an important news story, the kind usually assigned to a man. He sent me to cover the trial of a lieutenant commander, accused of stealing from North Africa enough ammunition to start a second American Revolution.

My story of the trial's first day landed on Page One, inky Utopia for reporters.

COURTROOM TURNS INTO ARSENAL
AT NAVY OFFICER'S TRIAL FOR THEFT

One of the strangest cases in the history of the Navy unfolded yesterday in the quiet court chamber of the New York Navy Yard in Brooklyn.

The floor of the courtroom became strewn with machine guns, automatic rifles and bayonets, unpacked from a wooden box as the Navy uncovered a small part of its evidence in the court-martial charges it is bringing against Lieut. Comdr. ———, 36 years old, of Forest Hills, for theft of Government property, violation of the customs statutes and bringing live ammunition into this country.

Officials say this case is unique in the annals of

Navy history in that no one individual has ever been accused of stealing so many items on so large a scale. Twelve charges with 101 specifications involving 180 stolen weapons are lodged against the defendant.

In the forty-two wooden cases that the Commander was accused of shipping here from North Africa as personal belongings are automatic machine guns, rifles, revolvers, pistols, anti-tank guns, hand grenades, mixed pyrotechnics and bayonets.

(I have quoted at length because I think it is significant that this particular story disturbed me. Courtroom, stealing, guns, court-martial, lawyer, judge, jury, guilty or not guilty. I, too, felt on trial.)

The pile of weapons on the second day rose almost to the courtroom ceiling as the Navy added evidence recovered from the Commander's treasure trove. (And instruments of death surrounded me in greater number.)

I returned to the office to write the story. I sat studying my notes. How will I begin? I wondered. The important thing that developed today was—the important thing is why, on this foul earth, did the young Commander steal? Didn't he know the risk he took? Why did he want the guns? Whom did he want to kill. Why . . .

Suddenly the typewriter surged up, struck me in the face. Desks, lamps and newspapers whirled in one crazy circle.

"I feel sick," I whispered to the reporter next to me.

"What's the matter?" His voice ground out in slow motion, megaphoned from a misty earth miles beyond my reach.

"I don't know," I moaned. "I've never felt this way before. Help me upstairs to the medical department, will you?"

He supported me as I spun dizzily to the elevator. He told the nurse, "She doesn't feel well." I could hardly talk.

The nurse placed me on a cot, thrust a thermometer in my mouth. When she removed it I asked weakly, "Do I have temperature?" I might be dying but if I had no temperature I would believe myself well.

"No," she said. "Where do you feel sick?"

"No place," I moaned. "Just dizzy."

"Probably just nerves," she said cheerfully. "You newspaper

people never take care of yourselves. Why don't you have a complete physical examination one of these days?"

"Just now I want to sleep," I sighed.

"Rest a few minutes, then go home," she ordered.

A new sensation was added—my right hand pulsed with an odd pins-and-needles feeling. But more devastating than physical pain was the blow struck at my pride when I asked the editor if I might give my notes to another reporter. I felt too sick to write.

I had never failed on a story. I boasted my stamina stood as strong as a man's. Now I felt someone had crippled me.

When I recovered from this attack (I think it must have been a slight stroke from high blood pressure) I determined to seek a doctor of the mind as the young nose and throat specialist suggested.

Informing family and friends I might consider psychoanalysis, I asked what they thought (always I must ask what others thought). I encountered skepticism, jeers, outright disapproval.

"You're the last person on earth to need a psychiatrist. You get along with everyone."

"Do you have to *pay* someone to listen to you?"

"You're crazy if you go to a psychiatrist."

"You can't possibly afford it."

No, I could not afford it if I continued to buy five or six dresses each season, jump into taxis, eat at expensive restaurants. But I also could not afford to live feeling as if I wanted to die.

The public held two extreme viewpoints on psychoanalysis. One coterie believed it diabolical nonsense, indulged in by pseudo-scientific Satans who spoke strange jargon. The other, a smaller group, lauded psychoanalysts as supermen who freed the spirit with the magic wand of words—one wave of the wand and the sick would rise healed, the wretched grow joyous.

The entertainment world dished out slices of psychoanalysis. There was *Night Must Fall* (I often felt I carried my head in a little hatbox just as the murderer bore his victim's), *Lady in the Dark* (what forgotten nursery song did I choke off?) and *Citizen Kane* (the sleighs of childhood, unused but forlornly cherished, vanished daily into my fires).

29

Psychoanalysis did seem here to stay although those I knew would not permit it to hold meaning in their lives. It is fine for others, they agreed, but not for you or me.

Well, I will dare it, I thought. I will become a pioneer in the brave new experiment, and if I die in the attempt, it will be death in the cause of advancing the knowledge of mankind. Thus I rationalized.

For the first time in my life, I defied my parents. There seemed nothing else to do. Perhaps it is a sign of health to show defiance of parents if one has always submitted to their will without question.

The first step took so much courage I postponed it for days. One morning, head pounding with pain, I crept into the city room hoping to find it deserted. One lone reporter, a few desks in front of me, managed to precede me.

I slid into my desk, sat there in a silence which, for once, seemed welcome. I wanted to phone from the office, rather than the apartment. I felt safer in the city room, my real home.

The black mouthpiece of the telephone yawned at me like the grin of some sinister savage. One rhythm of my heart beat, "Dial, dial." Another retorted, "Don't dial. Don't dial."

I pulled out of my pocketbook a telephone number carefully copied the night before. Unlike most of my rushed actions, I had written this number slowly, despairingly.

Before picking up the receiver I shot a surreptitious look around the office. I hoped the reporter, burrowing his way through stacks of yellowed clippings, would not be able to hear.

He must have felt my eyes on him, for he turned, forsaking research, to indulge in a moment of mock anger. He roared, "Damn this old babe whose obituary I have been politely requested to write!"

"Who is she?" I was grateful for the interruption. I could delay the call.

"Just another lucky dame whose grandfather left her sixty million dollars when she was twenty-one," he said disgustedly. "She's now eighty-eight. I'll bet she hasn't spent a penny of it."

"Are you burying her today?"

"She's not dead yet but she can't last too long," he replied gleefully. "Looks about the other side of Methusaleh, doesn't she?"

He held up the photograph of $60,000,000—gaunt old woman smothered by mink coat, shapeless hat clutching at wrinkled face.

"Wonder who she'll leave her money to?" he mused. "Never married."

I never married either, I thought, but then I never possessed millions to make up for it. Did money bring happiness? Many persons insisted it did. Bread first, and then worry about a man's soul, they said. How could you expect a starving man to develop soul? Happiness comes correlated with cream and butter and eggs and fresh fruit.

But here was sixty million dollars—and a thin face pursed in pain. Here was cream and butter and eggs and fresh fruit *and* unhappiness. What was the answer?

"Would sixty million dollars make you happy?" I called out.

"Couldn't take it," he answered, grinning. "I'd have a helluva time deciding which of my five houses to sleep in every night."

"Five houses and five beds—think of that!" I marveled.

"Five houses—but that means a lot more beds," he corrected. "Maybe ten beds in each house. What a problem!" He sighed and turned to the clippings.

Just one house would be nice, I thought. Why was I different from other girls I knew in high school and college? Why didn't I, too, get married and live and love in a chintz-filled cottage? Why couldn't I settle for one man "in a cabin meant for two, underneath a sky of blue"?

The reporter strolled to the files.

"Is she in it?" I asked, as he walked back with the social register.

"Yes, indeed," he groaned. "Do you know how to read this stuff quickly?"

"Sorry," I apologized. "My career did not include a course in interpreting abbreviations in the social register." I did not want to tell him my eyes ached so I could not focus them on the tiny type.

"I'll decipher it myself," he said.

31

I'll decipher myself, myself, I thought. Fight, fight, fight by yourself. But despair is a poor weapon with which to fight life. Despair is like slapping your enemy with a puff of spun-sugar candy. This is the age of experts. When in doubt, don't guess, don't generalize. Beat a path to the door of the expert. Life is too complex for one simple soul to solve its mysteries. But the expert knows. The expert for the tormented is the psychoanalyst. He should be able to arm you with some more formidable weapon than despair.

Slowly I dialed the number. A feminine voice answered. I asked to speak to the doctor, stammering my name.

A cheerful masculine voice said, "Hello, Lucy. It's good to hear from you. How's your father?"

"He's fine, thanks," I whispered. Each time something important occurred I would half-lose my voice. The madder I felt the hoarser I sounded.

"I-I'd like to come up and talk to you about analysis," I managed to croak.

"Come this afternoon at three if you can," he said.

He was one of the country's leading psychoanalysts and one of my father's relatives. My father's wrath at my desire to start analysis did not loom so fearful that it kept me from consulting a relative. After all, Dad has tried to teach me to be practical.

When I entered the analyst's office he shook my hand, made me feel he was glad to see me.

"You're the only analyst I know and I think I need help," I told him.

He inquired about the family, my job. He asked, "Are you married?"

"No," I replied, squirming inside, "but I have lots of dates."

"Are the men you go out with different from those you liked in high school?"

"I guess so," I answered, not certain what he meant. "I used to date athletes. Now I prefer more intellectual males."

I added facetiously, "The kind who can spell." Flippancy may be a lance tilted in the face of fear.

I decided to waste no more of his expensive time which, I

later realized, he gave free. I asked, "Do you think I need to be analyzed?" hoping he would say no.

"Yes, I do," he replied gravely. "I can't take you because it isn't advisable to treat relatives. But I'm going to try to get someone. It's difficult because the good analysts are busy, but let's try."

Within several days he referred me to a gruff, friendly analyst who wanted $15 a session, more than I felt I could afford.

"Get your family to help you out," this analyst urged.

"I won't take a cent from them," I said stubbornly. If they would not support me philosophically, I could not ask them to do so financially.

I called up other analysts. They would not even speak to me on the telephone, too busy with patients. I felt a mixture of relief and anger; relief I could postpone analysis, anger that no one would accept me now that I proffered myself as a psychoanalytic guinea pig.

One friend of mine believed fanatically in psychoanalysis. To him Freud was more important than George Washington, Abraham Lincoln and Franklin D. Roosevelt all rolled together. He learned of my search and kept earnest track.

One day he phoned to announce that an analyst, a friend of his, was about to return to civilian life from the Army.

"Why don't you become his first postwar patient?" he suggested.

"You ask him, Bob," I said nervously. "He's your friend."

"I'm going to bowl with him tonight and you can come along and speak for yourself," he offered.

"What's this man's name?" I asked. I knew enough to check his ability. He was a "fine and capable man," reported my father's relative.

That night Bob and I set out for the bowling alley. It was only a prosaic building on Lexington Avenue but, for me, its alleys held hint of turning into the furrowed fields of the promised land. This analyst had to take me, I thought, unless the demand was so great that patients had signed up in advance before he joined the armed forces.

We walked into a large room resounding with the sharp

crack of bowling balls against ten-pins. Bob waved to a lone figure standing in a far alley.

"Why, he's in uniform!" I gasped. I had not pictured a psychoanalyst dressed like a soldier.

"He isn't out of the Army, yet," Bob explained.

We walked over. The analyst wore a major's insignia.

"John, this is Lucy," said Bob. Introduction was simple, direct.

We shook hands. I was so excited I scarcely saw him. He was a slender man in his middle forties, with a sensitive, pleasant face. I was conscious of expressive, appraising blue eyes and a sympathetic smile.

I had a hunch the two of them had talked me over that afternoon and John knew why I had come to the alley.

I sat down in a spectator seat.

"Aren't you bowling?" John asked courteously.

"No, thanks," I muttered.

Me, bowl with a psychoanalyst? That would be the day of triumph, indeed. I shook with such fear it took all my strength to grasp the pencil with which I kept score.

John bowled with assurance and competence. He defeated Bob easily.

After several games, we adjourned to a bar. I sat across the table from John, waiting for some signal to show it was time to ask about analysis. He did not mention the subject. Instead, the three of us discussed the latest movies.

Fortified by the last swallows of a Scotch and soda, I thought, "Here goes."

"Would you consider taking me as a patient when you get out of the Army?" I blurted.

As casually as though I had asked for a match, he replied, "All right. As soon as I find a place to live."

"I can afford only $10 an hour only three times a week," I said apologetically.

"We can start with that," he agreed.

The next few days my feelings seesawed between the fear that because of the housing shortage he would find no apartment and the fear someone would give him space and I would be compelled to start analysis. I told no one of my venture.

I was afraid the reporters would make fun of me, as some still do.

Then Bob informed me John had found a brownstone house in the East 70's. He gave me the telephone number. I called, made my first appointment.

All this I told John, mostly in a whisper. It took up my second fifty minutes. I hurled a few last words to sum up my plight.

"I'm here in despair, all else having failed," I declared defiantly.

"That's why most people come," he said.

Chapter III

MEANING OF A TEAR

FOR THE FIRST several sessions I sat rigid on the couch, shoulders as erect as a patriot facing a firing squad.

I will not lie down, I thought. I know the position is natural for analysis because it relaxes you and allows you to think more freely, but I will not do it.

John did not urge me. We sat opposite each other as I questioned him further about theories of analysis. Occasionally I threw in a word about how much my sinus hurt.

One rainy May morning I dragged myself to his office. The sinus had launched an all-out attack. My stomach felt queasy from nasal mucous that had dripped its way downward from nose to throat to digestive tract.

I whimpered a weak hello. I felt too depressed to toss even one question at him. The couch looked luxurious, its pillow inviting. With a sigh I sank down slowly.

The couch did not feel too comfortable. Evidently analysts do not wish patients to relax so deeply they fall asleep, I thought. But it is better than hospital cot.

There was silence.

"What are you thinking?" John asked softly.

I was worrying lest my shoes dirty the couch. It did not seem good manners to rest one's feet on furniture, even if that was accepted as high style for psychiatry.

"Nothing," I muttered.

"Nothing?" he asked gently.

"Well . . ." I stopped.

A window fronting the courtyard stood open. Through it rang the noise of riveting, the birth of a building next door. In a nearby apartment a pianist experimented with a rhythmic arrangement of *The Man I Love*. The sounds formed strange counterpoint. Analysis seems to be counterpoint in dialogue, I thought. John asked a question, wished an answer. He wanted to know what I was thinking about.

Why should he care? What could possibly interest him or anyone else in what I thought? The only thing that mattered was that I talk about people far more important than I.

"It doesn't seem right to talk about myself," I objected. "We reporters look with scorn on the writer who puts everything in the first person. The 'I' doesn't belong."

We jeered at correspondents who wrote, "I spoke today to . . ." or "I and the Army landed at . . ."

"Perhaps the 'I' doesn't belong in reporting but it belongs here," John said.

"It seems egotistical," I mumbled.

"Everyone should be interested in himself, first," John said. "The people who refuse to think about themselves realistically never understand themselves or anyone else."

He added reflectively, "Perhaps you were never allowed to talk about yourself and now you feel nobody cares what you say."

Nobody cares? How often I felt nobody cared. Everyone but I seemed to have someone who cared.

"Maybe you don't care about yourself," he said.

"What difference does that make?" I asked sharply. I had never worried whether I liked myself or not.

"If you do not like yourself, you cannot like anyone else," he said.

I was too surprised to answer. The first tears in years flowed to my eyes. I dabbed them away quickly with the hand farthest from his sight, hoping he would not notice.

I heard a half-choked voice say angrily, "How could I like myself? I'm full of snails and puppy dog tails."

"That's what little boys are made of," he said. "You're a girl."

"Yes, I'm a girl," I repeated dully, wondered why I mentioned that old nursery rhyme.

"Maybe you don't know what you are supposed to be."

I know what I'm supposed to be, I felt like snapping. A girl, of course. What is he trying to do? Make me think I'm crazy?

"What are you thinking of now?" John's low voice urged me to talk.

"Nothing," I said sullenly. But perhaps I should make some reply. It was not good manners to be rude. (Always things done because they were "right," not because I felt like doing them.)

"What do you mean I don't know what I'm supposed to be?" When in doubt, seize the question to shoot out.

"Perhaps, as the rhyme you remembered suggested, you want to be something else in your unconscious," he said.

There it exploded—that secret and sinister word, *Unconscious*. It stood for the shame and sorrow of men's minds. I wanted no part of it.

But first I must lessen its threat by knowing more about it.

"What is the difference between the conscious and the unconscious?" I demanded. I had read descriptions but I wanted John to put the meaning into the spoken word.

"The mind may be compared to an ocean in which, at times, waves bring matter that has been buried up to the top, or conscious," he explained. "At other times, things on the surface sink to the depths, or unconscious, there to lie buried. In analysis you bring to the surface some of the buried matter that has been causing emotional storms."

"What could be disturbing me except physical illness?" I asked. It was my body that hurt.

"Experiences of childhood related to physical troubles," he said.

"And if I can't remember them?"

"That won't matter. The feelings are still with you."

"My childhood was happy," I assured him. "I never went hungry or worried about money or was ashamed of clothes."

He can forget this nonsense, I thought. When I was a child our family lived in peace and contentment in a large apartment just off Central Park. Each summer we moved to a bungalow on the estate of my grandparents (really great-uncle and great-aunt, but we thought of them as grandparents, calling them Grumpy and Granny, because they brought up Mother.)

They dwelled in the thirty-room white mansion known as "the big house." Centerpiece of one hundred acres, it stood majestically flanked by rolling lawn, rose garden, fish pond, apple orchard, tennis court and three-hole golf course.

I dated my life as starting when I was six, I told John. It was then my parents decided to buy a home in a Westchester town named after the larch trees which flourished along its wide, main avenue. They chose a newly built, three-story house not far from Long Island Sound. In winter when no leaves blocked the view, we could peer out attic windows, glimpse patches of blue.

The two-toned house divided horizontally into red brick as lower half, white stucco for the upper two floors. Green windows gave it a Christmas look. It spread out as a palace compared to our city apartment and cramped bungalow.

My father kept adding trees and bushes. He transplanted a magnolia, several tall maples and small spruces. Left to his own, he would have transformed our lawn into a suburban jungle.

Mother took charge of the flowers, directing the gardener where and what to plant. I liked the velvetness and vibrant colors of pansies that bordered the back walk, as well as the privilege of picking as many as I pleased (never "don't" on plucking a pansy, for, bless 'em, they replaced themselves promptly).

I approved of everything about the new house except the attic. It was haunted.

"Something up there is creaking and stepping around," I complained to Mother.

"Mice," she said. She set traps, caught several tiny ones.

But I knew ghosts lived there, too, ready to destroy me when I ventured alone above the third floor. They also occupied a black cave of a house down the street. Each time I walked past that empty house, I fled to the opposite side of the street to escape evil within. No one would buy this house, confirming my belief ghosts frightened tenants away.

Our parents treated us to exciting vacations in Atlantic City which became my fairyland. The hotel minarets and spires were to me the castles of this century. I stood entranced by the sparkle and glitter of the treasures in lush shops, the palatial movie theaters bordering the boardwalk, the piers stretching out hungrily to the sea and the net hauls bringing close for mortal eye the mysterious wriggling creatures of the deep.

It was a magic city where anything could happen and did. One morning as my brother and I ambled down the boardwalk bound for chocolate ice cream at the Traymore Hotel, a man with a camera grabbed us.

"Will you pose with this gentleman?" he asked, nodding at a dignified, white-haired man of portly size and impressive mustache.

"Of course," we chorused, delighted to allow an outsider to photograph us. Let Mother suggest we get together for a family picture and we would each flee to a different corner of the village.

The mustached gentleman draped one arm around me, the other around my brother. He smiled benignly for the camera. A bulb flashed in front of our startled eyes. Then the gentleman let down his arms.

"Thank you, my children," he said gravely.

"Who is he?" I whispered to the photographer.

"That's Colonel Ruppert. He owns the New York Yankees. Our local paper wanted a picture of him with some kids. Buy a copy tomorrow and see yourselves in print."

My practical eleven-year-old mind worked rapidly. For two years I had been an ardent fan of the New York Giants. But I realized a Yankee player, even though in the other league, counted for something in the baseball world.

I tugged at Mr. Ruppert's sleeve, said shyly, "I'm a baseball fan, sir, but I don't know much about the Yankees. The Giants are my team."

He laughed. "We'll see you learn about the Yankees."

He took a small notebook from his pocket and asked our names and address. My brother and I each received a baseball autographed by the entire Yankee team a few weeks later.

"This almost made me switch league allegiance, but not quite," I told John with a chuckle. "I had too deep a crush on Mel Ott and Bill Terry to give them up for the Yankee team."

"You were quite a tomboy, weren't you?" he remarked.

"I liked baseball better than other sports," I said wistfully. "I must have been pretty good, too, because I was the only girl the boys let play on their sandlot team.

"I faithfully kept a book of players, owners, managers of the teams, or anyone who was of prominence in the baseball world of 1928 and 1929. The preface stated frankly, 'My favorite ball team of both leagues is namely the New York Giants and, to whom it may concern, I will cheer them, and only them, on to win the pennant.'

"On September 4, 1929, I wrote sadly, 'The race to claim the pennant is practically over. The Chicago Cubs have clinched the lead; the Pirates come second, while our Giants are in third place.' "

"It's interesting that you chose a team with the name 'Giants,' " said John.

"What do you mean?" I asked.

"A little girl afraid of many things might unconsciously cling to a team of Giants," he said.

No such thing, I thought. I was not afraid of anything. I like the Giants—well, because I liked them. They were my heroes.

I worshipped other heroes, too. My imagination worked overtime as I dreamed up endless romances, then acted them out.

My first co-dreamer and co-actor was my grandmother's nephew, a young man who lived near us. Because of six months' seniority he earned the right to select the roles. He chose to play the magician, Merlin, and designated me the slave whom Merlin hypnotized to carry out commands, usually the slaying of vast armies of would-be conquerors.

A willing slave, too, until one afternoon out of the corner of my eye I saw the bakery truck drive up to deliver fresh bread and cake. This must have been a day when I ate a meager lunch.

At that moment Merlin was weaving a spell over me. "Abracadabra—Kalamazoo. Do as I tell you—do—do—do."

My eyes wandered from Merlin's piercing brown orbs to the delivery truck which, by then, had halted in front of our bungalow. Fantasy or fact? Stomach or soul?

Soul wound up second best. "Excuse me, Merlin," I apologized, breaking in on his spell. "The cake has come."

"Cake!" he screamed in wrath. "What do you mean—talking to me of cake? I'm a famous magician and you are only a slave. Obey me!"

"I'm hungry," I wailed, setting off across the lawn on the run.

"Come back, foul child," he yelled in magicianly rage. "Or I'll not forgive thee, ever."

I don't think he did. When I returned, pangs of hunger eased, he had disappeared for the day into the apple orchard. Thereafter, when I suggested playing Merlin and slave, he laughed hollowly, said I was fit only for the sandbox. Now, when he takes me dancing occasionally, he steps on my feet but hard, as though remembering how I deserted magic for mundane dough.

When we moved to Larchmont I found a playmate down the block named Virginia, Ginny for short. She liked fantasy as much as I did, but, unlike Merlin, also liked food. We reached perfect agreement on the moment to halt acting and race to the corner for chocolate ice cream.

On our front lawn drooped a weeping willow, practically the sole tree my father had not transplanted from elsewhere. Its sad, flowing branches sheltered alternately the lost cave where the kidnapped princess hid or the pirates' den in which rich treasure lay buried. Occasionally Ginny and I felt professional enough to stage a show. We charged one penny admission to my unwilling brother and sisters, a command audience.

When they showed restlessness (when they got up and walked away) we would haul them on stage, giving them minor parts.

During the analysis I talked often of Ginny, my best friend during adolescent years.

"She was a tomboy, too," I said proudly to John. Tomboy stood as acme of accomplishment for a girl.

Ginny lived with an aunt and uncle. Her aunt, a former actress, alternated dramatic moments between high humor and deep despair at Ginny's behavior. She complained bitterly of her niece's affinity for mud.

"That child cannot resist turning white clothes into black," she moaned.

"Buy navy blue," was my practical suggestion. Mother had long given up dressing me in pale colors.

One day Ginny's aunt received a phone call from the mother of one of the pupils at the private school Ginny attended. "You'd better call a doctor," the mother advised, "I can see the schoolyard from where I live and your little niece is balanced precariously on the five-inch ledge of a large pond, partially frozen over. It should be a matter of seconds before she falls in."

The voice went on, "I can't understand it. No one seems to be trying to help her. Wait a minute! It's all right, now. By sheer luck she fell toward the railing and she's hanging there. I see one of the teachers walking over. Now he's helping her off the ledge and away from the pond."

When Virginia walked into the house that afternoon, schoolbooks under arm, her aunt asked angrily, "Haven't you any brains? What were you doing on the edge of a half-frozen pond?"

Ginny stiffened her petite figure. She smoothed back blond hair, replied disdainfully, "That was the easiest bet I ever won." Her aunt, with a sigh, allowed her to keep the quarter.

Ginny and I even played football when the boys in the block lacked a full team. Ginny could kick a football clear over our house, no mean achievement for a girl. We played tackle football until both boys and girls grew old enough to become embarrassed because tackling proved so pleasurable. Then we settled for touch football where a push on the shoulder served as substitute for a hearty hug around the waist. (How I hated to chase the football when it flew into the neighbor's yard, for underneath the flowers lay a bulldog buried when it died despairingly of old age.)

Ginny and I would take Sunday morning walks to the beach. We would perch on rocks, look dreamily out over Long Island Sound. We juggled the boys we knew as marital possibilities, usually wound up by discarding all, settling for an unknown Prince.

We were overjoyed when, instead of looking at the water, we found ourselves on it. My father bought a twenty-six foot cabin cruiser on which he took us fishing and swimming. Sometimes we would even spend the night aboard the boat, for it had two double bunks, galley and bathroom.

"I helped run it," I told John proudly. "I pulled up the anchor and caught the mooring. Just like a boy." I felt my parents were proud of me for doing things as well as a boy.

I winced as I thought of times when I missed snagging the mooring with the narrow, unmanageable boathook and Dad, amid curses, would swing the boat around for me to try again. Or, when I would haul the anchor aboard all fouled up in seaweed. Or, when I would spin the anchor off with huge splash but it did not catch on ocean bottom and, before we could bait hooks, we had drifted fifty feet from the original place of anchorage. (Away from the only point in the entire Long Island Sound where fish were biting, according to my outraged father.)

I felt completely redeemed as crew the day one of our guests, forcing me to relinquish the honor, spun the anchor off the boat with huge splash. He turned around expecting approval for his herculean prowess.

My father's face showed a mixture of anger and laughter. He clasped his hand to his forehead, groaned, "My anchor!" Our confident guest had neglected one small chore, the tying of one end of the anchor line to the boat. Many a small boat, no doubt, has possessed an absent-minded crew member who cost the captain one anchor.

I liked the stormy, gray days when gulls squawked by with lonely cry. "This is living," I would feel. The rest of the world could collapse, for all I cared. The rhythm of the waves tossed us to the sky, to the sea, to the sky, to the sea, in lulling splendor.

In winter we would fly on skates over the very water we sailed in summer. Arm in arm with schoolmates we skimmed along the ice-crusted harbor. Skating gave me a sense of personal speed and power second to no other sport. I might move faster in boat or car but without the same feel of bodily control.

As I looked back at childhood these were the events and feelings I recalled at first, chiefly the pursuit of pleasure. I felt I had grown up free from care.

I told John my mother and father thought enough of me to hire a private tutor for the first year of schooling. This stern spinster gave me strict training in memorizing and handwriting.

For second grade my parents sent me to a progressive school. Once a private house, it stood in the Manor, the exclusive part of town, a stone's throw from the beach.

It was a school where . . .

Suddenly a scene flashed into memory, forgotten for twenty-one years. I stood alone in the street outside that school. January's ice-wind snapped in from the water. I waited for Mother to pick me up, as she usually did, to drive me home for lunch.

I was still there, long after lunch hour, my face blood-red from the cold. A teacher walked by, asked why I stood in the street.

"My mother's forgotten me," I told her, teeth chattering.

She led me indoors. She found out Mother had telephoned, asking that I eat at school as she was unable to call for me. The switchboard girl had neglected to tell me. As apology the school fed me a mammoth meal including double dessert.

But that could not remove the hurt in my heart. I was convinced Mother had finally forsaken me. She liked my brother and sister much better. She never would have left either of them standing alone in the street.

"Why is it always me?" I wondered, then and now.

Maybe I should tell John what I have remembered, I thought. Analysts expect you to talk about everything. I wondered, too, why, of the thousands of things that had happened to me I would choose years later to remember that day's events.

I lived through the experience once more, describing it to John. As I put it into words a strange thing happened. I started to sob and could not stop. I sobbed as though making up for all the tears I could not shed that day I felt abandoned.

And the words that came out in anger to my amazement were: "Why did she hate me so? What did I do to her that she should hate me?"

"She didn't hate you," he answered softly.

"Yes, she did," I insisted. "My mother hated me. And I hated her!"

I stopped, stunned. What was I saying? What right had he to pull out feelings better left unrevealed?

No nice girl should hate her mother or feel her mother hates her. Nice girls are brought up to respect parents, not to answer them back or alarm them or make them unhappy. Besides, I hated no one. I tried to love everyone. Even when I sat at my desk, frantic at the thought of having to get out a story, if reporters strolled over for aimless chatter, I stopped work. Some small fury inside might want to protest the invasion but I bottled it up, smiled with what I trust resembled pleasure. It shocked me when anyone unfurled rudeness.

Hate inside me? Never. Yet, how could I, who demanded explanation for everything, explain why, in one unguarded moment, I felt I had exposed a dart of hatred once hurled at me that had remained quivering inside ever since?

I reached for the box of tissues on the table next to the couch, placed there along with cigarettes for the convenience of patients. I blew my nose, flicked away tears.

"I'm sorry," I apologized. "I didn't mean to cry." I scorned tears.

"Maybe it's time you cried," he said. "Maybe you have wanted to cry all these years and couldn't."

That's nice of him, I thought. No one ever encouraged me to cry.

As I stood up, I felt strangely light-headed. My hands flew to my nose.

"Gosh!" I exclaimed, "I can breathe."

Then I said sharply, missing the peculiar pain of it, "Where's my sinus?"

"Perhaps it cleared up as your tears came out," he said quietly.

"I can't believe it," I marveled. "Look!" I breathed deeply through nostrils that had been clogged for several years, showing off like a baby taking first steps. I felt as if a thick gag had been torn from my mouth, heavy chains lifted from my ankles.

John's sensitive face held an expression of thoughtfulness, as though he once endured similar misery and suffered with me, but to a lesser degree.

"You probably have wanted to cry but couldn't," he said. "Perhaps the tear ducts became dammed up and, in turn, affected your nasal passages."

"That's direct relationship between the physical and the emotional, isn't it?" I suddenly understood the feel of the word psychosomatic.

"There usually is that relationship," he remarked.

As I walked down the steps I felt, literally, as though a great weight had risen from my chest. I breathed in the warm summer air. I stopped before a dress store to window-shop, a luxury in my rushed life.

I wondered if the world would be happier if people who felt like it cried more freely. I thought of the young Russian who gave up America to return to Russia from which he originally fled in a plane. He wrote in the diary which he left behind (part of him must have wanted to remain here) that in a dream he saw himself crying.

He commented, "But how could that be? I have never cried." Perhaps he wished he could.

What is my sinus? I wondered. Is it a nasal condition caused by climate? A broken bone obstructing the passageway? Unshed tears? Inheritance of my father's illness?

"The cause of any one thing is everything," John had said when I asked him the cause of the sinus.

He often repeated that when I asked for a simple explanation. ("Simple" is foolish, I came to know.)

I had always demanded "the" answer, and quickly. Perhaps

there was no one answer. Perhaps I would have to wait a long time before I could find even one of many answers.

A disturbing thought skittered into mind. I had visualized childhood as blissful, yet my adult life seethed with unhappiness. With the first dim awareness that childhood was not completely happy, I felt better, physically and psychologically.

Could I have been mistaken about myself all these years? And was I paying a fairly high price for the mistake?

Chapter IV

TRUST BEGINS

THE SUDDEN EASING of the sinus was the dramatic part of the analysis. All else happened so slowly that I was tempted a thousand times to give up in despair.

I felt I was searching for a nugget of gold but first must move mountains.

"What am I here for?" I would ask John angrily. "What must I do?"

"Face yourself," John would answer quietly but firmly. "You must stop running away from yourself."

"What do you mean—face myself?" I would demand.

"See yourself as you really are," he said. " 'The truth shall make you free.' "

I know what I'm really like, I thought. Is that what I'm here for? Seems a waste of time and money.

"What do you think I'm like?" I asked defiantly.

"It doesn't matter what I think—you must come to know."

"Well, can't you help me out?" I demanded.

"For one thing, you have a lot of anger in you which you've never expressed," he said.

"I'm not angry—you're mistaken. Why do you think I'm angry?" His criticism stepped up a small rage inside me. I tried not to show it.

"By the way you act here," he answered.

"I think I act very well here." Why was he picking on me?

"You whisper, for one thing."

Was that all he meant? I felt relieved. "I don't whisper," I shouted hoarsely.

"You whisper as though you were scared to death. I'm not going to kill you."

What a crazy thing for him to say, I thought. Later, I knew differently.

I realized I whispered. People would often ask me to repeat when they did not hear. That increased my fury so I could hardly get words out. The night before I had met a cousin's new husband. We sat a few chairs apart at the dinner table. At one point, trying to conduct a conversation over and above the voices of others, he complained, "I can't hear you. What did you say?"

I whispered back, "Why don't you listen, you jerk?" and smiled sweetly. He still did not hear, so we remained friends.

I apologized to John. "I know I whisper. I'm sorry I lied to you."

"That's all right," he said, as though it was all right. "You will reverse yourself here, if it's the truth you're after."

"I'm so ashamed of whispering I don't want to admit it," I confessed.

"Do you have any idea why you whisper?"

"No," I muttered. My throat, sore from sinus drip, hurt when I talked. I could not read fairy stories to my nieces and nephews because my throat pained after the first page. At times I completely lost my voice. I would sit on the beach in July minus voice.

"Maybe you whisper when you are frightened," John suggested.

"Maybe," I agreed to be polite, and let go the thought. I cared not why I whispered. I was just ashamed I did.

Hoping to embarrass him for criticising my voice, even though he did it in kindly fashion, I said reproachfully, "I think you have a very nice voice."

Sometimes I felt it did not matter what he said, only that he said it. I wanted to hear a reassuring sound rather than any words.

A friend told me he was going to an analyst who would not talk to him.

"Sometimes he won't say a word for days," my friend remarked sadly.

"Even when you ask a question?"

"He won't say anything—he just waits for me to go on talking," he explained.

"How do you feel?" I asked.

"I want to kill him," my friend said violently.

I could never survive such an analyst, I thought. The important thing in my life was to feel someone cared enough to answer, someone gave indication he knew I was alive.

John did this and more. He did not judge me or get angry at me. Incidents I mentioned to test his tolerance, expecting him to flare up in wrath, he accepted calmly.

I admitted I once stole candy, an act I regretted ever since. A poor woman owned a small store where Mother often shopped for magazines and candy, saying, "Charge it."

One day, walking to school alone for fifth grade class, I thought, "I want some candy." I entered the store, eyed hungrily the rows of tempting chocolates. Which should it be? Crunchy nut-chocolates, creamy tootsie-rolls, sweet chocolate, raisins imbedded in chocolate? I selected tootsie rolls for the chewy feel as they melted against my tongue.

"Charge it," I ordered, just like Mother. Several days later I did the same thing.

One afternoon Mother called me, waving a bill.

"Have you been charging candy?" she demanded.

Panic surged through my stomach. Carloads of candy lay available at home. Mother would never understand why I needed more. She would be furious.

"No, I haven't," I lied. Guilt swept through me, not only for lying but for depriving the poor woman of money. But my need to lie at that moment because of fear of Mother's wrath stirred stronger than concern for anyone else.

Mother paid the bill, undoubtedly knowing I lied and, perhaps, understanding why. I felt too ashamed ever to return to that store.

In telling John of this I protested, "I didn't really steal. I simply charged candy and then denied it."

"That's the same as stealing," he said.

"Yes," I agreed ruefully. "All I knew was that I *had* to have that candy."

"Candy is sweet; it may stand for love to children who crave affection," he said. "If they can't get love any other way they'll steal things that stand for love."

I began to feel what might drive men to steal. They need what they steal, what it stands for, far more than they care what anyone thinks of them for stealing.

John expressed no fury that I stole, seeming to understand why. Under his sympathetic guidance I dared gradually to expose some of the carefully guarded secrets of my life.

The nation was shocked not so long ago to discover that a man in Brooklyn had shut himself away in a closet for ten years. He kept alive by eating food shoved through a small opening by his mother.

Not many of us go to that extreme in refusing to face the world, I thought. But we may closet up thoughts or feelings, hoarding panic until the day we die. Some cannot contain the panic. It breaks through in furious rebellion to push them into a dream world more bearable than reality.

"The man in Brooklyn took to a closet—you hurl yourself at the world," John said when I mentioned the closet episode.

My breakneck pace was an office joke. Veteran reporters, used to speed, would caution, "Slow up."

Sometimes on my way out of John's office, I would crash into a banister that led upstairs.

"You're in so much of a hurry," he would chuckle.

"Who? Me? Never." I would rub my thigh, black with bruises from the latest brush with the kitchen cabinet.

"I guess I do hurry," I sighed. "But there's so much to be done."

"And is it really that important?"

I turned to give him an angry look. He sat to my right. I could not see him unless I switched my head sideways.

"Well, *I* think it is," I retorted, implying I did not give a headline what *he* thought.

"Got so much to do," I would repeat stubbornly. People were always saying in admiration, "Never saw anyone who gets so much done!" I'm getting things done, I would tell myself proudly (unaware the important things would forever remain undone until I could take the time to find out what they were).

"You can get everything done and still take it easy," he said.

"People can't be busy *and* take it easy." Whom was he trying to fool?

"Who do you mean by 'people'?"

"Oh—just people," I said lamely.

"There's you and there's me. Don't you think the term 'people' is a little vague?"

"We use it a lot in reporting," I said defensively. "The voice of the people, you know." People seemed such a solid word behind which to hide an uncertain identity.

Then he asked what I thought was a stupid question. "Do you know why you chose a career?"

"I've always liked to write," I said, starting again to feel angry.

"Do you like your work?" he asked.

"Of course." Emphatically.

"You're competing in a man's world."

"But I like men."

"Then why, at the age of twenty-nine, aren't you married to one?"

"It isn't because I didn't have the chance," I snapped. "I wouldn't marry the Messiah!"

"Why do you think you never married?"

I pretended to ponder. I felt he was asking an unfair question.

"I guess because I never found anyone I loved enough," I said sharply. "I'm still waiting for the elusive Mr. Right."

"It's a matter both of seeking and being sought," he said.

"Why does any woman choose a career?" I asked sulkily.

"Maybe because unconsciously she doesn't like playing a woman's role." His voice was low.

I asked hesitatingly, "The unconscious—it's a very important thing, isn't it?"

"It's more important than some are willing to admit," he

51

said. "We think we control our behavior but the unconscious often controls us. We may be, in a sense, slaves to our unconscious."

"But we know what we should do," I said, puzzled.

"Knowing isn't enough," he explained. "A murderer may know he is wrong when he kills but he must kill. He is driven to kill."

This took time for me to understand. But John allowed me to set my own pace. I flitted from one subject to another—horse racing, international crisis, economic theory.

I had to waste time to be able to feel safe enough with John to look at myself. Waste played an important part in my life.

For the "truth" he kept urging me to face could simmer out only as faith in him mounted. Because he had relieved pain I started to trust him—as an animal, whose wounds have been cleansed, licks the hand of the healer.

Chapter V

THE UNCONSCIOUS

THE CITY EDITOR telephoned me at home one morning asking me to leave immediately to interview a young violinist who had just arrived in this country.

I called John to cancel my session. I told him when I started I might have to break appointments because of sudden assignments on conventions.

"Sometimes I cover conferences in places like St. Louis or Detroit," I explained.

"That's all right," he said. He respected the irregularity as part of the reality of my life. He did not ask me to conform to any rigidity in his. The cancelled hours were lost to him, too, for an analyst cannot fill time suddenly.

I felt angry at breaking the appointment, though I knew I owed first allegiance to the job for which I received weekly pay.

I peered out the window, saw a murky sky ready to burst with rain. I felt too upset to bother with umbrella or raincoat. I seized only the scrap of paper on which I had scribbled the violinist's address.

If it rains I will take a taxi, I thought. But I will start out by bus because I do not have much money.

I stood on the corner waiting for a bus, hoping no one in Manhattan loathed buses as I did. All through grammar school I lived in terror of missing the bus which meant a black mark for showing up late to school, five miles away, and laughter on the faces of other children as I crept into my seat after the last bell. In nightmares I still race to the corner only to see the bus pull away slowly.

To reach the apartment where the violinist was staying I had to transfer from downtown to crosstown bus. As I bolted from the first bus the sky started to pour out its fury. Taxis skimmed by filled with luckier souls.

Pelted by the rain and wind, I stood skin-soaked when the bus lumbered up five minutes later. I climbed on, fought my way to a vacant seat. The woman next to me wrenched herself in two with a wracking cough. Why do I always land beside people who sneeze, sniffle or seem to be choking to death? I wondered. I wrung out the ends of my hair, hanging in Raggedy Ann rivulets.

Blocks passed in agonizing slowness. Fifth, Madison, Park— I stood up in fury. I was east-bound when I should be on my way west. Isn't life hard enough without my making it tougher, I thought.

I slithered off at Lexington. I dashed across the street, daring cars to strike me. After another wet wait I boarded a bus headed in the correct direction.

I interviewed the violinist, returned to the office in a taxi. I wrote the story of how the Nazis, with their cruel ingenuity, forced him to pick up hundreds of land mines, knowing there could be for him no greater torture than to expect his sensitive fingers to be blown off any minute.

I sat at my desk, depressed. I realized something had propelled me east when I was supposed to go west. The appalling fact was that during the bus rides my dripping hand had clutched the small, soggy piece of paper on which I had written "west."

Something had been more important than what lay before my eyes. Could this be what John meant by the unconscious? I knew I resented the assignment. Could it be that my deeper desire—not to cover the story but to go to the analyst (eastward to the analyst, not westward to the violinist)—flamed so strong it overpowered my conscious wish to work? I almost did not reach my destination. By the time I arrived, I had punished myself thoroughly for daring to give in to my impulse to flee.

Other vague, uneasy feelings often stirred me. I thought of them as moods, depressions.

The first Sunday after war ended in Japan, I rushed into the city room, early as usual. A few reporters sat scattered throughout the colossal classroom of desks, advance guard of the small staff that reports to work on Sunday, a relatively newsless day in New York.

This Sunday, however, was different from all other Sundays. This was the first Sunday of peace in four frightened years.

I sat down only to be summoned by the editor. I hurried across the huge room to the rhythm of the haphazard tap of a typewriter.

The editor was a scholar, a gentleman, a sculptor and a poet. No woman reporter could ask for a more charming combination of qualities in a boss.

"Good afternoon," he welcomed me. "How would you like to go to Central Park and . . ."

"Central Park!" The words exploded from me like expletives.

"Get a piece on whether the park has changed now that war is over. It ought to be a . . ."

He stopped. My dismay had registered.

"What's wrong?" he asked courteously. "Don't you like the park?"

"It isn't that," I muttered. I could not tell him why I dreaded Central Park because I did not know. Ironically, I was always being sent there. The first day of spring, the day war started, the many holidays with special ceremonies—all found me in the park, describing for our gentle readers what now occurred in Manhattan's glorified garden spot. I had come to detest every crumb set out for every bloated pigeon. Each smug duck floating on the stagnant park ponds I considered a personal enemy.

"It's a beautiful day," the editor said soothingly. "You don't want to sit in this stuffy room and rewrite sermons, do you?'

"I guess not," I sighed. I headed for the park.

I plopped down on the first empty seat. I scowled at sailors who passed armed with pretty girls. Two women next to me started in loud voices to berate an alcoholic friend. Maybe the animals will present more peace, I thought, heading for the zoo.

I wandered from camel to zebra, glaring at caged animals who looked more depressed than I felt.

"What do *you* think of this first Sunday after VJ-Day?" I hissed at Rose, the hippopotamus.

Next to me a small boy laughed gleefully. "Lookit the elephunt!"

Stupid brat, I thought. Doesn't know the difference between an elephant and hippopotamus.

I swallowed anger, thinking, I must get a story. I saw a policeman, thought, "I'll ask him some questions."

"Do you notice anything different about the park now that peace is here?" I queried one of Manhattan's finest. I expected "no" as reply.

"Certainly," he boomed. "We've lost our commandos. Why, we had more dead Japanese here than on Okinawa. But I haven't seen one kid fire a wooden gun today."

I had my story. No longer did legions of youthful commandos charge up the grassy hills of Central Park with whoops of "ack-ack" and cries of "The marines have landed!" Peace plucked at the hearts of children.

Although carnage of war had ended I felt no peace. Children laughed at animals and I hated them for laughing.

When I told John how depressed I became each time I was dispatched to the park, he asked, "What do you think about in connection with the park?"

"Just that I hate it," I replied. He waited for me to go on.

"Well, it was one of the first places I must have seen in my life," I recalled. "When I was a baby we lived just off it. My father would wheel me around the reservoir in my carriage. Mother used to tell me how proud he was. . . ."

I stopped talking, went on thinking. You were such a pretty baby, Mother would say. I would feel, But now, you mean, I'm such a bad girl. I'm not a pretty baby now. No longer is my father proud of me, no matter how many important stories I write.

The park also served as my first playground. I remembered the tinkle of the merry-go-round and the freckle-faced, stalwart boy who ran it. I fell in love with him when I was five and he fourteen. When I ran out of nickels and could no longer afford to ride the horses I would stand and look at him longingly (perhaps one reason I like to play the horses today).

Years later, on my first newspaper assignment in the park, I walked straight to the merry-go-round, searching for Lochinvar of the wooden mounties, knowing, of course, I would find no one who remotely resembled him. My first love remained forever lost.

My daydreams reminded me how forsaken I felt. I lost Lochinvar, I lost my childhood, I lost, perhaps, what I never had. My conscious might struggle to cheer me up but something stronger—the unconscious—dragged me down to despair.

The thought of possessing an unconscious over which I lacked control frightened me. I did not want to admit anything so terrifying could influence my life.

"What kind of feelings are in my unconscious?" I asked John fearfully.

"You will find out by thinking through to them," he said.

"How do I do that?" I was not sure I even wanted to try.

"By talking," he said. "Let thoughts flow freely."

Words did not come as easy on the couch as on paper. I found it hard to set sail on conversation.

"If I said everything that came to my mind I'd feel like a damn fool," I objected.

"If you feel like a damn fool inside, you'd better get it out because that's the only way you'll get over feeling like a damn fool," John said.

Other patients, I trust, found it easier to spin off thoughts. What held true for me did not necessarily hold true for the one who followed or preceded me in John's office. This I cannot say too strongly.

Upon entering the room I would usually comment on the weather. "Beautiful spring day, isn't it?" Or, "Gosh, it's lousy out."

But discussion of the weather, which meant postponing the time when I would have to talk about myself, could last only a few minutes. Then I would tremble inwardly with fear, think, what do I say now? I would search for a cigarette.

When I first began analysis my hands shook so violently I did not try lighting a cigarette. As I felt more at ease I could smoke, but always one of my own. As I felt even freer, I opened John's cigarette box, announcing loudly, "I'm borrowing a cigarette." (Sometimes even when I had some of my own, for it felt nice to be able to take from him.)

After a few puffs I would think, What will I say? I must start somewhere. I cannot lie here in silence.

Something inside kept whispering, "Don't let him talk you into revealing yourself. Control! Control! You have already told him too much."

I had to control my thoughts, afraid to let them fly free for fear of where they might lead. Everything must make sense and sound logical. (Perhaps, because underneath nothing made sense?)

I knew I wasted money because I was too frightened to talk of things that troubled me. Terror is costly in more ways than one.

I tried giving myself pep talks. He is a doctor, a doctor, a doctor, I kept telling myself. You must describe things of which you are ashamed, even if it kills you. You can lie your whole life on this couch trying to appease him and please him and give him a pretty picture of yourself but you will not help yourself to feel better.

Let him think you a damn fool, an idiot, a baby. The important thing, so he tells you, is that *you* learn to know what you feel and think. Try to tell him what thoughts scream through your mind, no matter how crazy they are.

But they are *so* crazy. How can I tell him the shadow of that desk lamp on the wall makes me think: "There, is a *goblin*.

The goblins will get-cha if you don't watch out. Goblins, gobbleins, gobble-gobble, how I hate to watch people gobble up food because they remind me of goblins who will get me if I don't watch out."

He wanted me to say everything that came to mind. Particularly important, I knew, were references to childhood fears such as goblins (giant goblins with fiendish grins).

But I did not want to talk. I felt I was bad when I talked. Voices of the past rang clear, ordering me to hold my tongue.

At first I rationalized I could not talk because my throat hurt. But as the sinus cleared up and my gasps and whispers changed to firmer tone, I lost that excuse.

Then I claimed I had difficulty recalling details of childhood.

"I just cannot remember a thing," I would complain. "A friend of mine boasts a memory of total recall. Mine is total non-recall."

One thought leading to another is technically called "association." For instance, we need toothpowder. Our thinking goes, so the advertisers hope—toothpowder, Bob Hope, he makes us laugh, we like him, he tells us to buy Pepsodent, because we like him we buy Pepsodent toothpowder. In analysis, thoughts travel the same way, although the substance to which they lead, rather than toothpowder, may be gunpowder in our lives.

John did not mention the word "association." Instead, he asked, "What are you thinking about?" or "What comes to mind?" Never did he use jargon to impress me with knowledge I could not understand. He never referred to the "id," "ego" or "superego," those tri-partite divisions of mind often cited by the enlightened and the frightened. At first I brought up esoteric words, but as I listened to his simple, honest language I felt ashamed, tried to be less intellectual, less patronizing.

I came to know that my thoughts would steer, true as an arrow, to the heart of my troubles, tracing the torments of my life. Not the first or second thought but sometimes the fourth or fifth or sixth held real meaning.

Associations started to reveal amazing facets of my life. One morning I lay on the couch not knowing what to say. I heard the groaning rhythm of carpet sweeper pushed back and forth across a rug.

""That's a queer sound," I mused. "I remember hearing it when I was little. We had a nurse and cook once when I was about three. They were sisters. . . ."

Something troubled me about them. They hated me, I felt. I recalled one afternoon on the lawn in front of our bungalow when I had been racing around the grass. I dashed over to the nurse.

"I'd like a drink of water," I panted.

"Go away," she ordered. "Can't you see I'm talking to my sister?"

"But I'm thirsty."

"Go away!" Crack! She slapped my face.

I burst into tears. "I'll tell my father on you," I sobbed (not mother, but father).

"You tell and I'll kill you," she threatened. "My sister and I will kill you."

I dried my tears quickly, too terrified to say a word. A few weeks later I saw the two women packing valises. I ran to Mother, asked what had happened.

"They're leaving," she said. "We fired them. They were fresh."

I am lost, I thought. They have been fired and they will think I told and now they *will* kill me. I ran and hid in the bedroom until they left. For weeks I trembled lest they steal back at night to kill me.

As I told this to John, I started to cry. "I didn't tell on them," I sobbed, half in fear, half in rage.

All through the years the frightened, lonely part of me expected the wicked sisters to return to do murder. I understood now why Henry James's *The Turn of the Screw* held such morbid interest for me. I, too, fought the ghost of a wicked governess.

Associations prompted by a prosaic carpet sweeper had led back to an experience that would forever frighten me no matter to which corner of the earth I fled.

"How could Mother have chosen such wicked employes?" I stormed.

"People who are emotionally disturbed are apt to surround themselves with other emotionally disturbed people because that is all they know," he said. "We seek what is familiar. We are most comfortable with what we know."

"What do I know?" I asked sharply.

"Keep talking and you will learn," he said.

"I thought we learned from experience," I retorted.

"Did *you?*" he asked quietly.

No, I thought. Experience is a poor teacher for the emotionally confused. It adds nothing but further misery. I could never profit from experience because one experience after the other was a repetition of the original mistake.

I learned not to underestimate the power of my unconscious. It was not a sometime thing, but lived with me, directing not only the functions of my heart and liver but thoughts and deeds. It tried to help me live happily but if I overloaded it with too many intense feelings, it spilled over into the conscious, as though saying to it, "You have to assume some of the burden. I've got too much."

I possessed no such thing as a random thought—every little thought had a meaning all its own. Each one threaded through to the totality that was me.

Thoughts might flow, one from another, in what might seem crazy-quilt logic, but which made sense to my unconscious.

"Even the disconnected thoughts of a very disturbed person are meaningful to him," said John.

The non-sense (nonsense) in my life often held more meaning than what I had been taught was "sense." The little foolishnesses, the remarks uttered "without a thought," the slips of the tongue, the innuendos, the wisecracks—these betrayed how I felt. They might embarrass me, but they showed honest feelings. They were most apt to escape when I was tired or slightly high, when the guards of the conscious stood less vigilantly at the doors of the unconscious.

It was then I might call someone by the wrong name and feel ashamed, remembering how furious I felt when Mother would confuse her daughters.

"How are you, darling?" she would greet me as I entered a room.

Two minutes later she would say absentmindedly, "Now, Sue, you . . ."

"Mother," I would protest. "I'm Lucy, not Susan or Sally." I would think angrily, cannot I have even an identity of my own?

When someone called me by another's name, I knew something stirred his unconscious to the extent that it took over his conscious for the moment. He was telling me, for some reason known only to him, he would prefer me to be this other person, or prefer me not to be at all. It was not complimentary. To the rose itself, another name is not so sweet.

Sometimes associations led nowhere, for I blocked them. They might prove too dangerous. While visiting an aunt who lives in the bungalow where I spent the first six summers of my life, I sat staring at a diamond-shaped rock jutting five feet above the ground.

I felt hypnotized by its mica gleam. Nostalgic feelings swept through me.

"There's something about that rock," I muttered. "Something happened on it or behind it or around it."

I tried to remember while I gazed at it, and later on the couch. All I could feel was that, for some reason, it was important to me. Perhaps I shall never know why.

As I started to unreel my life I mentioned incidents haphazardly. I would talk about a person I had seen the day before, then refer to an event in college, then mention my father, then ask John to explain the word "compulsion."

Time jumbled all experiences. There seemed no past, present or future, just a maze of feeling.

The thoughts jumped to mind, apparently just by chance. Later, as I could fit them into the flow of my life, I saw there had been a definite reason for recalling each one.

I remembered what had been important to me, the pain and the pleasure. I remembered people I loved, feared, envied, hated. I recalled events that had been frightening or delightful.

Everything held meaning. I hated bright red—there was a reason why. I loved green—that had a reason, too. I did not like scrambled eggs—for a very definite reason. I was frightened of high places—for a reason. The reasons were important, dangerous; that was one reason I forgot them.

I had thought I controlled my actions but I was controlled by the past. I did what I had to do, what I was driven to do. Only as I could recognize the power of the unconscious would I stand the chance to become captain of my soul. The more I knew of my unconscious, the more control I would possess over myself. Forewarned is forearmed in the psychic sense, too.

If I could pay attention to my associations, which reflected the subtle spin between conscious and unconscious, I could pick up the threads of daily living that led back to childhood. Then I could spin these threads into a different kind of pattern, one in which there would be more harmony between the warp of the unconscious and the woof of the conscious.

"The unconscious works with the conscious, is that right?" I asked John, trying to understand the relationship.

"United they stand, divided they fall," he replied.

Chapter VI

DOUBLE-CROSSED BY DREAMS

ONE MORNING I FOUND it particularly difficult to talk. I will tell John a dream, I thought. Freud called dreams the gateway to the unconscious. Perhaps they will help reach my recalcitrant unconscious.

I dug hastily into the dreams of the week for a pleasant one.

I recalled one in which I whirled around the floor at a party at our house (we were always holding parties; it took only a friend's visit to serve as excuse for inviting in neighbors). In the dream, as in reality, I was dancing my head (not feet, but head) off.

Handsome young men cut in as the orchestra played swing. Suddenly a tall stranger marched over to me, led me into the sun porch that bordered our parlor. A stranger, and yet not a stranger, for he reminded me vaguely of someone.

"You're mine," he said. "I've come from afar to marry you. Will you marry me?"

"Of course," I breathed. "I've been waiting for you."

Just like in Cinderella, my prince showed up. I must tell Mother, I thought. She will be delighted I have found someone who loves me.

I rushed into the parlor to find it darkened and deserted. "I must find Mother," I thought. I searched the house, dashing from room to room. They were all empty (no furniture, no human beings). I raced up the final flight of stairs to the attic. There I found Mother sitting on a bed in the maid's small room.

"Why are you here?" I asked.

"Everyone has gone home," she said as though drugged. "I came up here to rest."

"I've the most wonderful news for you, Mother." I sat down and put my arms around her.

"What is it, dear?" she asked, only half-listening.

"I'm engaged to be married," I announced joyously. "He came tonight. I've found love at last."

Mother stared at me sadly—queer look, I thought, for such welcome news.

"Oh, dear!" she complained. "He's a Southerner. But go ahead and marry him anyhow."

What did Mother mean? Of course I would marry him, Southerner or no. Wasn't I in love with him?

I woke thus in a state of delight. At least in my dream I had found love and marriage.

I remarked wistfully to John, "The dream had a happy ending. I found my prince."

John waited for me to continue. I knew a dream must not be accepted at face value. There was more to it than met the first association.

I bit my lips in perplexity. "I must admit there is one thing I don't understand."

"What is that?"

"The man in the dream reminds me of a young reporter I know." I was fond of this reporter, though consciously I had never dared face how deeply he stirred me.

"This reporter is not a Southerner," I added, bewildered. "He comes from the West."

"What does 'Southerner' mean to you?" John asked.

"It doesn't mean anything special," I said, trying to sound liberal. "I think of the individual. I can't just generalize about a Southerner."

"I can," he said. "My conception of a Southerner might be a prejudiced person who hates Negroes and Jews. A Bilbo."

"I know some very nice Southerners," I said defiantly. Several good friends were born in the South. My brother attended the University of Virginia and I had enjoyed proms there. My sister, too, went for a year to a Southern college.

John asked a strange question. "What does your mother think about Southerners."

"Mother?" I said in surprise. "I don't think she thinks much about Southerners, but I'll ask her."

"No, don't," he said. "What do *you* think she thinks about them?"

"Oh, she'd probably say a Southerner was someone who fought the Northerners in the Civil War," I said breezily.

"Very good!" he said, approval in his voice. I could not understand the approval but I was glad to have it. I would keep trying. Evidently he did not want my liberal theories—he wanted my opinions about what my mother thought.

Then I heard him say, "By Southerner, your mother meant enemy, didn't she?"

Something clicked into place inside me as tears started to my eyes. "He's a Southerner—enemy—but go ahead and marry him anyhow," became translated into: "He's an enemy—man—but go ahead and marry him anyhow."

Man to me meant enemy. I could deceive myself by believing I got along well with men but inside me, where Southerners once meant enemies (so the history books told me), I felt men were enemies.

This lovely dream revealed a deep distrust and fear of men. It also represented a wish. I wished, in spite of my fear, I could marry one. I resented the fact that, at an age when most girls were married, I still stood single—and singular.

"I don't understand it," I protested to John. "I seem to get along well with men."

"Can you get along with one man?" he asked.

64

That remark hits below the belt, I thought. But he must mean it for my own good. He knows what he is doing even if it hurts me.

I did have to admit I was not able to go with one man for long. I always broke away when one or both of us became serious. I would then plunge into writing, find extra work to fill up idle hours.

Deciding to find sunshine in this gloomy session that started out with a dream that was pleasant before we took it apart, I said, "Well, I may have kidded myself I liked men, but I really like writing. I like the excitement of the newspaper world. It's so glamorous and . . ."

I stopped. I could not explain what was happening but I knew I was not being honest.

"Those blasted deadlines!" I burst out. "I hate them."

"A second ago you said you liked newspaper work," John reminded me. "Which is it?"

"I don't know," I wailed. "I thought I liked it but I also feel terrified of it." The one consistent thing about myself now seemed to be inconsistency.

I would return in panic from covering an assignment, wanting only to get the story out of the way before, somehow, I would be unable to write. The deadline might be three hours distant but another deadline rumbled inside me, immediate and threatening.

I fled the slowness of a weekly newspaper to work on a daily. It seemed as though I could never move fast enough. ("Hurry, hurry, child.")

For the first time, I was able to sense I had been running. "Why did I run so fast?" I asked John in dismay.

"To forget," he answered.

"Forget what?"

"That's what you're finding out here. Dreams will help you."

"My stinking unconscious!" I muttered.

John said, somewhat sternly for him, "The unconscious is not supposed to be beautiful. It's a Vesuvius that erupts and spills out repressed fears so you can feel better."

He added, "Only by facing your unhappiness will you become happy."

"Such a paradox," I scoffed.

"The truth is sometimes found in a paradox," he said softly.

I decided to tell another dream, one that puzzled me. I woke up filled with fear, not knowing why I felt disaster near.

Again I was planning to get married (so many dreams touched marriage, which I both wished for and feared—dreams showed the wish and the fear inseparable). The shadowy figure of the man reminded me of several I knew, rather than any one.

"We must live in a house," he said.

"Of course," I agreed, although I felt in strange contradiction we did not have to live in a house. A house was too good for us: a tent, perhaps, or maybe a trailer.

He walked to a telephone, which, oddly enough, was not connected and called a renting agent. When he hung up he said loftily, "He will pick us up in a car any minute." Before he finished speaking, in dream time, the car arrived.

We rode in silence through dark streets. I could feel myself asking myself, "Where are all the people? Must life always be a world alone for me?"

The car stopped before a wreck of a house. The broken glass of its windows formed menacing patterns. The roof sloped crazily to one side, as though any moment it might slide to the miserable earth.

"I can't go in there," I whimpered.

"Get out," the renting agent ordered.

I stumbled up a rocky path. I peered in the front door. To my surprise, I looked into a living room decorated in warm, gay colors and simple, graceful furniture. In the center of one wall rose a huge, salmon-pink fireplace reaching to the ceiling.

"Why, it's a lovely living room," I gasped. "I could live here always." I turned to my fiancé to tell him this. He had disappeared. But the renting agent remained by my side.

"Keep going," he insisted. "See the rest of the house."

"For me this is enough," I said. "What could be more beautiful than this room?"

I was entranced by the fireplace. I touched lovingly the smooth pink plaster that formed its outlines. It felt soft, seductive.

"Move on," ordered the agent. I was afraid of him. I walked out of the parlor, into the kitchen.

Here I could hardly believe my eyes. I expected to see a gleaming, spotless kitchen. Instead this was a witch's hovel. The bare ground served as floor. Mud stained the walls dark-brown.

A chipped, dirt-encrusted sink ran the length of one wall, piled to overflowing with filthy dishes. Food half-chewed splattered the dishes. Spiders and cockroaches crawled in and out of the rotted food, leaving tracks in the refuse. I wanted to scream.

"Get me out of here," I sobbed. "Let me go home!"

I woke up sobbing. As I told John the dream I found it hard to keep from crying. I blew my nose several times.

"I can't get over how wonderful I felt in the parlor with its luxurious fireplace and then . . ." I gulped. "And then how sick I felt in that kitchen. It was horrible!"

I put my hands across my eyes to blot out the revolting scene.

"Is that how you feel about kitchens?" John asked.

As though speaking in a trance I said, "Women belong in kitchens. Women are . . ."

I could not go on. I felt like choking.

"Take your time," John said calmly. "Women are what?"

"Women are sloppy and dirty!" I almost spit out the words. "I feel about women the way I felt about that kitchen," I added softly. "Men are nice, like that modern living room."

"You envy men," he said.

"I sure do!" My agreement was fervent. "I always wished I were a boy. I wanted to be a baseball player." I added jokingly, "I'm only fooling."

"Are you?" he asked in a serious voice.

I was to find out often when I thought I joked, I told truth, afraid to speak it except in jest.

No matter how strenuously I might try to hide it from myself during the day, at night my unconscious revealed I esteemed men, even though they were enemies, and disliked women. There were many other feelings I could not hide from dreams, if I would but look at them.

At first talking about dreams seemed a game I could play. I thought, This really has nothing to do with me. I openly debunked dreams.

I dismissed one with, "Oh, it's only a dream," when John asked me to describe it in detail.

"Do you mean you don't think your dreams are part of you?" he asked, as though I could not possibly be that stupid. "*You* dream them."

"Of course they're part of me," I said hastily. I must learn to believe they are, I told myself.

Of many dreams I wanted no part. There was one I thought particularly mad. I was married, although no man appeared as husband. I was going to have a baby.

"I guess one goes to a hospital," I thought. I rushed out into the night. Taxis whizzed by refusing to stop. Finally one pulled up. A bearded old man leaned out leering nastily. "Where'ya goin'?"

"To the hospital, please," I whispered. "I'm going to have a baby."

"Oh—a baby," he said, his face taking on a gruesome smile. "Get in."

I stepped in to find only floorboard. I stretched out, feeling I would die. The taxi banged up and down as though traveling over a field furrowed ten feet high.

"Will we never get there?" I sobbed.

"Take your time, madam," the driver said, turning around and grinning. "Hospitals never close."

"Hospitals have time but I haven't," I groaned.

"Here we are," he said, opening the door. I fell out on the pavement, picked myself up and hurried inside without paying. A nurse beckoned to me, said, "We have a place for you."

She pushed me into a small room where iron bars guarded the window. It held a white cot. "This is a jail, not a hospital," I thought.

A doctor entered, ordered, "Lie down." I lay down, thought, "Now I die."

Then the nurse was bending over me. "You had a nice baby. It was born at the age of forty-nine. You lucky girl!"

My baby was forty-nine years old. What could be nicer? I woke up feeling pleased.

"Isn't that a crazy dream?" I asked John. "How could a baby be born at the age of forty-nine?"

"What about forty-nine?" he asked.

"What difference does it make what age I chose?" I retorted.

"Each detail is important in terms of your past. It holds meaning for you whether or not you face it."

"Let me see," I stalled. "Something important happened in the lives of my parents when one of them was forty-nine."

"What else?"

I could think no further, which meant I did not *want* to think further. "I don't know," I said stubbornly.

He helped out. "I can think of lots of things. The forty-niners. Or seven times seven. Or the age in a woman's life . . ."

That wizard of a doctor, I thought. "That's it," I said, feeling as though I wanted to cry. "Forty-nine or fifty."

"What about forty-nine or fifty?" he asked again.

I felt embarrassed. "I've always heard at that age, a woman's sex life doesn't bother her any more." I added, "She doesn't have to worry about getting caught and having babies."

"So, you might wish your baby born at an age when it would not have to face problems of sex that have been so threatening to you," he said.

I do not like being exposed this way, I thought. It is not fair.

Then he asked, deliberately, but kindly, "Didn't it ever occur to you that you did not like being a girl?"

"No," I said quickly.

"Look at your dreams," he said.

"I guess I don't like being a woman," I muttered. I burst out, "But it isn't only that. I hate being! It's being born at all I resent."

"The only other thing you could have been was a man, so you like to think you'd prefer that," he said.

"I hate myself!" I said, tears flowing. It felt good to be able to admit it.

"People who do not like themselves cannot like anyone else," he reminded me again.

"I doubt if I ever have liked anyone," I retorted.

What had I been betrayed into saying? I thought I liked everyone. Why were my dreams double-crossing me?

Why did they hold so much death? Night after night I fled strange, horrible creatures of fantasy, all bent on one mission in life—to murder me. Down the endless corridors of dreamland I dashed, seeking to escape death. Atom bombs exploded in my ears, men hurled knives at me, railroad trains thundered down as I raced wildly from track to track. I would wake exhausted, thankful I still lived.

Only last night I spent the nocturnal hours fighting for my life. I fled through the narrow halls of the city apartment where I lived as a child and which I had not seen in twenty-two years. A disheveled maniac of a woman chased me, gun in hand. I paused to peer into a room where a group of doctors surrounded a small girl, cutting her up. I recognized the room as the one in which once I had undergone an operation (a minor one—the lancing of a boil on the thigh). In the corner stood a man made of chocolate. "That's the chocolate Uncle Eddie brought when I had the operation," I thought. I remembered, my uncle was the only one I wanted near me when I had the operation. I liked him. Then the mad woman was upon me and I had to run.

She caught up with me; pulled the trigger. Nothing happened. I turned around to see how close she stood. She held a dagger, drew back her hand to fling it.

"Put that down," I screamed in terror.

Again she caught up with me. The dagger had disappeared. She grabbed me by the throat, choking me. In one of those miraculous dream-escapes I pulled away as a doctor cornered the woman. He led her, screaming in frustration, off to an institution.

"You've saved my life," I gasped, kissing the doctor.

I woke up feeling my life had been saved. As I told John this dream I said half facetiously (not daring yet to be grateful to anyone), "That's almost what you're doing—saving my life."

"Whom did the woman look like?" he asked.

"Funny," I said, thinking about that, "she reminds me of a friend of mine at college who was pretty and jolly but . . ." I stopped. I did not want to say more.

"And . . ." his pleasant voice urged me on.

"I always felt this friend looked like my mother, and not only like my mother, but me."

"Maybe the woman in the dream was the 'bad' side of you, the side you feel is wicked and should be locked up," he suggested.

"It *was* me," I said, knowing. "Both the crazy woman and the one fleeing. I was fighting my own bad impulses, feeling at the same time I would be killed because of them. And you, the doctor, came along just in time and saved me, as you're doing now."

There were other less violent but just as threatening dreams in which I missed the newspaper deadline, failed to get a story or was fired. The danger of each day was reflected a thousand-fold in the danger of the night. What did it all mean?

"I don't understand my dreams very well," I complained to John.

"Perhaps that's one reason they are so full of violence," he said.

If my conflicts were clear, he meant, there would be no need for the unconscious to protect me in dreams. For, dreams, too, are part of nature's scheme to help us survive. They serve as safety valves, permitting in some measure the escape of violent feelings and thoughts.

Something that happened during the day usually sparked the firecracker of a dream. My unconscious selected from the hundreds of thoughts that spun through my mind those that were important and from them fashioned the dream.

One day I got lost on an assignment in lower New York searching for an obscure address. That night I dreamed I wandered lost in "the woods."

"The woods" of my childhood surrounded our bungalow, stretching out for miles in perilous blackness, dark even in daylight. Many times, walking through them with my father and grandfather, I skipped bravely ahead, then raced back in terror at the spurt of sudden noise behind slithery bush. Death lurked underneath the silent stones and clawing grasses.

In the dream I dashed wildly up and down a path that led deeper into snarled underbrush. I felt trapped, sucked away

71

from humanity, the unnatural world of nature seeking to destroy me.

Just as I reached a clearing, a tall man wearing a cloak which hid his face stepped across the path. He held up a long, thin hand.

"Go no further," he ordered.

"Who are you?" I asked. "You have no right to order me when I don't know you."

"You know me," he said, laughing like a fiend. I tried to run past, but he grabbed me, started to choke me.

"He wanted to kill me, to make sure I wouldn't be free," I said, describing this dream to John. I felt like a hurt child who does not understand the reason for brutality.

"Who do you think wants to kill you?" John asked thoughtfully.

"I don't know," I answered, puzzled. I was expert in figuring out the murderer in mystery stories which I read by the dozens, but stumped when it came to my own life. I did not think, really, anyone wanted to murder me.

"You operate in daily living as though you would live or die by every action," John remarked. "Look at the fury with which you rush around."

When he said the word "die," I felt he plunged a knife into my body. I started to weep. He was right. Someone, at some time, meant to kill me. But who? When?

"I don't know why I suddenly thought of this, but I am very much afraid of the night," I confessed through tears.

The dark hours brought torture, each brush of the wind on the window a stab, each creak of the floor a whip across the breast. Who, what? whispered the night air. Often I would wait for dawn to suck the room of terror; then I could fall asleep. Sometimes I left a light burning to frighten away anyone who might break in. Break into what? I owned nothing anyone would value.

"I put away all sharp things, like scissors and hatpins, before I go to bed," I admitted.

"Why do you think you do that?"

"Because I'm afraid I will get up during the night while I'm sleeping and stab myself," I said slowly, feeling the words to be true.

"Or murder someone else?" John asked.

"Me—murder?" I laughed.

Whom would I want to murder? I bore nobody malice. I winced when someone swatted a fly. A drop of blood sent me into shudders. It was lunacy to believe I would hurt anyone or anyone would hurt me—except in dreams.

"What do my dreams mean?" I asked John worriedly.

"They show your real wishes—the ones that have been dangerous to you—and your real fears," he said.

My daydreams, those wisps of sun-fancy I dismissed as silly (who gets what he wishes for, anyhow?) were wishes of a fashion. In them I might be the champion woman golf player of the universe or married to a millionaire and no one would look at me with horror.

But my deepest wishes, the devastating wishes that tore me apart, had long been censored by the sentinels of the conscious. The clues to the panic-puzzle of my troubled life lay buried deep in the substance of dreams.

I might fool myself during the day but not at night when I slept. I could hide my dreams from myself but I could not hide myself from my dreams. They searched into the shadows of my life.

Shreds of the truth drifted to me slowly from dreams. There was nothing quite so devastating as a dream if I could catch hold of what it was trying to tell me. If I laughed it off or explained it away dream-book style, it meant I was afraid of it. Not remembering was a way of denying it.

What dreams were made of was not content but what came to mind as I thought of them. It did not matter whether I fell downstairs or was left a million dollars or walked the streets in a nightgown, but what that meant to the whole of my life.

A dream focused the quality of my life in one chaotic picture. By spinning out recollection after recollection, from one dream I could unreel many feelings.

Dreams brought me nearer the truth, helping me to know what James Stephens meant: "What the heart understands today, the mind will understand tomorrow."

For me, the mind tried to understand first, for the heart was afraid. Spun out of my life, peopled with my gods and devils, dreams showed what I feared and revealed deeper desires. In them I did not have to turn the other cheek or love my neighbor or honor my mother and father. I could hate and kill or love whom I willed. There was no one to say nature nay. My dream life, the other side of the coin of living, showed what I dared not face in the sun.

Chapter VII

LOVE

IN MY DREAMS death drummed away at me. Kill—or be killed! Flee, for you have committed a fiendish crime. They are after you, so run quickly, for this time you may not escape.

"What is the matter with me?" I raged at John. "Why do I feel all the time I am in the wrong in my dreams?"

He was silent.

"What crime did I commit?" I stormed.

"You committed no crime," he said softly. "It is not a matter of commission, but omission. You did not receive the gift of love from your parents."

My head whirled, trying to make sense of this. I had always believed myself loved.

My father gave me spacious shelter, cars, a college education, vacations. My mother fed me, shopped with me for expensive dresses and coats. What with the four of us children each carting home our own friends after school, the house was usually jammed from cellar playroom to attic step. Yet my parents rarely objected to the noise whether it was our feet shuffling to the latest Armstrong record or our voices raised in cops-and-robbers scream.

"I'm sure my parents loved me," I protested. "They denied me nothing."

"Was it a love that set you free?" he asked.

I wanted to hear more of this amazing theory. "Do you think that is what has been wrong with my life—in a nutshell?"

"You can't put things in a nutshell," he said. "Life is more than a nutshell."

Not for nuts like me, I thought crazily, who stand ready to seize one thing as answer to everything. My feeble mind cannot encompass the whole.

"I know love," I said defiantly, masculine faces revolving through memory. "I've fallen in love several times."

"I wouldn't call what you feel 'love.'"

"What is it, then?" I asked, puzzled.

"Hunger based on emotional need," he replied. "Love is a gift. I think of love as noun, rather than verb. The Bible speaks of 'love' as a noun. It says, 'God is love.'"

He also referred to a passage in Corinthians. "Love suffereth long and is kind; love envieth not; love vaunteth not itself, is not puffed up; doth not behave itself unseemly, seeketh not her own, is not easily provoked, thinketh no evil."

Love flows out of the feeling of one's fullness, he said. Hunger, which many mistake for love, stems from emptiness. It is more of a demand than a gift.

"Love is acceptance, understanding, tenderness," he said. "It does not strangle, grab or possess. It sees the other person not as a god or idol but as a human being, possessing the strengths and weaknesses of all human beings."

Love does not ask to be served, but only where it may serve. Quiet, gentle, trusting, it is composed of affection and desire without anxiety.

This was a new kind of love to me.

"Who's got *that* kind of love?" I demanded.

"We're concerned here with those who haven't got it," he rebuked me.

I always assumed love was a sweeping, passionate feeling, full of mystery and wonder—haunting, dramatic, consuming, like my first real kiss at the age of ten.

"It was a lovely kiss," I told John wistfully.

The boy who bestowed it was host at a birthday party to which he dutifully invited sixth-grade classmates. Unanimously we voted to play the popular kissing game, "spin the bottle."

After an evening of eats and platonic pecks on the cheek, guests prepared to go home. The host evidently felt entitled to a bonus for his birthday. He led me into the darkened sun porch. He pulled me down on the couch and proceeded to kiss me on the mouth with a thoroughness and warmth I never dreamed existed. The feeling frightened me.

"No!" I struggled to my feet. He tried to draw me down again but I fought him off.

"Please!" I summoned the injured innocence of an insulted ten-year-old. "I have to go home."

He shrugged his shoulders, a miniature man-of-the-world rebuked.

"Okay," he said breezily. Now I held no more attraction than a lump of mud. "I'll get your coat."

But from that night on, I knew what a kiss could mean. For the next few years I was too busy competing with boys on the baseball field to kiss them. You did not kiss a boy whom you tagged out as he slid into third base and who rose from the bag cursing you. Nor one who, when he pitched, threw such fast, wicked curves that you struck out, cursing him.

My first important love affairs were conducted on paper. During seventh and eighth grades we thrived on mash messages. The noise of notes jumping from desk to desk crackled daily through the classroom. A system rigid as the U. S. Postal Service prevailed. Everyone knew which boy had a crush on which girl and cooperated by speeding love on its way. A total of all the words in all the notes dispatched in class would have far outnumbered the words in our textbooks. The words in the notes, I wager, held more meaning to us, too, than those in the books.

Some I hoarded as treasures of first love. One reads: "Listen, Sis: I've been going around in circles long enough. If I'm going to lose sleep it's going to be for a worth while purpose. Two weeks ago I was your only one. If I can't have you, no one else will. I will give you 24 hours to give all the rest the gate."

Another, unsigned, puzzles me. It asks:

"Did you by any chance mean what you said Friday night?"

I cannot remember who wrote it or what I said Friday night (although I can make a fairly good guess it was "I love you best").

If a teacher deemed the class too distracted by note-passing, she would interfere with the communications system. Our geography teacher stopped a boy in the middle of a stammering recollection of products that come from Brazil. She walked over to a girl who was trying hastily to cram a note between South and North America.

The teacher stretched out her hand. With a sigh of defeat, the girl relinquished the note unread. The teacher tore it up. Then she addressed by name the boy we knew had sent it.

"I just want you to know," she remarked dryly, "that your note traveled the length of this room in record speed. Now, all of you, pay more attention to your lesson."

I did not fall deeply in love in high school although I might have contemplated marrying several boys if they had dared become more serious. But even then my parents' desire that I go to college would have probably prevailed.

Freshman year at college I plunged into my first serious boy-girl romance. In accordance with its progressive approach to education and living, the college permitted freshmen to own cars. I stored mine in town, four miles way. The garage owner, when overwhelmed by calls to deliver cars to college, would press into service any man who stood by.

One day I slid behind the wheel to drive the temporary chauffeur back to town. I noticed he was not a garage "regular" but a sturdy, blond young man, wearing open shirt and tweed trousers.

"Hello," I said cheerfully.

"Hi," he answered, not smiling.

Sourpuss, I thought. He doesn't want to talk. Then I thought, But he sure has a nice build. (Athletes, again.)

We drove in silence. Suddenly he asked, "Do you like it here?"

"I guess so," I replied, gratified to hear his voice. I turned to find him staring at me. Take a good look, brother, I thought.

"What do you do?" I asked.

"I play professional football in the fall," he said, as though ashamed. "But I'm looking for a regular job."

"It's nice to be able to play football," I said enviously.

"There's a game every Sunday when the weather's good,"

he remarked. I wondered whether that constituted an invitation.

I stopped at the garage to let him off. He opened the door of the car, started to step out, then turned abruptly.

"Would you think I was fresh if I asked you to go out with me tonight?" he said.

He added, "I have my own car," telling me he did not want me for my car.

The girls at college often discussed the danger of dating boys from town because they were supposed to be "fast," but as usual, I paid no attention to what girls said.

"I would like to," I replied. "Especially if you can dance."

"I dance," he said. "I'll call for you at eight."

That evening we sped along country roads, mountains embracing each side of us. Moonlight glanced off the car's chromium.

"Where are we going?" I asked guardedly. I had the reputation of the college to maintain even if I flaunted the opinion of girls.

"A place where we can dance," he said.

I studied his face, the American youth of posters—cleft chin, clear eyes, firm lips. (I saw him, and yet did I ever see anyone? Was I not too driven to know what I saw?)

We passed the usual college hangout, State Line, half in New York, half in Vermont. The collar city, Troy, soon lay behind us. Finally he stopped the car in the town of Mechanicville. We walked into a neon-lit tavern.

"This has a band," he said. "I thought you'd like live music." We found an empty table, sat down.

I hope he can dance, I thought grimly. But any boy this handsome probably moves like a derrick. The law of compensation.

A small orchestra started to dole out musical justice to tunes from the current Broadway hit, *Roberta*. I thought, not Goodman, but good.

"Dance?" he asked.

I stood up bravely. He could step on my feet; I would not care. At least I could listen to the music. We moved off together on the dance floor.

After that I never heard another note all night. He moved easily, confidently, in perfect rhythm. I should have guessed a football player would possess the grace to dance like a god, I thought.

When the orchestra paused for time out, he suggested, "Let's have a drink."

I felt like replying, "Who needs drink? One drink and I'll explode with feeling." I confessed, "I don't know what to order because I don't drink much."

"Have a sloe gin fizz," he suggested. "It tastes like fruit juice."

My first sloe gin appeared. I felt pleasantly wicked indulging in the rosy-hued drink. (Now I order sloe gin or bacardi for the color as well as the taste.)

Our feet flew even more freely after the drink. We danced until the band packed up. Reluctantly we headed for college.

The mountains were turning turquoise in the mist of early morning, melting one into the other. We rolled past silent hillside houses where men and women rested from farm chores. I felt no one had a right to be awake. The hour belonged alone to the star-flecked sky which hid the secrets of centuries from the men of this moment on earth.

Just before we reached college he turned off a side road, drove up a steep hill. At the top he stopped car and motor.

I felt the roughness of his coat as he slid an arm behind me. I wanted to pull down a star, clasp it to my breast.

His fingers tightened on my shoulder. I struggled away from searching lips.

"No," I said firmly.

"What's the matter?" he asked.

"Not the first date," I pleaded. The virginal code did not permit you to kiss until at least second date. "I don't kiss fellows on the first date—ever," I explained.

"You don't?" He let go of me. "That went out with the ark, I thought."

"Take it or leave it," I announced haughtily.

"What difference does it make when you kiss a fellow if you like him?" he said, as if I spoke nonsense. "If you don't like him you can go out with him a million times and not want to kiss him at all. Don't you like me?" He reached for me again.

This is a hilltop on which a famous revolutionary battle was fought, I thought.

"Please show me the monument," I begged. "It's over there, isn't it?" I pointed out into darkness.

"It's just a rock with names on it," he grumbled. But he opened the car door. We trampled over dewy grass which surrendered as we tread it.

He struck a match. I read off names of men who died in battle more than one hundred and sixty years before.

"Finished with the roll-call?" he asked.

I shivered, pre-dawn coolness.

"Come on," he said gallantly. "I'll take you home."

I wanted very much to kiss him that night but I felt I must keep the Code. He would respect me all the more.

I had no excuse on the second date when we again stopped on that hill. The kiss was memorable. I was breathless when we drew apart.

We danced and kissed away that year, at lakeside amusement centers in fall and spring, indoor cafés in winter. The band in Mechanicville serenaded us with *Smoke Gets in Your Eyes* each time we entered.

I stubbornly refused to go beyond the kiss even though I often felt torn by hunger. I was too terrified of becoming a "bad girl" to give in to desire.

One college friend asked frankly if I had "surrendered my honor" to this boy with whom everyone knew I was going steady.

"No," I said, blushing.

"No fooling!" she said in horror (to my amazement). "Why don't you give in?"

"It wouldn't be right," I said firmly.

"Do you neck with him?"

"Of course."

"You sit with him in moonlit woods and open fields, under the stars and the deep blue sky, and you neck with him—is that right?" she said sarcastically.

"What's wrong with that?" I asked, indignant. "I'm not made of wood."

"No, but you must think he is. Why don't you leave him alone if you don't intend to give up your precious virtue?"

"That's my business," I said angrily.

"I'm honest with myself, that's all." She shrugged her shoulders. "I freely admit if I loved a man I would sleep with him." She added jauntily, "The world doesn't spin just for you. Who's going to care whether or not you get knocked off?"

"I care," I said, shocked.

"You should be caring about more important things," she scoffed.

"What's more important than sex?" Righteous indignation stirred my voice to high pitch.

"If you have character, or use the right contraceptives, why a lot of things," she said scornfully. "Drama. Literature. Government."

"Those interest me, too. Just because I don't give all to a man doesn't mean I can't be interested in other things."

Wondering about her strange (to me) attitude, I asked, "Who brought you up?"

"An aunt," she said. "Mother was busy on the stage most of the time."

"That's the trouble," I said reproachfully. "You never had a mother's care."

She declared fervently, "Thank God."

I did what I had to do (as people usually do what they have to do) but I should have been spanked for the torture through which I put the boy and myself. I did not blame him when he demanded a showdown.

"You won't marry me and you won't sleep with me—what is this?" he asked. He said he did not want to see me again.

"And our date for tomorrow night is off," he announced defiantly. He knew I had been looking forward to a dance on the shores of a small, picturesque lake nearby.

"I guess it is," I said sadly. We parted forever.

The next morning another boy from town who had been trying to date me for months called up. News of the quarrel had evidently reached him. He asked if I would go to the dance with him.

"Yes, thank you very much," I said gratefully. A gentleman, if not a scholar, had come to my rescue.

He proved a solid dancer, a keeper of steady rhythm. But I felt lonely, missing the familiarity of the boy I had lost.

Suddenly I stiffened, for across the dance floor toward us strode the man who had chosen to leave me forever. He tapped my escort-for-the-night on the shoulder.

"If you don't give her up this second I'll flatten you out on the floor," he said. (One of the most romantic of all situations to a woman.)

My terrorized date gave in without asking my opinion. He evidently did not want to risk a punch in the nose from a professional football player.

Virtue again triumphed. My hero accepted me at my own terms.

I wanted to marry him but the family persuaded me to finish college first. He took a job in a village twenty miles away. Distance led to detachment. I started to go out with other boys. He called up one night to tell me he intended to marry someone else. I shall never know whether we could have been happy. He would not have cared about Shakespeare or Freud but that might not have mattered.

The next year brought a breezy young automobile salesman, also from town, into my life. Irrepressible and fun loving, he was a fanatic about speed. I recall evenings when we tested out a new salesroom car, screaming along the highway at ninety miles per hour. If my parents had ever found out, I would have been transferred immediately to a city college.

A friend of mine at college dated a friend of his from town. The four of us enjoyed many evenings dancing in roadside restaurants and exploring back roads. We hoped wistfully we all would get married but it did not end that way. Again I brought up the subject of marriage and again the family suggested I finish college first.

If in my heart I had wanted to marry either boy, I would have gone ahead in spite of parental protest as other girls were able to do. I did not want to defy my parents. Peace at their price, for me.

"You did not dare question their authority as you never dared question anyone's authority," John commented, after I told him of the two times I thought of marriage.

"They knew what was best for me," I said defensively.

"Love might have allowed you the choice," he said gently.

I had not known of love. But if I had mistaken hunger for love, I was not alone. If mine was neurotic love, great poets also were guilty of it.

They described love as an exciting, tempestuous emotion for which men gave up their lives or committed deeds of violence. The most famous love story of all, Romeo and Juliet, tells of need, not love. The very words, in the description by Friar Laurence, are of a desperate relationship:

> These violent delights have violent ends
> And in their triumph die, like fire and powder
> Which as they kiss consume.

"Why have I been incapable of your kind of love?" I asked John.

"The anxiety in your life prevented you from being able to love," he said.

"Anxiety? What is that?" I was learning a new language. John spoke words that, up until I met him, held no meaning for me.

"Anxiety is the physiological reaction to fear," he said. "It's a state of tension and apprehension that exists in those who possess fear."

"Fear? Fear of what?" I asked, mystified.

"Just fear, *period*," he answered. "It is always with you. Some things bring it out, others allay it or relieve it."

"And what destroys it?"

"The displacement of it by love. As the Bible says, 'Perfect love casteth out fear.' "

If a child is given love, his life holds little fear except that related to reality, he explained. But if a child grows up surrounded by fear he will fight fear with the weapon Nature gave him to preserve his life when he feels threatened—hate.

"Love's ally is confidence," John said. "Fear's ally is hate."

The hatred in life is due to men's fear, for they hate what they fear, he said. He told me to look at the hatreds expressed by people if I wanted to know what they truly feared.

"If there is fear, is there always anxiety?" I asked. The word "anxiety" intrigued me. I had heard it used by poet and musician to describe this age of ours, but had not thought of its pertinence to my life.

"If people possess a large degree of fear, they will possess anxiety," he said. "Remember—it is always a matter of degree. Everything is natural—in degree. Fear distorts it."

"How will I get rid of my anxiety?" I asked.

"By knowing it and living it through," he said. "When you no longer feel the need for it, you will give it up."

"When will that be?" I asked eagerly, as though to suggest "tomorrow?"

"When you replace it with safety," he replied.

That was another new word. "Safety" to me related chiefly to travel hazards.

"The neurotic never feels quite safe," John said.

"Will you please define neurotic?" I demanded. The term made me uncomfortable. When someone acted eccentric, I thought, "Oh, he's neurotic." But John used the word as a medical term like diabetic.

"A neurotic, to me, is a person physically and intellectually mature but emotionally still a child," he said.

"What conflict causes this?" I was still thinking of unhappiness in terms of "conflicts."

"No one situation or conflict causes neurosis. It is the result of many moments of fear and terror, of feeling unloved and unwanted."

"I never knew how I felt," I muttered. "Sometimes I felt needed, sometimes rejected."

"But always one or the other, always as though life held some sort of crisis?"

"Why, yes," I said slowly. In our family, life whirled from one crisis to another. I felt as though charged by a high tension wire.

It was as though I lived in a house battered by emotional

storms. I lived in fear of high emotion (yet, because that was all I knew, I must forever live in high emotion).

All through life anxiety had caused the ordinary to become the extraordinary. Small things were dramatized into productions. A mild dislike became deep hatred; friendship, passion. My reaction to anything was "wonderful" or "horrible."

As I walked home from work one night, I saw a small, gray cat lying in bloody death on city sidewalk. Other pedestrians passed the carcass without giving it second thought. I felt like throwing up. When I reached home, I could not put the cat out of mind. In the morning, although it had been carted away, I could still see its red tongue sticking out in deathlike defiance and felt the texture of spilled blood as though it were mine. My anxiety had distorted the importance of a cat's death.

Anxiety was my unseen albatross. I could not see it or touch it but only feel it as it touched me. When it stole over me, displacing calm, it made me nervous, irritable, unable to control feelings. It created the feeling of being "driven," not knowing why I did things but only that I must do them.

Anxiety took terrific toll. When I possessed anxiety (when it dispossessed me) I could feel my stomach repudiating the rest of my body. Anxiety prepared the way for my sleeplessness, indigestion, sinus, susceptibility to disease.

Anxiety could weaken any part of the body—stomach, heart, bones, muscle. It might slowly destroy me, psychologically and physically. A large amount of anxiety is not normal to nature, John said, and nature, when thwarted, will take revenge. (Nature prefers people to be peaceful, I came to feel.)

Not everyone's anxiety was expressed like mine, John explained. Anxiety could take the shape either of excessive emotion or apparent lack of emotion. I imparted the feeling of living in high wind because of strong emotions. Others, of opposite manner, were lethargic in anxiety, as if existing in dead calm.

"Neither gives a sense of living," John replied when I asked about the two extremes.

"But the people who seem the most driven also seem to be the ones who get the most done," I said.

"Necessity is the mother of invention, but anxiety is the

mother of necessity," he philosophized. "What men do may be a result of anxiety, but they do not enjoy what they do if anxiety is present."

Necessity presided over my life, but behind her, like a worried, prodding mother, stood the specter of anxiety, made up of all the feelings I had buried over the years because I was afraid. Anxiety stemmed from the unconscious—my vast, deep lake of long-lost feelings. Lost in one sense, but not in another, for, torn from original moorings, they were tied up in other places.

In analysis, I might hope to return the feelings where they belonged, to face them and realize I no longer needed many of them. Then I would not have to disguise them, transfer them or deny them—all of which deceit brought me unhappiness.

"Do you think I'll ever be able to get rid of my anxiety?" I asked John.

"You will lose it gradually," he said. "But first you must know the difference between 'in love with' and 'love.' "

I had used the words "in love with" to describe my feelings. "I'm in love with so-and-so"; never, "I love—"

"It will take you a while to know," he said.

I started to understand slowly that a world of difference lay between the love that John meant (sometimes called mature love) and what I had believed to be love (infantile love).

Love makes the world go 'round, I always glibly assumed. Now I wondered if one reason the world goes 'round in war and hatred might be because so many men thought of love as I had, not a love that sets free but one that possesses.

At the same time many sought the love I sought, not the ephemeral love of the fairy tale but a more substantial love, one that would bring inner peace.

Headlines roar of international strife but between the headlines may lie a cry for love, masked by hatred because there has been no love, I thought. Maybe one reason the world is so concerned with death is because it is so starved for love.

Each child needs a calm, consistent love to guide him and help him overcome natural fears which, in themselves, are dangerous enough, John declared. Each child needs a love

86

that will not hurt and will protect him from all hurt. Each child needs a love that strengthens.

John said, as though I must remember this, above all else: "To a child, no love is death."

No love equals death.

Chapter VIII

Murder Starts at Home

The word "death" terrified me. I was so frightened of it I had to ignore it, putting the morbid thought out of mind.

When I complained to John of dreading an assignment or feeling ill, he would say, "You won't die."

Of course I won't die, I felt like snapping. Why must he remind me of death?

It took months before I could speak of death and then only in a general sense.

"Death is such an unpleasant subject," I muttered. "I've always tried to avoid it."

"Your dreams don't want to let you forget it," John reminded me.

Those damned dreams, I thought. Then I told myself, Heed your dreams if you want to feel better. Remember, they help you to know yourself.

One night I dreamed I sat in a funeral parlor attending services for someone I loved, not knowing who, not wanting to find out.

"I don't want to look at the body," I kept saying. "No one can force me to look at it."

The director of the funeral parlor floated toward me, took me firmly by the arm, shoved me up the aisle toward the coffin.

"Look at your pretty friend," he ordered.

I covered my eyes with my hands. "I won't look. You can't make me."

"Sissy," he scoffed.

I took my hands away from my eyes slowly. I looked into the coffin, saw the slim body of a pale young man, stranger to me. With a shock, I noticed one leg was gone, the trouser folded under his back.

"Poor boy," I thought. "Maimed and dead." I woke up, tears in my eyes.

I told the dream to John, saying, "This boy was a complete stranger to me. Why should I dream a stranger was dead?"

"What comes to mind about him?" John asked.

"He was young and blond and . . ." I was puzzled by one thing. "That leg. I knew someone once whose leg . . ."

I felt like crying. "Poor Mimi," I said sadly after a few gulps. "That boy reminded me of Mimi, an old friend of mine. He went through so many operations on his leg that we often wondered how he had any leg left to stand on." The "stranger" was not a stranger after all.

A frail, esthetic boy, Mimi's gay spirit made up in strength for his sickly body. He sang and laughed as he played base-ball or danced with us. One day Mimi went to the hospital. Just another of his regular operations, we thought. But this time Mimi left the hospital in a casket.

Over the years I missed Mimi, so much, perhaps, I could remember him only in a dream.

A few months after I started analysis, I lost a second friend. I raced into John's one morning, collapsed on the couch in tears. It was rare for me to show deep emotion without first asking twenty questions.

"A good friend of mine just died." I sobbed in explanation.

Bee and I had been constant companions through grammar and high school—on tennis court, golf course and double date. She was a tall, attractive, athletic girl who could make a piano rock with rhythm; my arrangements followed the more conventional chords.

Many dewy mornings I pried her from breakfast for a set of tennis on the school court before 9 A.M. algebra class. Often we dashed to her house for quick lunch before returning to the tennis court for a few more sets before 1 P.M. history class.

After school, and after more tennis, we would wind up at her house for a sandwich to puzzle over homework, compare feelings about the boys in class.

"Pick me up at Bee's," I would instruct Mother who would call for me since we lived several miles from the school.

"Shouldn't Bee's family charge you room and board?" Mother would jest.

"Oh, they're glad to have me," I said loftily.

I was not certain Bee's family approved but I knew Bee needed me for moral support. Her battles with her mother made mine with my mother look like mild maneuvers.

One of their storms nearly wrecked a school play in which Bee starred. I had been dragooned into a small role, my first stage appearance. I thought that inasmuch as I would lose Bee as tennis partner while she rehearsed, I might just as well act, too.

The evening of the performance as I dressed for the part, not much of an effort as I played a girl my own age in contemporary culture, the telephone rang.

Bee's familiar voice sounded in unfamiliar pitch. She sobbed, "My mother won't let me wear the dress I picked out. I can't go on tonight."

"You must!" I was horrified, thinking of the disappointment of myself and seven other girls if the play sailed into oblivion before we got a chance to perform it.

"I won't," she cried.

"Let me speak to your mother," I said. When her mother came to the phone, I pleaded with her.

"Please help Bee to get dressed. We need her. We can't put on the play without her." Real pathos flooded my voice. No acting then.

"She's a bad girl," said her mother angrily. "She won't obey me."

I had been defeated too often by those very words to be able to cope with them. I ran to my mother, at that moment an emotional rock of Gibraltar, explained the crisis.

"You've got to help us, Mother," I begged as if lives depended on it.

She called up Bee's mother, tried in vain to reason with her. She hung up, announced, "We'll drive over to the house and see what we can do."

My father, against his better judgment, planned to attend

the play. My brother, knowing creature, fled in advance to the movies; my sisters prepared to go to bed. Mother asked Dad to take our other car and meet us at school. She and I drove ahead.

We found Bee and her mother both in tears—and Bee in her underwear. Mother led Bee's mother into the parlor. I dragged Bee upstairs to her room and pulled over her head a dark blue dress I saw flung on the bed. I never did find out if it was the one she wanted to wear or the one her mother wanted (how little girls will tear themselves apart over a dress—only, of course, it is not just the dress).

After the curtain fell and we bowed graciously to "an enthusiastic audience," I raced to find my parents. They must be proud of me, I thought, in this, my first public appearance.

I caught a glimpse of my father in the parental mob. When I reached his side he said crossly, "Let's go. It's late."

"How was I?" I asked excitedly. I expected him to say he now stood ready to put me through the Academy of Dramatic Arts.

"Couldn't hear a word you said," he replied. "Get your mother and let's go home."

"Couldn't hear?" I gasped. "Where were you sitting? In the balcony?"

"Third row, center," he said. "Are you ready to go?"

Thus ended my dramatic career.

Bee provided me with solace, too. One disillusioning day in the spring of eighth grade, I was walking to the tennis court, racket in hand, when a girl in my class accosted me. She was a tough, embittered child, who had few friends because of her sharp tongue.

"Teacher's pet!" she sneered, spinning me with such force that the tennis racket clattered to the ground. "You're just too damned sweet to live."

I was speechless. No stranger ever spoke crueler words. Well, this was a girl, and what could I expect? Women were always trying to put me in my place. I held back tears, picked up my racket and walked to the court.

Bee was bouncing a ball up and down, waiting impatiently. I told her what happened.

"Don't let it bother you," she said. "She's just jealous. I always say, 'consider the source.'"

Wise words, those, except then I did not know how to use them.

Bee gave up drama, or rather exchanged it for drama of a more personal, devastating nature. She endured two unhappy marriages; then lost a baby a few months before birth.

Over the years Mother grew fond of Bee, accepting her almost as a daughter when Bee's parents died. Now it was Bee's turn to eat at our house.

One afternoon I returned to the city room after interviewing Mary Margaret McBride for a feature story for the radio page. I found a message to call Mother.

"Doesn't she know better when I'm at work?" I thought. Personal calls at the office irritated me. I possessed only enough energy to do work, not enough to cope with the troubles of others. But I called her back.

"Lucy," she began, and I knew something must be wrong, for she and Dad usually called me "dear," saving my name for moments when they were upset (no wonder I disliked my name).

"I don't want to frighten you," Mother said, "but you have to know this. Bee was hit by a car, taken to a hospital and died there."

I started to cry. But I felt glad it was Mother who broke disaster to me. It meant she cared enough to want to be the one to tell me.

Bee had entered a sanitarium for a few weeks' rest. The day before she was scheduled to leave, she walked to town alone. While crossing a main highway, she saw a car bearing down on her. She dashed in front of it, then changed her mind, started back. The confused driver swerved and struck her. The court later ruled the fault was Bee's, convinced the car was not speeding.

I determined not to cry at her funeral. I wondered, indeed, whether tears could be left, for I had wept almost constantly since her death. It seemed incredible she could be destroyed so violently. Like Mimi, she appeared so to enjoy life, always telling funny stories or wisecracking. I never knew that some like Bee, who must always show to the world a merry, joyous face, may be slowly dying inside.

We arrived early at the funeral parlor in Yonkers (Mother and I, always early for everything, even a funeral) so we stopped for coffee at a small restaurant. Someone started the juke-box. From this fountain of music rolled tune after tune that Bee once played on the piano.

Suddenly I heard the haunting strains of *Someone to Watch Over Me,* which Bee and I always considered the finest short melody of Gershwin's tragic life. I wonder if somewhere Bee is greeting Gershwin, telling him how much she loved his music, I thought. My tears streamed into the coffee. It was little consolation to think Bee would have preferred Gershwin for funeral march instead of the somber dirge we later heard.

(Sometimes, walking along the street, I would see a face with sparkling brown eyes and high cheekbones. "There's Bee," I would say, start to wave. Then I would pull back. "Bee is dead, you idiot." This was part of my refusal to face death. I did not want to admit Bee was dead in spite of the reality of her death.)

"Why couldn't I have done something for her?" I asked John. I might have saved her life if I could have helped her reach an analyst.

I visited her just before she went to the sanitarium. I stood alarmed by the stricken look in her eyes, a helpless, pleading expression I had never seen there before. She did not put her misery into words. I dared not interpret. I had strength, then, only to save my soul. A man who is drowning cannot rescue another who drowns beside him.

"Part of me died with her," I told John.

"Do you feel relieved it was not you?" he asked.

I was stunned. How did he know? I felt I had escaped death miraculously (the way I felt when I read the obituary columns). Although I loved Bee, I was glad it had not been I who died. I excused this intolerable feeling by saying, "Well, part of me died with her."

"Haven't you ever felt you wanted to die?" John asked.

Why did he keep talking of death? My head throbbed. Did he want me to die, too? Sometimes I felt everyone wished me dead. And that I wished myself dead. And, not only that, but I wished others dead. Death jammed in wholesale massacre.

The one person I felt wanted me to live was my grandmother. She was a stately woman with a strong, queenly face. Some members of the family considered her a matriarch and tyrant, for she held the purse-strings over the small fortune my grandfather, an immigrant from Germany, acquired in Wall Street before his death.

To me, she was a fairy godmother. With one wave of her dollar-laden wand she transformed me into a gleaming princess. She gave me my favorite evening gown, a silver lamé dream of a dress with tight bodice and flowing skirt. I stubbornly keep it wrapped in black paper so it will not tarnish although I have long outgrown it. I wore it at my début which she arranged for me at the Savoy-Plaza Hotel.

She always insisted I spend part of Christmas vacation in her elaborate Park Avenue apartment where original Corots mixed with antique Chinese vases. There a butler would serve me meals, a maid help me dress for opera or Broadway show.

"I want Lucy with me," she would announce to my parents.

"Do you want to go?" Mother would ask.

"Of course," I said eagerly. I would be crazy not to want to visit an elegant dwelling where I would be treated like royalty instead of ugly duckling.

Granny and I held long philosophical conversations. She told me, "You cannot do anything original, for there isn't anything new under the sun, but you can try to think of a different way to do it." (As I am now trying to do.) She would smile as though to say, This is what I believe, but you must do what you must do. She never raised her voice with me although I heard it could roar with others.

Several times during analysis I would say to John vehemently, "I want to be a lady."

"What does 'lady' mean to you?" he would ask.

"I don't know," I replied, really not knowing.

One morning, talking about Granny, I said proudly, "*She* was a lady. She liked me and wanted me to be a lady, too.

"She wanted so much for me," I added wistfully. "She really

93

liked me. And she smelled so sweet all the time. Shalimar scent." (Funny that I recalled the perfume.)

My grandmother was a lady. Much as I tried to be like her, I felt I had failed. Failed her, failed myself. (I never bothered with perfume.)

When I graduated from college she handed me a diamond wrist-watch, her wedding gift from her husband.

"Diamonds for me?" I was stunned at such a glamorous present. "I can't take this!"

"I want you to have it," she said. That ended the matter.

The day after she died we drove to the apartment where I had spent merry holidays. The servants, who once greeted me with a smile, looked sorrowful. Mournful relatives sat in Granny's velvet chairs, continuously wiping eyes. I could not seem to shed one tear.

"Go in and see her," urged an aunt.

"See her?" I did not understand. She was dead.

"Do you want to see the body?" Mother asked.

"Heavens, no." I shuddered. I had never seen a dead body.

"You should," insisted my aunt. "She's never looked so beautiful."

If she was still beautiful, perhaps I would not mind seeing her, I thought. My aunt must know. I trusted her; she had always shown me kindness.

I walked into Granny's bedroom. The dark gray carpet looked the same. So did the lace curtains framed by blue silk drapes. So did the Louis XVI chairs. So did the Empire bed with its blue coverlet.

But Granny looked different. Usually when I entered she would smile happily, wait for me to kiss her, then hug me, enfolding me with warmth and perfume. This time she does not move, I thought. She is dead. Stone dead. White lace covers stone-dead lady.

I ran from the room. I am never coming back to this now-hideous apartment, I thought. I never did.

I could not even cry at her funeral. I tried to explain to myself why I could not cry for the person who asked less and gave me more than anyone else.

At the cemetery I looked with scornful eye on relatives who

sobbed. Even my father, whom I had never seen cry, sniffled. I stared up at trees, stiff, silent in February chill. My only sensation was a shiver as the cold wind shook me.

"Why couldn't I cry?" I asked John dully.

"Perhaps you were too afraid to cry," he said.

Why should I have been afraid? Afraid of what? She was my friend.

And I had lost her. I had lost my best friend. Now no one would want me to throw my arms around them any more. I felt deserted, lost.

It was then I cried. In John's sympathetic presence I spilled the tears I could not shed at Granny's funeral. There I had known if I once started I could not stop. I would cry so much I just better not start at all. To protect myself from breaking down in front of strange people who did not know how much Granny meant to me, I kept icy and detached, like the February weather which took her away.

I pretended, "This is not my Granny at all. This is some stranger they are putting in the coffin and on whom they are hurling all that dirt. My Granny will be with me always."

As she has been, in a way. Forgive me, Granny, for not crying at your funeral. I missed you too much.

"She was one person who wanted me to live," I said to John, drying tears.

"You seem to feel someone wants to murder you," he observed.

I could not escape the strange feeling (like in my dreams, yet not like in dreams) that something threatened my life. Death lurked just around the corner.

It even pervaded John's office, the place I now thought safe. One morning I crawled there, bent over double with the acute cramps that had accompanied the menstrual period ever since I was ten. (Even at that age I was in a hurry to grow up.)

The day of high school Regents examination in chemistry, pain cut into me so sharply I could not hold myself up at a desk.

"What will I do?" I asked the teacher in shame.

My face must have conveyed suffering. She ordered, "Go to

the teachers' lounge and lie down." I staggered across the hall; fell on the couch.

She appeared in a few minutes to explain unless I took the examination that morning I would have to wait until following mid-term. The school did not want to compel me, a senior, to return for another year. If I felt well enough to write the examination lying down, she would send in a teacher as special monitor.

I agreed, gratefully. I would have written it standing on my head. Flat on my back, stomach burning away, I scribbled answers to questions about chemistry, a subject I loathed (who cares about the composition of air, trouble enough just breathing it). I got the highest mark in the class, to walk off with the science prize (infallible memory on facts outside self).

A month later I could hardly stand, but I did, in a long white chiffon gown at graduation. As salutatorian, I delivered an address comparing the New Deal to a baseball game. I also received prizes for the highest marks in English, science, and total Regents examinations and, of course, the American Legion medal for the best sport (that I *had* to win, as though apologizing to my classmates for selfishness in marching off with most of the prizes).

Inside, I ached in more ways than one (all pain tied together), probably the unhappiest girl in the auditorium that night in spite of the prizes.

Now, twelve years later, still suffering the same monthly agony, I moaned to John, "I'm here, though I'm dying of the curse."

He did not even offer aspirin. I thought bitterly of days when Mother would wrap me in a blanket, put a hot water bottle at my feet, a cup of tea beside me and the latest movie magazine in my lap. I was miserable in comfort. (It seemed when I was ill I got the most care and attention.)

Instead, John said unsympathetically, "Those women who refer to menstruation as 'the curse' seem to have the most pain."

"Just a coincidence," I groaned. What an unfeeling creature, to be talking of other women as I lay dying.

96

"If you must know," I said angrily, "that's what most of the girls in college called it."

"I'm sure there were some girls who didn't."

"All my friends did," I retorted.

"Your friends were probably the ones who had difficulty in a psychological sense with accepting it as part of their lives."

He did not seem to pay attention as I insisted the term "the curse" had become part of the culture, that most women of my age called it that although some older women referred to it as "the period" or "under the weather."

I felt too sick to debate. It was not nice to discuss the topic, anyhow. He was a man and women did not talk about "those things" with men. I never would have mentioned it except that I was deathly ill.

I believed I had been brave in staggering to his office for the regular session. Instead of admiration for courage, I received criticism for pain.

"Haven't you got an aspirin?" I asked in my best Camille-tone.

"I'll get you one." He sounded amused.

He left the room to return with an aspirin, a glass of water and an expression which clearly told me I was making a fuss out of all proportion to the importance of the matter. I gulped the aspirin, thanked him for his trouble.

"I'm really dying," I assured him.

"You know you're not," he said.

"Well, I feel like dying," I muttered.

"That's different!" he said. "That's only a feeling. If there were a sudden earthquake, you'd be on your feet pretty quick."

Was there a difference between actually dying and feeling as though you were dying? Were words that important? Had I blithely adopted the expression "the curse," believing it to be popular, when it actually conveyed real feeling? Did I call the period "the curse" because I felt it *was* a curse, because I envied boys and wished I were dead because I was not born a boy? Some girls bleed profusely for days and eventually become anemic; their way, perhaps, of slowly dying unconsciously, John said.

Discomfort is not death, he wanted me to know, and pain

is not death, even though to me they often stood for death. When I shivered with cold and felt like dying, I might be uncomfortable, but that did not mean I would die.

My preoccupation with dying seemed strong judged by the words I used, the dreams I spun.

"If all the blood I shed in dreams poured out of my body, I sure would be dead," I said to John. "Last night I had another violent dream."

"Let's hear it."

I dreamed I visited the beach club where as a child I swam during summers, a palatial estate jutting out into the Sound. In the dream, as often I had done in real life, I plunged into the water. Surfacing, I found my back bloody and clawed as though someone underseas dug into it with giant fork.

"Two of the cuts were enormous," I said to John, image of the gaping wounds flashing through mind. "Like an anchor. No, not like an anchor. Like a fish-hook! That's what I was! A fish—hooked!"

"Poor fish," I said sadly. "So often I feel like the poor fish I watched flopping around the bottom of our boat, bloody and helpless after we caught them."

I always hated to hook a fish. I wanted no part of death—for fish or me. But my father seemed to enjoy fishing so I fished to please him.

The dream brought other recollections. "I hurt myself quite badly one day at that club," I reminisced. "Funny. I haven't thought of it since until just this minute."

One summer day, just like in the dream, I went for a swim. I was not a strong swimmer but I could manage to keep afloat for an eighth of a mile if I remembered to swim slowly. This day I ventured out quite far before I turned back. I felt relieved to near the float.

I started to climb out of the water. I stepped on the rusty chain that fastened the float to the ocean bottom. As I lifted my foot to the float the sole of it dripped blood. I had cut it on barnacles clamped to the chain below the water's surface.

The lifeguard, sitting in a rowboat nearby, noticed the blood pouring out. He rowed me to shore quickly. He would not let me walk on the sand, but carried me to a deck chair. I felt embarrassed by this attention. I did not want people staring at me because I was bleeding.

My stomach throbbed more violently than my foot. I wanted to throw up, but I thought, I'm giving the guard enough trouble. He won't thank me for vomiting.

He poured iodine in the cut. I winced as it stung open tissue. He bandaged it and ordered, "Go to a doctor right away. You need several stitches in this cut and it ought to be more thoroughly cleaned out."

"Thanks." I clenched my teeth.

Shoe in hand, I limped to a telephone, called a taxi. I waited on a bench outside the club, wondering if now I would die. When the taxi driver asked what happened I said jauntily, "Oh, I got a little cut." I lifted the foot; blood had seeped through, spattering the white bandage.

When we reached our house I paid the taxi and ran inside as quickly as I could maneuver on one foot. Only the cook was home, an outspoken young woman whom I adored because she designed rich desserts and because she liked me.

I burst into the kitchen. Mae looked up from rolling crust for chocolate pie. She saw the fright on my face.

"What's the matter, child?" she asked, putting the pin down.

"I cut my foot at the club," I whispered. "It hurts like sin but I won't go to a doctor." I started to cry. "I don't want to be sewn up."

"Go into the living room and let me look at it," she said.

I limped to our plush mulberry couch. She followed with a basin of hot water, iodine and bandages. I turned my head the other way as she removed the lifeguard's dressing. She placed my foot in warm water. I felt drugged, reaction from pain.

I love her, was my drowsy thought. She will not let me die.

She studied the wound, parting broken skin with gentle hands. "Whew, what a cut!" she exclaimed.

"I don't want to see it," I said fiercely.

"You should go to a doctor," she pleaded. "It goes across half your foot and it's so deep I can see the bone."

"I won't go to a doctor," I said stubbornly. "I'll lie here

and die first!" (So I would have. Is it any wonder I chose psychoanalysis instead of surgery?)

"Well, I'll do the best I can." She swabbed the cut with iodine. I can bear pain now, I thought, for she will take care of me.

"You'll have to give up baseball and tennis and keep this foot up on a chair," she warned.

"Of course," I agreed hastily. Anything, so she would not insist on a doctor.

I marvel my parents did not haul me to one (they did for everything else). I did not tell them how dangerous a cut I received and I swore Mae to secrecy. But they might have guessed at trouble because I remained in the house for a week. For me to stay quiet half a day meant something wrong.

I felt Mae saved my life. I might have died if rust from the chain had infected the cut.

"She, too, wanted me to live. Not like others who did not care whether I lived or died," I told John vehemently.

"What others?" he asked.

"My mother and father," I whispered.

"That's all that counts in a child's life," he said. "There are no 'others.'"

"Why did I feel they didn't care?" I asked.

"Because at times you felt they hated you and wanted to kill you," he said.

"That's hard to believe," I gasped. "I felt they hated me. But that they wanted to kill . . ."

"Not actually kill you," he said, "but they made you feel at moments their lives might be easier without you."

I thought of Mother storming, "You make me wish I weren't born." Or saying angrily, "I wish I were dead!" I remembered the words, "weren't born" and "dead," the feeling that, angered and annoyed, she looked at me as though she truly despised me.

I remembered with sudden fear "looks that could kill," shot out by both parents. I remembered them calling me "that crazy kid," staring at me at times as though I were crazy. I remembered other thoughtless, unkind words, no different from those spoken daily in countless homes.

But it was incredible that my parents wanted to kill me. I often felt they thought me stupid, crazy, but not that they wished me dead.

Shortly after this, I was covering a meeting in Memphis where a psychiatrist discussed the psychological importance of feeding in the lives of children. As I took notes, my eyes blinked tears.

I knew tears started at the sound of words meaningful to me. What about "feeding"?

I thought: feeding, eggs, they tried to poison me, my parents tried to murder me, a doctor snatched me from death, they are my enemies, they get angry at me all the time, they hate me, everybody hates me.

Every so often my parents mentioned the time Mother fed me my first egg. I threw it up, ran a high temperature. She called a doctor, to rescue me from the jaws of death, I felt. Now Mother and Dad talked of this with a chuckle. Family joke, I thought ironically. Yet, was it a joke to me, then or now, thirty years later, when my dreams had to absorb the death I could not consciously feel?

After returning from Memphis, I lay on the couch, silent. I wanted to speak of the egg, yet I was afraid. It is not easy to tell anyone you suspect your parents wanted to poison you.

I started off by saying sullenly, "I remembered about an egg when I was away."

He politely waited for me to explain. No "Hurry, Hurry," or "Well, get it out," or "Why do you move so slowly—are you sick?" Just restful, pleasant wait. Sometimes so pleasant I could not bear it and had to break it furiously with words.

"I felt for a moment as though my parents wanted to kill me," I said, "but it's completely crazy, of course."

I told him of my thoughts. I asked, "Does it make sense to you?"

"Your parents never really tried to kill you," he said, "but in your unhappiness it seemed to you as though they wanted to. Intellectually you know they did not, but in your inner, unrealistic world you felt at times they wished you dead."

He continued, "It is hard for children to distinguish between

101

a real threat and an unconscious threat. When the parent rages, an unhappy child may interpret it as intent to murder."

He added, "Some parents do kill children."

See your daily newspaper, I thought.

"But some parents who do not kill their children possess the same feelings as those who do and it is those feelings the children absorb," John explained.

Words spoken in violence and hate often shield intent to murder, unconscious, but murder nonetheless, I thought grimly.

"Children are the barometer of the feeling of parents," he said. "If a child is happy you know his parents possessed little need to feed on him emotionally."

We do not eat people to keep from starving, I thought, but some may "eat" their children in an emotional sense. When these children grow up they will "eat" others to feed their emotional starvation.

I knew some who walked and talked like humans but seemed little more than zombies. (Zombie may have been one name applied to the psychotic of an early culture.) Parents may slowly kill children psychologically, draining them of ability to feel or think.

The fears of parents become indelibly impressed on children, John said. Long before a child may have thought of stealing, for instance, a parent may be afraid that the child will steal (because the parent unconsciously has wanted to steal). He will drive home the arguments against stealing so violently that the child feels he *must* steal. He steals to save his own life, unconsciously carrying out his parents' wishes.

Many murderers are unconsciously carrying out the wishes and fears of their parents, John believed. ("You'll kill me some day, you nasty child," says a parent, unconsciously asking the child to kill him and also making the child feel, "I blame you for my misery and I wish you were dead.")

The need of some to die is so great they must find a way to die, John said. Their parents unconsciously wished them dead so intensely they must die.

Death is the real drama of life, I thought. Those who must die, either by suicide or murder, star in the greatest tragedy of all, but long before they die. The original drama took place when they were murdered, in a sense, as children. They received not love, but hate.

"Children know whether parents love them," John said. "It is only as they grow up they learn to hide the knowledge they have been hated."

We are back at love, I thought. Perhaps we never really get away from it.

"All children need love to survive psychologically," said John. "Only love can carry a baby through to strong maturity.

"A man does not need love to grow physically or intellectually, but he needs it to grow emotionally. When, as an infant, he does not receive love, his psychological life as an adult may become so fearful he cannot bear it."

Rebuked by parents, the child in his hunger for love turns to those nearest, John said. It may be brother, sister, neighbor or the world, for emotional hunger knows no bounds.

One who has lacked love goes in eternal search of it. He may seek fame and fortune, he may murder, he may closet himself from everyone—all in desperate desire for love. Life for the unhappy is an endless search for "the good parent," one who will truly love him instead of making him afraid, John said.

Some children (too many, perhaps,) stand in hidden corners crying out their hearts, rage-choked. They gaze up in distrust and confusion at the person who is their god, and who, they feel, hates them. Others stand too frightened for tears.

As a child I was ashamed of tears. A brave girl doesn't cry even when a wild pitch drives into her stomach and the pain flares up like fire. Not even when her parents, whom she loves more than anyone else in the world, slap her, does a girl cry.

"I'm sure they didn't know they hurt me when they occasionally slapped me," I told John.

"But it wasn't the slap that hurt you—it was something more than the slap, wasn't it?"

What is there more than a slap? I thought. What indignity tears through a child's thin soul with sharper stab than a slap? Even a beautiful face will feel ugly if slapped enough.

"What do you mean?" I asked.

"It's the whole feeling of the parent for the child," he explained. "Sometimes a slap is good for a child if he feels underneath the parent loves him. But if fear is present, everything the parent does becomes distorted."

Consistency is important, John said. The parent who is consistently cruel gives the child a better break than one who soothes one moment and rages the next, for then the child is confused, not knowing what to expect. He lives always on the promise of being appeased, flies into panic when he receives rage instead. With an always brutal parent, the child at least may build up a realistic defense, look elsewhere for affection.

Usually it is not one parent but both who bring either calm or chaos into the life of a child, John held. Parents either pull together in behalf of the child or, unconsciously, work together against his interests, even though they may tell themselves otherwise. ("I know what's best for you, don't question me." Never asking, "Have I questioned myself?")

The average child fears his parents to a certain degree but it is a realistic fear, the kind that keeps him from thrusting his fingers into the fire because his parents have told him fire will destroy him. It is fear mixed with a liberal taste of trust. To the unhappy child, however, fear outweighs trust.

The parent must trust the child, for that is how the child learns to trust himself, John said. The parent who will not trust a child to learn some things by himself is, in a sense, destroying him.

Some mothers who outwardly must overprotect children, inwardly may want to destroy them. ("Put on your rubbers because if you get your feet wet and catch pneumonia and die, I will have been responsible for your death and that would be too much guilt for me to bear because, at times, I have wished you dead.")

Such parents are so afraid they may harm the child (the fear and the wish, again intertwined) they must exaggerate how much they care, as though saying, in overprotecting manner, "See, I really don't want you to die." But the child knows, and is afraid.

No parent wants to hate a child, John said. The parent does

104

what he has to do because of his unconscious hatred of himself and his own parents. Parents often blame children for much that went wrong in their own lives, using the children as emotional buffers.

"Your parents asked much of you," he said. "In a sense, they expected you to bring them the happiness they were not able to get from their parents. When you could not do this—for no child can—they sometimes became angry at you."

Some children are so petrified of parents that when they grow up they dare not try to live by themselves. Eventually they must be taken care of by others in mental hospitals, jails and specialized hospitals.

Luckily, I was not so frightened as some, although childhood terrors as I could recall them showed I lived in fear.

One summer my parents moved me from my regular bedroom to sleep on the screened porch because it was cooler. Early every morning I heard weird tapping, a subtle rat-tat-tat outside the porch window. Terrified, I would bury my head in the blanket, try to drown out the tapping. One morning when I could bear the panic no longer I called to my father, sleeping in the next room. He staggered in sleepily.

"What's the matter?" he yawned.

"There's a terrible noise every morning right outside this window," I moaned, pointing toward the trees.

He peered out, listened. The noise had stopped (noises always seem to stop, do they not, when someone draws near to hear?).

"I can't hear anything," he said. "Go back to sleep."

He tucked the blanket around my neck, walked away, closed the door behind him.

The noise began again, as if to mock my show of fear. I slid deep into the bed. I pretended my father sat on the edge to protect me from whoever sought to kill me.

When I told my parents because of the noise I wanted to return to my own room, they said, "Don't be a sissy. It's just your imagination."

"They think I'm crazy," I thought. "They think I'm hearing noises." I wondered, "Am I crazy? Is there no noise outside?"

I remained on the porch the rest of the summer, waking each morning to listen in fright to the sound of steady tapping. It stopped only when I moved back to my room.

A few months later I was walking past the massive red-brick Catholic convent next door. Black-uniformed nuns shepherding children to day school were a familiar sight. They often waved or stopped to chat with us. They even permitted us to cut through their lawn.

Two nuns smiled at me.

"How are you?" I asked them.

"I'm fine," said one. Then, indicating the other, "But she is not so well."

"You don't sleep where I sleep," the second nun reproved her. She addressed me. "My room is near the attic and every morning a woodpecker wakes me pecking on the tin cross on top of the building. I'm going to have to do something about that bird."

I felt sudden shock. Woodpecker! I am not crazy, I thought jubilantly, even though my parents had not believed me.

A small bird, mistaking the tin cross for a tree, had stirred the terror in my life, made me wonder who wanted to kill me. Even prayers at night spoke of death. I recalled the line, "If I should die before I wake." I thought, I must even think of dying before going to sleep.

I would also feel like dying each time Mother refused what I thought was a fair request.

"Please let me stay just a half hour later," I would beg after she ordered me to be home at nine o'clock. No other girl abandoned a party that early. I was ashamed because I always had to be the first to dig out my coat. I felt different enough from the rest without that added indignity.

I would want to die, too, when I felt my parents did not care enough to listen. I would burst into the house with what I considered important news—a class trip to the Metropolitan Museum or my making guard on the basketball team. They would appear to hear but I could tell they were not really interested.

"Isn't that nice?" they would say.

I thought, They are saying isn't that nice just to be nice. I know they do not care. I would feel beaten.

Life may hold so much psychic brutality that, in terms of hardship to the body, one suffers just as intensely as though whipped, I thought. Children who live on Park Avenue may be victims of as serious an emotional beating as those in East Side slums.

Where did all this desperation start? I wondered. Cain held so much fury he had to murder his brother, so it must have begun with Adam and Eve.

"Who's to blame?" I asked John. For children do not spring full-blown with fear from the womb.

"Look at the women of the nation and you will know that nation," said John. "We speak of 'men' and 'women' but they are 'sons of mothers' and 'daughters of mothers.'"

It is true, then, I thought. The hand that rocks the cradle rules the world. Women bring hate or love to the world.

I could bring love to no one. I was too busy fleeing the shadow of death. I trusted no one and allowed none to trust me. I feared even those to whom I was close for the moment. Always I must flee.

While reading the Bible, something I never did before analysis, I found the line, "The wicked flee when no man pursueth."

I did not have to write down these words, as I did others. I would remember them always, I thought.

I repeated them to John. "I have a feeling they are important to me," I said. "Why should I feel wicked?"

"Perhaps because you want to murder," he said gently, casually.

Preposterous, I thought angrily. He knows I love everyone. But I wondered, do I love people according to his definition of love? I am sweet to them but, underneath, do I genuinely care for them? Is not my chief concern they approve of me?

"What makes you think I want to murder?" I asked John skeptically. I would hear him out, anyhow.

"The unhappy person wages a continuous battle against the unconscious fear of death," he said. "He wishes to murder, he fears being killed by someone else and he fears he will kill himself.

"Suicide is part murder, revenge on those who hurt you, just as murder is part suicide, for a murderer knows he risks losing his life," he explained.

So they all go together, I thought. Blood. Period. My blood and the blood of those I hate. B-l-o-o-d. Blood red. Perhaps that is why I have hated that color all my life. I will wear rose and pink but I will not wear blood-red. Reminds me too much of death.

Not only the death I fear for myself but the death I fear I will inflict on others if I am not careful. For I am afraid. I have always been afraid. And what had John said about fear? "We fight fear with anger."

If I lived in fear, I would naturally fight it with the only weapon I possessed. Anger.

"Nature gave anger to the first man in the jungle so he might survive," John had said. "Anger gave man added strength to fight off enemies."

He added, "The threat of being devoured by animals has disappeared but another threat exists today. Destruction from within."

Many do not know how to fight this kind of fear, I thought. Guns and axes are of no avail, although some still seek to battle with such outmoded weapons. We no longer live in jungles but there are those of us who must use jungle methods because we know no other means of saving our lives.

I had never resorted to gun or axe. Instead I turned fury inward. Because I felt no one cared, I wanted to die.

Now I could also know I felt mad enough to murder.

Chapter IX

DEATH IN SMALL DOSES

THOU SHALT NOT KILL.

But every day some do kill. Daughters kill mothers, fathers kill sons, husbands kill wives.

Every day thousands of people feel like killing but do not

kill. Some are able to admit to themselves they would like to murder. Others dare not face the feeling.

I was one of those too terrified even to feel murder. I hid from myself and the world the murderous wishes that throbbed in my heart. No one must know my secret—especially myself.

Murder was out of the question (the one question in my life I could not ask or answer).

"How can I admit murder?" I asked John wildly. "It's wrong to murder."

"Here it's not a question of morals but of what you feel," he said.

He wants me to face not what is "right" or "wrong" but what exists in me, I kept telling myself. He does not want me to think in terms of what I "should" or "should not" do but what I feel like doing. For unless I do, I will be unable to build a life based on purpose, instead of deceit.

The day the worst storm in history struck the city I covered a meeting in lower New York. I emerged from the building in late afternoon to find the city still tormented by the fury of wind and rain.

The streets looked as if madmen had raced down them, slashing viciously at window and door. Glass graveled the sidewalk. Slabs of store windows disfigured the ground, scattered like giant jigsaw puzzles.

Through this debris I scurried, trying to reach the safety of a subway. I bucked a violent wind that turned my staunch umbrella inside out. I noticed vaguely that crowds stood huddled to one side of the street. The stretch on which I walked yawned empty.

"Look out, girlie," a man yelled at me. "Want to get killed?" He pointed to a large sign above me, groaning in the gale.

"Thanks," I yelled back sarcastically.

I cursed to myself. "Isn't life hard enough without this guy telling me I'm going to get killed?"

I bolted into the subway as though witches rode me. My temper rose to titanic level. I fumed as I told John about it the next day.

"I feel enough like dying without someone reminding me of it," I snapped. "I wanted to kill that man."

"Do you hear what you are saying?" John asked.

"Why, yes," I said, surprised at his question. "I said, 'I wanted to kill that man.' "

"Do you mean it?' he asked.

"You know I don't mean it," I said teasingly. "Why on earth would . . ." I stopped.

I tried to remember how I felt. I wanted to explode like a fierce firecracker. First I felt terror, then anger, then hatred, then murder. All this toward a man who warned me of danger. "I wanted to kill that man," I had said.

To escape my violent feelings I had started to run (as I had run away from them all my life). But that did not mean the feelings did not exist. It meant only I would not face them.

When I flung out a flip remark such as "I could kill that man," did I not mean it? (Just as I felt my parents had meant it when they spoke thoughtlessly to me.)

Feelings of murder oozed slowly to the surface of my consciousness. They burst as mere bubbles of awareness.

One day I returned from visiting a diagnostic center for emotionally disturbed children. (John did not believe much emphasis should be placed on "diagnosis." He felt those who possess convictions about the nature of emotional illness know the important thing is to offer a child trust and guidance. "What else is there?" he asked rhetorically.)

The director of the center told of one boy who set fire to a barn. Under sodium amytal, the so-called truth serum, the boy talked freely, revealing the wish to kill his stepfather.

I trembled as I heard this. Never, never, must I allow myself to be put under sodium amytal, I thought.

I wondered, then, why do I feel so frightened? Am I afraid of what my unconscious might reveal? Do I know that I feel no different, underneath, from this boy, except instead of setting a barn on fire, my way of expressing murder is to set the world on fire—with words? Words born of murder.

I attended a party given by the city's newspaper women. Celebrities showed up at the Waldorf's Starlight Roof to perform for the ladies who occasionally gave them a break in feature story and column.

"Sid Caesar was wonderful," I raved to John. "So was Irene Dunne."

Miss Dunne told us she had just returned from London where she had been presented to the King and Queen. She smiled coyly. "You girls better watch out. I'm going to start writing a column for a newspaper in Podunk, so look to your laurels." She spoke with humor and charm.

But there was one performer who upset me. Should I tell John about him? I better, I thought, because it is usually the things I do not tell him at first that later appear to have been the most important.

"I didn't like one man although everyone else laughed," I admitted.

"Why didn't you like him?"

"He sang a parody about Lizzie Borden. It made me furious." I sounded my anger.

"Why?"

"Because I didn't think it was funny," I explained.

"Maybe you didn't think it was funny because you, too, felt like killing your parents," John suggested.

Was that why I could not laugh? Did I feel too much like Lizzie Borden to be able to take a joke at her expense?

Could I remember that, as a little girl, when my parents raged at me I would feel, "I could kill you, too, and some day when I grow up and get big I will kill you because you hate me and you threatened me first?"

Could I know that when I "got big," I had to forget such ignoble feelings, for society does not laud its Lizzie Bordens even though it may laugh at them in envy?

Could I know that the murderous feelings that seethed in me were revealed by my dreams? For dreams could not be deceived. They showed how hard my unconscious was forced to work to save my life because I felt so wicked.

Could I know that I had transferred my desire to commit murder to books on murder, movies on murder, newspaper accounts of murder?

Could I know that the feelings that drive some men to kill, which exist in everyone to a certain degree, stirred in my life? That, with the same intensity I felt my parents wanted to murder me, so also I wanted to murder them before they had the chance to kill?

I recalled one time I felt mad enough to kill Mother. I was eleven. I closeted myself in my room to compose a poem for Mother's Day.

At the appropriate moment I handed it to her, blushing. She read it through, looked up, pleased.

She said, "This is a good poem." Then she laughed nervously. "Where did you copy it?"

I was too stunned to answer. She must be joking, I thought. Feeling like a prisoner, I stuttered, "I—I wrote it myself. Last night."

By that time she was thinking of something else. I was sure she had not heard me. I thought, What's the difference? She would never believe me anyhow.

Now I know Mother was probably embarrassed by my flowery tribute. But all I could feel then was:

"She has everything—my father, my brother, my sisters—and she cannot let me have even one lousy little poem as my own without accusing me of stealing."

For one of my first parties mother bought me a light green chiffon dress, ruffled from waist to hem, so I might make what I hoped would be an unforgettable impression on three older men, fourteen-year-old cadets from Peekskill Military Academy. I remember how carefully I slipped the dress over my head before I started downstairs to be driven to the party.

Our stairs were split in two sections by a small landing. Often I would pause there to peer out the window to see who played ball in the back yard. If I liked the company I would continue down. If I considered it boring I would return to reading.

This night as I reached the landing, Mother called up, "Lucy, it's cold. I hope you're wearing your heavy underwear."

I stared out the window into blackness. A fib would do no good. She could easily peek under the green chiffon, see I wore the sheer.

"Gosh, no," I protested. "This is a party, not a sleigh ride."

"Put it on," she ordered, "or you don't go."

"You can't mean it?" I asked in alarm.

"You heard me," she said.

112

I hurled myself back into my room, angrily threw off the rayon underwear. I struggled into hideous flannels with sleeves to the elbows and legs to the knees. I tried to pin up the underwear so it would not show. By the time I left the room I looked like a walking pincushion.

Early in the party I made out well, even though several safety pins worked open to jab me occasionally. I kept pushing invading underwear up under frothy chiffon, hoping no one would take me for a victim of seven-year itch.

The party turned rough as we raced around a circle of chairs playing the musical game, "Going to Jerusalem." Another girl and I dashed for the same chair. Down went the chair and down went the underwear.

I made an impression, but not the one I sought. Later, in the solitude of an upstairs bedroom in this strange house, I cried in rage because Mother would not understand why I did not want to wear long, heavy underwear even if the night were cold. I thought, When I grow up I will never humiliate my little girl this way.

As I grew older, Mother and I fought some vicious verbal battles, usually over my wanting to go to a movie or to a friend's house when she wanted me to stay home. Choking back fury at defeat I would race upstairs to my room, to lock myself in after slamming the door hard. I would grab magazine or book and try to concentrate on the words. But I would feel underneath I was a wicked girl. (Could I think it so strange that now I could not tolerate sitting alone in my apartment, shut away from everyone, still feeling "bad"? Could I not see I was still running away but in different fashion, racing across a continent instead of upstairs and into my room?)

Sometimes Mother would whistle or hum to drown out my words and I would want to scream in anguish. (No wonder when I was depressed and the person next to me on a bus started to whistle, I winced and felt like choking him.)

I would feel like murder each time my parents lost their temper at me or the other children. But I would bury my feelings, think, they must be right, for they are my gods, my superbeings. I must be a very wicked little girl, indeed, to draw their anger.

It must never occur to me that occasionally something might be wrong inside them. For that would mean my utter destruction. If I displeased them, who would take care of me? Half a loaf of love is better than none. I needed them alive even though at times, I might wish them dead.

Therefore, I had to pretend to myself I loved them (when part of me hated) as I had to pretend to the world I loved it (when part of me hated).

This explained why in later years I sympathized with criminals. I felt I must help them to be understood by the public to pay them back for doing my dirty work. I envied them, too. They not only were able to rebel but they could admit their guilt. I could only let mine slowly destroy me.

Sometimes murder escaped in roundabout ways. Through my fingers, perhaps. I was always spilling liquid contents of glasses across clean tablecloths. Throughout childhood and adolescence I left behind a literal trail of ink. An ink bottle in my hand was as good as half on the floor.

My father grew hoarse bawling me out. Fountain pens, ostensibly designed to contain ink for others, betrayed me. One time a pen spattered the sheets as I wrote a letter.

"Even in bed you spill ink," Dad roared. "Is no place safe?"

Only once did I feel penitent. Father had just left the house to remarry. Mother tried to raise our spirits with new décor. She allowed me to choose for my room soft gray paint, maroon curtains. For her bedroom she bought gay, flowered wallpaper.

One evening I sauntered into her room to fill my pen from the ink bottle on her desk. I unscrewed the top hurriedly. Ink geysered into the air and onto the wallpaper. With horror I watched it black out purple flowers, overrun pale green leaves. In maddening slowness it oozed downward to the green rug.

Mother walked in at that moment, stared at the still-moving ink. She sat down slowly on the large double bed whose purple and green spread matched the wallpaper. She looked utterly defeated.

114

"I'm sorry," I muttered, shaking with fear. "I didn't mean to do it."

"That's all right," she comforted me. "I know you didn't." She knew I felt as troubled as she.

Because of the desire to kill, my guilt was great. (Thou shalt not kill!) I felt doubly guilty because I made Mother suffer even before I was born. When she was pregnant, doctors cut open her abdomen after she complained of acute pain. They found nothing wrong, sewed her up. A few months later I arrived on schedule. But Mother might have died. She had endured agony for me. I was an ungrateful, nasty child to cause her so much unhappiness, to dislike her after she suffered so on my account.

An early childhood memory brought out many of my distorted feelings about Mother. When I was four years old my father took me to the old Battery aquarium. We walked into a room filled with tanks in which cavorted graceful, fancy fishes.

Suddenly I looked up at the ceiling. An enormous dead turtle filled the entire room with black death. I stared at it in horror.

"It's going to fall on me! It's going to fall on me!" I wanted to scream to my father. Instead, I tugged at his coat and whispered, "Let's get out of here."

Years later I was sent to the Aquarium on assignment. My first act was to look fearfully at the ceiling. It stretched bare. Only in my mind had the turtle hung suspended all the years.

The turtle stood for many things: my fear of Mother, my hatred, my wish that she, like the turtle, might die, my guilt for such a horrible wish. I felt any moment the turtle might come alive and snap me up (one of my deepest terrors seemed to be fear of the mouth from which anger poured forth and where teeth gleamed sharp, ready to devour).

Because of guilt I punished myself for crimes never committed. A young woman from whom I once sublet an apartment in New York jumped out of a hotel window killing herself. Several days later I threw away a few dress hangers I took from the closet of her apartment. At the time I thought, She will not need all of these.

I told John of my deed. "I couldn't stand having the hangers around. They reminded me of her death."

"You weren't responsible for it," he said.

I had stolen from her (a lesser crime than killing), felt guilty about that. While she lived it did not seem to matter, but when she died my feelings became confused. Because of my wish to die, my murderous feelings toward my parents and toward her (she had made me feel uncomfortable when I met her, quizzing me suspiciously, I felt, about my references) I had to punish myself for the larger crime of which I was innocent.

I had carried guilt through the years for other crimes of which I was not guilty. I remembered a boy who lived down the block from us. He had been struck in the head with a baseball, never recovered consciousness. I did not know him before his accident, but I saw him many times after, standing at the window, staring out, unseeing, at children who rode bicycles in the yard below.

I often played with his sister but she would not talk much of him. She would say, "He's sick. We hope some day he will get better."

I would look up at the window and wave, although he would never wave back. His handsome serious face kept its vacant look. "Poor boy," I would sob inside. "Poor, poor boy."

As I told John about this shattered boy I insisted, "I didn't do it! I wasn't the one who threw the baseball." (As though protesting false innocence elsewhere; perhaps having felt at times like striking my brother?)

Because of guilt I felt I deserved to die. As much as I feared dying I also wished to die because I felt unworthy, friendless, guilty.

I had never faced how much I wanted to kill myself. My whole life was, in a sense, desperate flight to make sure I would not stop to commit suicide.

A friend called to ask me to eat with her.

"I can't," I wailed in panic. "I have to cover a story, write a book review, see people for cocktails and pick up theater tickets."

116

"Sounds like you won't have time to drop dead," she said dryly.

She's right, I thought. That is exactly what I have been doing with my life. I have filled it with endless activity so I will not have time to drop dead—because I am so afraid I *will* drop dead (run, run, little lamb, so you will not slaughter yourself).

I was scared to death to ride in an airplane because I was certain the plane would crash. Friends of mine had been killed in smash-ups. Why should I believe my life safer than theirs?

Instead, I rode trains, but each time I boarded one I felt I would never return. I feared for my life even on the comparative safety of a train. (More people get killed, perhaps, when there is a train wreck but the wrecks occur less frequently than in the air.)

When I cut my finger I doused it with iodine to prevent germs from infecting it. (People had died thus, too.) Crossing the street, I cursed at drivers who careened close; they wanted to kill me by pinning me against the curb, I thought.

This was part of the wish for death. I unconsciously hoped I might die and be relieved of the pain of living, but, not having the courage or desperation to take my life, I wished someone else might do it for me.

At the same time, my strongest instinct, self-preservation, fought the idea of dying, finding it repulsive.

A dream showed this. In it I was bleeding to death from a wound in my arm. A doctor stuffed cotton in the wound to stop the bleeding.

"That doctor was you," I told John. "You were trying to keep me from dying."

"You won't die," he said reassuringly.

"But I think I want to, at times," I said. "Even though I've never been able to admit it. When I think of the number of times I've hated living. . . ."

"You also want to live."

Yes, I wanted to live. I had to live, even though I wished I might die.

I could not bear to be near sick people, for I wanted to conserve what little strength I possessed rather than take an added chance I would catch something and die. I could not understand how any girl would want to be a nurse. "That's the last job I could hold," I protested to John.

"Some like it," he observed.

Though I complained loudly of pain, I would never give in to sickness. I would work even though I felt like dying. Many were the stories, a few front page, I wrote sitting at my desk with throat raw as though cut and head splitting as though cracked open. One time, when the late Mayor La Guardia spoke at Washington Market, I could hardly stand. I crept close to the building, leaned against its cold stone as support.

"I sure have been punishing myself," I complained to John.

"You covered up your rage from yourself and others by appeasing people so they would not kill you or suspect you might want to destroy them," he said.

"Why did I do that?" I asked.

"That is the way you fought to survive," he explained. "Survival comes first with each one of us."

Over the years I had forgotten the many hours I spent attempting to save my life from what I saw as threats to it.

My memory had been a fickle tool. I recalled only what served me, exiled danger to the unconscious.

As I could look back with an eye not quite as myopic as before, I could see that one thread ran through my life, constant as breathing itself. I unconsciously chose what I thought would be most useful in saving my life.

I acted to save my skin. All else was embellishment. If I would not understand this, I would truly be deceiving myself. I could search and re-search until the day I died but it would not lead to truth.

The need to survive lies at the bottom of the well of truth. I was driven by the life force, which John described as holding both the will to survive and procreate. Survival and sexuality stand interdependent—no more to be separated than mind and body.

Each one fights to survive. The woman who cannot marry, the man who marries eight or nine times, the alcoholic, the drug addict, all fulfill some need which if left unfulfilled would mean greater suffering. It is not only in concentration

118

camps that men resort to desperate measures to survive. They do it every day in peacetime.

The martyr survives by letting others kill him; the murderer by killing others; the suicide by killing himself. Many survive just by leading lives of "quiet desperation."

Each does what he needs to do to save his life, whether he knows better or not. The will to survive is greater than knowledge.

"All that a man hath will he give for his life," the Bible told me, if I but could have understood it.

All down my lifeline I made unconscious choices that, to me, represented the lesser of my fears, offered me more of a chance of survival.

As a girl, it was less terrifying to play baseball with boys than to face girls to remind me of hatred for myself. In school I competed for honors not because I enjoyed learning but because I feared the wrath of my parents if I did not get good marks. I entered a girls' college selected by my father rather than oppose him to go to the co-educational university which was my choice. After college it was less dangerous for me to leave home to work than to face either marriage or living with Mother.

In relationship with men, it was less fearful to know many casually than to know one intimately (the Don Juans of both sexes fear to be close to one person). I could hide behind a hundred pairs of trousers, yet not be responsible for any one pair.

I, a human being, a member of the animal kingdom, was interested, just as are the animals, in saving my own life. But unlike the animals which have real fears, such as attack by larger animals or death from starvation, my fears were often false. I was afraid of things that did not hold death but which symbolized death. I lived scared to death and scared of death.

Now I understood the meaning of my sinus. Because I had not been realistic about fear of death my body was taking a beating. It overworked its protective function trying to save my life from what it felt as destruction.

The young nose-and-throat specialist had been puzzled because the glands in my nose refused to reduce the swelling. No longer did it puzzle me.

The Lord (or nature) devised this mechanism as protection for the body. When cold air rushed into my nose, to protect the sensitive lungs from sudden blast, the glands in my nose were supposed to flash a signal to the membranes to swell up so that the air could enter only very slowly.

But cold chill filled my life all the time, not just during winter frost. I lived in an emotional climate where I felt I must combat constant iciness. My body reacted as it should to the danger. Nature did her part. But at the same time, she flashed me her storm signal—pain. She warned me something was wrong in the pain of the sinus (the symptom of fear).

My sinus and other illnesses were like death in small doses. I was punishing myself in what seemed a petty way compared to actual death but the illnesses held a part of death, just as inoculations contain a mild form of the infectious substance to protect against intense attack.

My unconscious tried to warn me in dreams that terror mounted. My body tried to warn me through physical ailments that I was destroying myself. I had been too frightened to pay attention until I saw my job, which had become my life, threatened.

Only then could I dare know of my inner drive for destruction. I had to become sicker before I could get better. I had to feel at wit's end before I could seek help.

Chapter X

SEX

ONE REASON I FELT WICKED and deserving of death was because I dared to possess sexual feelings. I felt I must apologize to the world for the strange hunger that stirred me.

At first it was even painful to say the word "sex." I would bring up the topic, drop it quickly like something stolen.

One morning I dared to say (defiantly), "I suppose I've got to talk about sex."

"Talk about anything you choose," John said.

"I've heard that in analysis you're supposed to talk about sex," I insisted.

"Will you please forget what you've always heard?" he asked. "Think for yourself. You don't have to rely on others."

"Other people seem more objective," I said weakly.

"There's no such thing as objectivity—merely a balance of biases."

"Let's skip sex," I mumbled. "I don't feel I have much to say, anyhow."

"It's the things you don't say that are important, too," he reminded me.

"I don't think I'm particularly afraid of sex." I tried to sound casual. "I just don't see any reason to discuss it at length."

"Everything that exists is to be talked about," John said. "What is, is."

Without an apparent reason in the world, I began to cry, softly but thoroughly.

"What's the matter?" he asked gently.

"I lied to you," I sobbed. "I'm scared to death of sex. Even saying the word makes me feel funny."

"You don't trust me, do you?" he asked.

"No," I said, truthful for a change. I knew now I lied when I was afraid truth would bring pain—I lied to people I did not trust.

"I'd expect you to have fear about sex," he said reassuringly.

"I must be scared to death of it," I admitted. "I even hate dirty jokes."

"We don't hate something unless it has special meaning for us," he said. "Take the Women's Christian Temperance Union. Liquor must play an important part in the lives of women who belong."

"But don't you think it's disgusting for people to tell dirty jokes?" I asked, my voice rising in wrath.

"I tell them sometimes," he said. "Why do you think it's disgusting?"

"Because it is." I was indignant. "It's putting sex on a low level."

"Maybe you get disturbed because you *feel* sex is on a low level," he suggested.

John did not talk about sex as most people I knew did, with shame and disgust, tempered with secret glee. He discussed it in the same tone of thoughtfulness he discussed all else.

"Doesn't sex disturb you?" I asked, struck by his composure in the face of such a tumultuous topic.

"Why should it?" he answered. "It's a natural function that thousands of people enjoy daily. It is neither noble nor disgusting. It just is, like the digestive system."

I could not understand this attitude. I would get upset and excited when I thought of sex. It did not even seem proper I think of it. Yet, here was John telling me to accept sex as part of life.

"You mean sex is all right?" I asked, in that joking tone which, underneath, holds not humor, but fear.

"When it is kept in its appropriate place," he said.

"And what is its appropriate place?"

"As a part of life, not the whole of it, which it often becomes for unhappy people," he replied.

Could it be that because I was so afraid of sex, it held importance in my life out of all proportion to reality—the fascination of forbidden fruit? Perhaps, I thought, when sex becomes all of life it can have no real meaning, for then there is nothing to which it can relate except emptiness. What should exist as an enjoyable, satisfying experience becomes a furious be-all with little resemblance to the kind of love John described.

"Sex to me has always been a secret thing," I admitted to John.

"You feel it belongs in the bathroom. You don't see it as a natural feeling belonging in every room of a house," he commented.

It was difficult to accept as natural that which I had never been permitted to accept as natural.

"I'm mixed up about sex and love," I said.

To me they were two different things. Love was romance,

white chiffon, *Stardust* and soft summer breezes. Sex was sordid, torn black blouses, the blues and sultry nights.

"Sex is only part of love," John said.

I never thought of love as part of sex or sex as part of love. It was always love *or* sex, just like black *or* white, good *or* bad.

Hate or love, good or bad, the balance of life tipping from one extreme to the other, and is it any wonder there may be madness in a world where never the scales are level? We are wicked, wicked little ones for daring to believe bodily pleasures are for us. It should be "Wisdom, child, wisdom," but it seems always to be "Aren't you ashamed?"

"Why *must* people romanticize love, make of it a dramatic, fiery thing if it should be calm and assured?" I asked John. (For me still the why to stem fear.)

"Because they are afraid of the greatest manifestation of love—sex," he said. "Some clothe sex with the glint of glamour to make it bearable because they fear it so much. They feel sex is bad."

"Sex headed the list in my 'bad' category of the 'good' and 'bad' divisions of life," I admitted.

"This concept in which love and sex are split makes for much unhappiness," John said.

The newspaper that morning carried the story of an old man's rape of a young girl, after which he strangled her.

"That man must have thought of sex and love as being worlds apart," I said. "He had to kill the girl to keep her from telling anyone because he thought sex so wicked."

"Some people cannot conceive of sex as being tender and part of love, but think of it, rather, as dirty and violent," said John. "Men rape and then murder because they are filled with hate, not love."

Perhaps, I thought ruefully, if ever I were able to accept sex as natural, I would not be disgusted with dirty jokes. I felt my disgust also disguised envy, because I could not enjoy sex I did not want anyone else to enjoy it.

My parents disapproved of kissing and necking. Anything else they rarely mentioned, ignoring it as though it did not exist, which, of course, made me all the more curious since my body told me it did. Why did they hide it? It must be sinister, indeed.

In high school some of us began exchanging shy kisses on dates. A feeling of adventure, "getting away from it all," flooded the early thirties. These were the hangover years of the gay, drunken twenties, although our crowd did not drink. We worshipped sports. To be a good athlete you forsook drink, forsooth. The important thing was to keep on the move so you had no time to think, for the truth might shock you. You might learn you had a body for other purpose than sports.

I never dared go beyond the kiss. Better to tolerate stomachaches resulting from prolonged kissing than the guilt of giving in to further wickedness.

The length of the kiss counted; endurance became the part that compensated for lack of the whole. I remember one kiss lasting from Harrison to Larchmont, a distance of five miles. If the car had not stopped and the driver yelled, "All out," my embraceable partner might have held it as far as New Rochelle, next town down the line.

"A kiss is just a kiss," said John once, as though it could be as casual as a handshake.

But to me a kiss had become far more than a kiss. It symbolized sex—exciting, wondrous, magnificent.

My kissing crimes were committed chiefly in the automobile, particularly its back seat. Romance rode with the wind in the rumble seat. Adolescent mores permitted the couple who climbed in to be cold (even in July) and to snuggle close. The boys would take turns driving so the couple in front would not feel cheated. Sometimes the owner of the car would not allow anyone else to drive, putting the value of auto above ardor for girl. He would grudgingly give up his chance at the rumble seat to the other couple's unashamed delight.

Thus I indulged in my share of kisses. But they were bestowed out of daring and rebellion, not with the feeling that kissing was pleasurable or natural. I fled from crush to crush because I felt "bad." I would exchange kisses with a boy, feel guilty, transfer to him the blame for my badness, give him up and go on to someone else.

Because of the straight and narrow lane I forced myself to

124

tread (and dread) all through high school and college, I deeply envied the primrose path tripped by less discriminating ladies.

When a young magazine editor asked what I would like most to do in life, expecting me to say join his staff, I replied sarcastically, "Work in a whorehouse."

"You've had one too many." He nodded at the third drink set on the table in front of us.

"Maybe." The drink enabled me to say what I thought. My flippancy, assumed to hide fear, often revealed honesty.

Part of me envied women who worked in houses where sex was their business. I had never been allowed to have sex for my business in any realistic sense. Unrealistically, in fantasy, however, it was almost the whole of my business (this is an example of how repression works, with the unconscious making up for a strict conscious). That a prostitute might be as emotionally disturbed as I, although expressing it in another way, I was still too frightened to see.

I was brought up to believe death preferable to "violation," not in those words, but often the words need never be spoken by parents—the feeling tells the story. Over the years I clung to virtue as though it were something of which to be proud. I might be as unvirtuous as I chose in the rest of life, but to my rigid mind as long as I did not give myself to a man that would justify hatred, envy, fear. Admitting to sexual feelings would be a fate worse than death and death in my life was a strong enough threat.

I became more and more ashamed of my body, feeling it had to be put out of sight and mind.

When John said, "Your body belongs to you alone, to do with as you choose," I felt stunned.

Somehow, it had never seemed mine to enjoy. I had always been ashamed of its functions.

"You're a big girl now and you must stop wetting your bed." (I received the spanking of my life at the age of two from Father and I never again wet the bed. But is this the way to teach children to grow up in confidence and calm?)

"Why, what a good girl! A nice bowel movement. You get a piece of candy for that." (Always, in later life, when I did not want to be a "good girl" or felt frustrated or angry, I

125

would become constipated, or when I was constipated, I would feel like a "bad girl.")

"Now, I don't want to frighten you, but all girls, when they get about your age, so they can later have babies, go through an unpleasant few days each month." (This introduction to what nature intended as normal intensified the feeling it is a "curse.")

"No nice girl lets boys make passes at her." (No nice girl feels proud of her body. No nice girl feels part of nature.)

The only time I took pleasure in my body was when I could dance, I told John. There was nothing like being summoned to the dance floor of a roadhouse by Jimmy Lunceford's or Glen Gray's orchestra. To whirl around the floor in the arms of a boy was one way I could express feelings and still believe I was a "good girl."

Dancing, at best, was no substitute for a real release of feeling. Sometimes it even increased frustration. But it was better than nothing (the answer to many of life's questions).

When my father and I went to Florida one year, I became friendly with a girl who lived in the house next to us on the beach near St. Petersburg. One night she asked if I wanted to go out with her.

"We're going to a dance marathon," she said seriously, as though to the Metropolitan Opera.

"What is that?" I asked.

"It's where dancers dance until they fall down and the ones left standing get the prize," Helen explained.

"Sounds wonderful." I was ecstatic.

We set off for an outdoor arena in which the marathon, now in its fifth day, was taking place. The stands were jammed with enthusiastic spectators who cheered on favorite couples as they gulped cokes and hot dogs.

"C'mon, Babe," I heard one of them shout as a husky lady and her partner darted past. "You can hold him up another round!"

Hungrily I watched dancers embracing each other, dragging in desperation around the wooden floor as the tired orchestra beat out a rhythm which few bothered to keep. To some in the audience this was a sorry spectacle of humanity

126

suffering to earn a few dollars. To me, I regret to say, it proved an entrancing sight. I could think of no life more perfect than one in which you danced away time forever. (How better to work off fear and fury than through your feet?)

Helen's handsome, older brother, with whom I was dying to dance, never invited me out, showing only disdain for a sister's friend. When Helen and I combed the beach for rare shells, he made fun of us.

"For heaven's sake, what are you searching for?" he demanded one afternoon when we returned empty-handed.

I explained that I sought one type (we had collected almost all others), a small, white conch shell, which, when held to the ear sounded the ocean's roar.

Early one morning this family left for their New Jersey home. They came over to say good-bye. My father woke me up, urged me to go to the door.

"I can't," I protested. "I'm not dressed." I did not want them to see me in a nightgown.

Dad bade them farewell as I hid in the bedroom. He returned, carrying in his hand a small, perfectly shaped white conch shell.

"For you," he said. "From Richard."

I don't think I have ever been more pleasantly amazed. Young men take funny ways to show they know you like them, I thought.

Richard would not dance with me but through the years I found other men who liked to sweep around dance floors. Often I will jokingly (?) ask a man who dances well if he will enter a marathon with me. Most of them ignore the question. They think I am teasing.

One friend stumbled over a rumba step recently when I suggested we go into a marathon.

"It's illegal in most states," he said sharply.

"Is it?" I was disappointed. How now would I ever get enough dancing? I was not trim or pretty enough to join a chorus.

"Besides," he added disgustedly, "who the hell would want to take that much punishment?"

A hungry little girl would, I thought, if she did not know

what else to do with her feelings. It would give her an acceptable way of releasing sexual emotions.

Before analysis I thought of sexual feelings as pertaining to the act of intercourse alone. I came to know that sexuality encompassed many of the feelings that had been part of my body since the day I was born.

The first feeling of sexuality that I experienced took place when, as a baby, I desired the warmth of my mother's body, John said, for to me, that was life.

"A baby, like a tiny puppy, needs the comfort of a larger body in order to survive," he said. "He then develops through the stages of growth in contentment. Denied a sure, warm love, however, he will seek the mothering of flesh all his life." (And if he hates, in his hate will lie anger because of unfulfilled infant hunger.)

Adults sometimes use advanced sexual feelings to fulfill earlier demands, he went on. This, however, cannot make up for the earlier loss, so people will continue to be unhappy no matter how frantically they use sex. Sex cannot solve the problem of anxiety although it may ease tension temporarily.

It is difficult for some to admit that excessive sexual activities may be attempts to make up for the physical and psychic comfort withheld as a baby, he said, for such infant desires would be abhorrent for the adult to confess. He displaces them on what, to him, represents adult love.

This was shown in a dream which spun itself out of an event of the day. An older man gave me a jovial hug in an attempt to keep me warm when we stood waiting for a taxi one chilly evening. It was merely a comforting, protective embrace.

I went home—to dream. In the dream we no longer stood on a street corner. We sat snug in my apartment. I mixed him a drink. As I brought it to him, I gently pushed him backward on the couch, leaned over and kissed him ardently several times.

I woke up ashamed. All that fantasy from just a friendly hug! Part of me had not been content to settle for the hug of reality. It demanded more. My original hunger, to be warm and protected as a baby needs protection, was translated into sexual feelings permissible to an adult.

128

The unconscious dared go no further. It could not go back to the original hunger for the mother's breast, because the unconscious, too, must censor a little. The raw truth may often be too dangerous to take. Dreams, while they showed me truth as deeply as anything could, also protected me from underlying truths that I was not strong enough to face. As I became safer, the nature of my dreams changed, revealing more of the deeper disturbances. Gradually I could dream of many things that once had been too dangerous to get through to a dream.

Gradually I started to see sexuality more as part of living, rather than as a sinister secret to be buried. I realized that, in a sense, my parents had expected me to live without any feelings of sexuality until I got married. Then, suddenly, sexuality would be permitted to change from "bad" to "good."

When some girls who have had puritanical childhoods get married, they assume they will be able to accept sexual relationships normally, but often have trouble, John said. They indulge in sex then not because it is right or because it is enjoyable but out of rebellion and curiosity. They are angry at their parents for having deprived them of the feeling that sex is natural. They may also get angry at their husbands, unable to shoulder alone the burden of guilt, projecting on the men some of the blame.

Conscience does make cowards of us, I thought; the kind of conscience, which, when arising from fear, keeps us from the bravery of freedom.

We absorb our feelings about sex from parents just as we absorb from them the quality of happiness or unhappiness, John said. As our parents feel sexually toward us, thus we feel sexually toward others. The seduction of the child by the parent plays an important part in the growth of the child. A certain amount of seduction is necessary to pave the way for relationship in later years with the opposite sex. It is also needed to induce a child to develop, for we are all, to a certain extent, seduced into learning. We learn for those who love us and whom we love (and this, too, I felt, is part of analysis).

Our family was not too affectionate. We never kissed each other on the mouth, only the cheek. It was unusual to exchange careless caresses. I never dared to hug my sisters and brother very often even though I felt like it.

Dad, to me, seemed outwardly the warmest, for I recall that most of my embraces came from him. When as a child I kissed and hugged him he did not push me away as Mother was apt to do.

Mother, I felt, found it difficult to accept affection. Sometimes when I kissed her I felt I was repulsive to her.

For months I had been telling John how deeply I despised bugs. I saw a cockroach crawling up the wall of my apartment, killed it by smashing my shoe against it, felt like vomiting. I dreamed of vicious, hairy bugs more loathsome than nature ever created.

"What is this terror of bugs?" I would beseech him. I was so terrified I would flee a flea.

"I think you transfer a lot of your feelings about other things to bugs," he said. "What comes to mind when you think of bugs?"

"Words like dirty and filthy and death. I don't like to kill bugs because they squish so. I can't stand the sight of them." My unconscious was not helping much.

Several weeks later, in discussing my mother, I mentioned again how I felt she always drew away from me when I would try to get close.

"When I kissed her, at times, she looked at me in disgust as if I were a bug she had just killed," I said.

Then I repeated slowly, "A bug she just killed! Me and bugs—Mother looked at both in disgust."

"As if your kiss might bring infection," John said.

In later years all I had remembered was the look of loathing. I did not want to admit it had been for me so I transferred it to innocent bugs, at the same time feeling at one with the bugs (she wanted us both dead). Whenever I saw a bug it reminded me of the "bad" in me that caused my mother to withdraw in repulsion, the "bad" she might some day kill as she killed a bug.

John did not seem alarmed at Mother's detachment. He said it was preferable to a parent who does not try to control physical feelings toward a child. He warned, however (again

130

stressing degree), that sometimes the relationship between parent and child may develop into too great a hunger or too great a detachment. When parents are emotionally upset, the seduction, along with all else in their lives, may assume too deep an importance, he said. It may be used with such a degree of intensity that, whether implied or actual, it literally drives the child out of his mind because of the guilt aroused in him. We often use the expression "scared out of his wits"; this may also mean "seduced out of his wits," I thought.

I remembered an aunt who terrified me when I was a child because I felt she swooped down on me in such physical hunger she would eat me alive, craving me as she would food. Children may become frightened of being devoured alive by parents who hunger for them (death and sexual feelings synonymous).

I told John about a father and small daughter I had observed in the park.

"I could eat you up, you darling!" gushed the father, grabbing the pretty three-year-old to his breast. She squealed with delight as he covered her face with kisses.

Five minutes later, irritated by her refusal to leave the park (she wanted to watch boys riding bicycles—and was the father, perhaps, a little jealous of the boys?) he slapped her. She burst into piteous wails. Could a father do this, I wondered, if he really loved his daughter, if he saw her as a small person entitled to respect, rather than an aborted part of him, one minute plaything, the next, slave? I have seen many parents, I thought, act this way to their children, showing hunger one minute (why, you darling child, I adore you), slapping them the next (stop annoying me).

When I asked about this behavior, John said that the parent may often repulse the child because of guilt about his sexual feelings toward the child.

"This inconsistency may tear little children to emotional pieces, for the children blame themselves for the rejection," he said.

(Children are extremely sensitive, I thought, but at the same time, nature makes it possible for them to withstand a large amount of cruelty before they crack.)

There is also a sexual hunger that denies affection, shown by the detached, repressed person afraid to express any feeling toward the child, John said. He shows his fear of sexuality by refusing to admit it exists, just as much a mockery of sex as excessive display. (Children of repressed parents may grow up as terrified as those whose parents devour them, emotionally speaking.)

Fear keeps people regressed at certain levels in their sexual development, John said. A frightened child will progress with difficulty to the next step of growth. Sometimes he will refuse to learn at all. If, because of fear, he is terrified of toilet functions, he will not only have trouble with them all his life but this fear will prevent his being able to cope easily with the rest of sexual development. If fear haunts one stage, it usually haunts them all.

The fear is followed by anger, then self-hatred. Some cannot even think of themselves as good enough for other people. They sink to what they feel is the level of animals, not daring to believe they deserve to be identified with the human race.

I dreamed once that I kissed a dog, told this to John in shocked tone.

"Don't feel ashamed," he reassured me. "Yours is only a dream. Some people actually have sexual intercourse with animals. They do not feel worthy of another person."

"Sometimes I don't feel worthy of living," I confessed.

"That's because there was so much fear in your life," he said. He added as though to himself, "Some people think starving is the worst thing in the world. I'm trying to do something about what I think are worse things—fear and hatred."

Everything is appropriate in degree and this holds true for sexual feeling, also, John kept reminding me, over and over. A certain amount of fear, a certain amount of sexuality, a certain amount of everything that exists. It is only when excessive fear is present that feelings loom disproportionate.

But no matter how afraid some of us are of sex, he reassured me, instincts, like a river, will flow on in spite of obstacles. When fear obstructs childhood, as rocks obstruct the middle of a river, the instincts, like the water, will flow around. But in so doing, they will create sound and fury, just as water does.

132

Many of us, because of our fear, become noisy about sexual feelings, I thought. The boisterous laughter at jokes about sex, the unabashed public prying into the sexual life of others as blatantly tabloided, the Winchellian column—these point to fear of sex. Those who accept sex casually and quietly feel no need to dramatize it in their own lives or in the lives of others.

Look at the time and energy spent in our culture in the telling of dirty jokes, I thought. Our laughter at them is one way of relieving inner fear about sex. The man who spun the world's first dirty joke possibly possessed a shade more fear than his contemporaries who, perhaps, did not need to make fun of sex. By analyzing the subjects that draw shamed laughter, we may find out what we most wish and then, because it is forbidden, fear.

Many verbal slips are of a sexual nature. An actress once entered a room intending to greet merry-makers with, "Hello, fellow thespians!" Instead she said gaily, "Hello, fellow lesbians!" The word "fork" has always frightened me because I am afraid one day I am going to say, instead, a word that sounds like it.

One of my expressions of fear of sex was to pretend noisily not to care. I dressed sloppily; a way of saying, "See? I don't care about my body," whereas, underneath, I cared deeply.

I was too afraid of sexual feelings to find jokes about sex funny. The humor that appealed to me was less dangerous to my psyche. My favorite type of joke was the cartoon, humor safe enough to be pictured.

One of my favorite cartoons shows a man rowing a small boat head-on into an ocean liner. A woman companion screams: "Look out, you'll run into that big boat!" The oarsman, stubbornly pulling harder than ever in the path of the liner, replies: "Let him look out. I've got the right of way." (Perhaps I laugh because this represents what I felt my parents were always doing, pulling full speed ahead on what I considered a disastrous course. I wished I could laugh instead of feeling it was a matter of life and death.)

Another pictures a sailboat with a man standing in the prow, hopelessly tangled in canvas and rope as he tries in vain to hoist sail. He calls out to three guests sitting in the stern laughing at him: "Believe it or not, this isn't as simple as it looks." (That is how I feel about life; I am tangled up, while onlookers laugh and insist, "It's really very simple." I wish I could reply, "It isn't as simple as it looks." I cannot laugh at my own absurdity but I can laugh at the absurdity of the man in the cartoon.)

In another two fishermen cast in a stream. The figure of a bear stands in the background, one hand on hip, the other planked against a tree. One fisherman whispers to the other: "It's the game warden. He thinks nobody'll notice him." (I chuckle at the game warden whose disguise is showing, hoping mine is not.)

Unconsciously I have selected cartoons that relate to water in some form. In my life, water symbolizes much feeling. My dreams overflow with oceans, rivers, streams, lakes.

"What does water mean to me?" I asked John.

"What do you think about when you think of water?" he replied.

"I like water because when I'm on my father's boat I have so much fun; my father likes water, too, he always seems relaxed on the water, he always likes me on the water, I wish that I could spend my whole life on the water." For years I joked that I intended to marry a tugboat captain so I would never have to give up the sea. My father and I and the sea—we are all caught together in my fantasy.

The sea symbolized my sexual feelings; to it I also transferred feelings of danger (sex was dangerous, the sea was dangerous). I thought of the sea and felt like crying. I thought of sex and tears came to my eyes.

I feared my sexual feelings not only for the opposite sex but also my own. Homosexuality raised its misunderstood head.

John shocked the primness in me by asking casually if I ever had any physical contact with a girl.

"Heavens, no!" I exclaimed, horrified. "I couldn't even bear touching a woman by mistake."

I disliked women and that was that (as if that was not enough). I wanted no part of them (little realizing I also disinherited myself). I did not like boys, either, I realize now.

134

I minded them less than girls but I lacked fondness for them as human beings. I could care about no one because I could not care about myself.

No wonder college held some of the miserable moments of my life. Catapulted from the warming world of tomboy into an icy all-girl world, I could think of no greater torture. Many nights I lay on my collegiate bed of psychic pain wishing my appendix would burst or that I would flunk out so I might go home. Homesickness is natural but my longing throbbed too deep. I was too frightened to accept independence.

I managed, nonetheless, to acquire several girl friends. I did not sink to the desperation of one girl at college, another who liked baseball. Our freshman year we listened to the World Series of 1938, eagerly cheering on the Giants who, that season, believe it or not, won the pennant.

During sophomore year I saw less of her, occupied as I was with romance and the need to study. One day another student remarked, "It's too bad about your friend," mentioning her name.

"What's the matter?" I asked, alarmed.

"She's had a nervous breakdown and her family put her in a sanitarium," she said.

"Good Lord," I gasped. I never thought anyone that young would go out of her mind.

After college I buried distaste for women as I latched on to a career. I lived more quietly with my hatred.

One evening while covering a national conference of social work in Cleveland I decided to seek entertainment with a masculine friend of mine, a male psychiatric social worker.

"Where'll we go?" I asked.

"Let's see a burlesque show," he said.

"I've never been!" I was shocked. "Besides, that's for men."

"A lot of women go," he insisted. "It will do you good if you've never seen one. After all, it's Americana."

He literally dragged me, fur coat and all, to the small theater. As he paid the entrance fee I stared in disgust at lobby photographs showing glamorous women half-draped in silk.

"Whatever he's paying, he's getting gypped," I thought.

I skulked down the aisle, hoping to high heaven no one else

from the conference was stupid enough to be there (so they would not see me, of course). I crouched low in a seat, with effort forced myself to look at the stage.

A dark pretty girl with flowing hair, wearing black brassiere and panties, was weaving her curved body in a strange, primitive fashion. Drums beat out a provocative rhythm. A clarinet caressed the low notes of *Mood Indigo*.

My disgust suddenly turned into another feeling—envy. Imagine feeling free enough, I thought, to appear on a stage and express how you felt. I lacked the courage to stand up and seduce openly, like Gypsy Rose Lee. Mine was a more devious, cowardly display of self—intellectual exhibitionism.

After the show, my escort turned to me and asked, "How did you like it?"

I felt I owed him honesty. "It was very interesting," I admitted. "I was fascinated in a way."

"By what?" he asked.

"By the dancing and the music," I said hastily. I did not feel like going into detail.

"That all?"

"And by the reaction of the audience. I was watching their faces. They certainly couldn't keep their eyes off the women."

"And you, too, perhaps, couldn't?" he said.

"What?" I turned in anger. "Why should I be interested?"

"Why not?" he said. "You're human. Aren't you interested in your own body and the bodies of other women?"

He made what I thought was a perceptive remark. "All week I've been listening to learned papers delivered by experts and almost everyone refers to our vast 'body of knowledge.' Don't you think people would be happier if they admitted they were really more interested in 'knowledge of body'?"

That night in bed I wondered about my feelings toward women. Did my hatred and disgust mask other feelings? John said disgust was fear, disguised. What disgusted me? Could it be the very things I desired but which I felt were evil and might destroy me?

I could not bear to kiss a woman on the lips although I could very easily kiss men. I turned my cheek when women

136

kissed me hello or goodbye. Could it be I was afraid because actually I wanted their kisses so very much (just as when I was little, I yearned for Mother to kiss me and reassure me, instead of being so busy all the time with the other children and the thousand-fold duties of her private life)?

My dreams occasionally showed hunger for women's caresses. In one my sister Sue and I ran out of our house, fleeing disaster. I turned to see the house in flames.

"Stop, Sue," I gasped. "We're safe. It's all gone."

She fell down to the ground, exhausted. I sank down beside her. "Are you all right?" I asked.

She started to cry. I put my arms around her to comfort her. This feels good, I thought. I hugged her tighter. Then I kissed her on the lips. This will help her, I thought. She needs love.

I was embarrassed to tell John about this dream. "I've never kissed Sue on the lips in my whole life." I added in wonder, "And why should it be Sue? I always thought I liked Sally better."

"I get the feeling from you that you're more comfortable with Sue than anyone else in your family," he said. "Therefore, in your dreams it is logical she is the one you would feel safe enough to love."

All of us go through a homosexual stage in growing up. Some who are frightened remain at this level, where they fear members of the same sex less than they do those of the opposite, more dangerous sex, John said. Men who need men and women who need women are settling for the lesser of their fears. Men who are homosexual fear men less than they do women (terrorized by their mothers). At the same time, their inner need for a woman is desperate, for they have been even more deprived of a good mother-son relationship than the man able to indulge in normal sexual relations. Both their need for women and their hatred of women are intense; they are truly among the troubled. Women who are attracted to women fear women less than they do men. Their relationship to their father held terror, and, afraid of men, they stay in the safety of women.

"Homosexuality, like other symptoms of unhappiness, indicates lack of mother-love," John said. "A girl, in homosexual fantasy, longs for the warmth of the mother's body. A boy, rejected by his mother, takes his father unconsciously as mother substitute."

Because of fear, society makes cruel fun of homosexuality, I thought. In this country we treat people who indulge in it almost as criminals. We are too afraid to look closely, to recognize it as sickness, just as tuberculosis or cancer is sickness.

Perhaps, some day, I thought, enough people will accept their own feelings so that they will no longer be frightened of homosexuality.

We pay a pretty price for our collective fear of sexuality, in dollars and cents as well as psychologically, for the cost of maintaining our mental hospitals and jails is staggering.

Society expects some to live without sex, both inside and outside institutions. When we punish criminals, unconsciously are we not wreaking on them the worst punishment of which we can conceive—depriving them of normal sexual relations? We become horrified when we hear that homosexual practices take place in prison (they exist in every large prison) and yet do we stop to think where these men are to put their sexual feelings? Would we rather they kill each other or themselves, as some do? The answer, alas, from many of us would be yes.

When I visited a reformatory in Massachusetts recently, where young women were serving sentences ranging from one to five years for such "crimes" as alcoholism, adultery, cohabitation and abortion, I protested to John against the persecution of these women for indulging in acts that thousands of women perform daily without ever "serving time." I was also angry because these girls were too poor to hire lawyers.

"Many women never land in prison because they can pay to keep out," I stormed. "It isn't fair. I feel as guilty as some of those girls. But I could afford to keep out of jail."

"It isn't the money," John said quietly. "Someone wrote, 'There but for the grace of God, go I.' He did not say, 'There but for money go I.' "

Some go to prison, he said, because unconsciously they seek to be punished. Some of these girls could have moved to

138

blue-law-less states or avoided getting into situations they knew would put them in prison.

Our criminals are often those who, underneath, have the strongest consciences, he held. They rebel partially in order to be found out and punished, not for a specific crime alone, but for what they feel is their crime of living.

I admitted that I felt some of the women seemed almost to enjoy being in prison, as though grateful for this chance to atone. I thought of one who appeared cheerful even though she faced the next five years locked up for the crime of abortion.

"That's a pretty stiff sentence," I said to her, thinking of women who suffered abortion without the extra punishment of going to jail.

"I don't mind taking my medicine," she said. "In fact, I feel better now that I'm here. I'm making up for the crime I committed."

She added, with nervous laugh, "It will be good not having a man around. Then I won't be tempted."

"Why were you tempted in the first place?" I asked.

"Because sex seemed all-important at the time," she said.

Unhappy people put so much emphasis on sex because sexuality is the core of life, and as unhappiness represents an unconscious threat to life they will often seize sex when they feel threatened, John said. They may grab at it wildly and blindly, not ever enjoying it but "using" it to save their lives, or they may go to the other extreme and refuse to indulge in it.

He mentioned a young man who claimed his ambition in life was "to screw every dame in the world." He added, with a laugh, "He hasn't quite made it." This boy, he explained, was, in a sense, fleeing from parents who had been very seductive toward him and, at the same time, was trying to rid himself of fear and guilt about sex.

The happy person (the emotionally well one) settles for one mate, John said. He will know that he may be attracted to others but it will not be a matter of life and death to him that he "possess" them.

Promiscuity is for the perplexed then, I thought.

Because of my fear I projected sexual feelings into the cinema world of Cinderella, using the substitute love that bombards us in movies, books, theater and song. That was what the lowdown blues (adjective well chosen) meant to me; when I heard them, I could revel in abandon, yet not feel too wicked.

The substitute love possesses little relation to reality but it exists because of the need for it by those, like me, who can bear sexual feeling no other way. Some of us, thus, can continue to dream and, for the moment, forget fear. Such solace is of no small measure to those who see the world as frightening.

Slowly, I started to feel that if I could not accept the right to my body as pleasurable, surely I could not accept anything else as pleasurable. Because this most pleasurable of pleasures held for me the connotation of "sin," pleasures in milder form also had taken on the tinge. I had difficulty at times enjoying myself at the theater because I felt I must continually punish myself for daring to feel pleasure in anything.

"Only the emotionally ill carry the fear of sexuality into adulthood," John warned.

Just as all living should be easy and relaxed, so should the feeling toward sex. The song, *Take It Easy*, with the sympathetic advice, "And if you can't take it easy, take it easy as you can," goes for life, goes for love, I thought, as contrasted with many of our jazz lyrics which mirror need rather than love: *I Wanna Be Loved, Someone to Watch Over Me* and *You've Got Me Crying For You*. This is talk not of giving but getting. It represents fear of sex by and for people who are too frightened to see that love, like the tortoise, is slow and sure, while hunger, like the hare, dances in haste and loses the race.

I had to relinquish my concept of "love," the one picked up in childhood when, at the age of twelve, I read every lurid romance magazine I could beg, steal or buy with pennies. Love was good, true and beautiful—sex, evil and black.

Love actually held in it many of the feelings of living of which one was sexual feeling. If my life could become happier, sex would take its appropriate place with all other feelings. But if I continued to be unhappy I was apt to give sex more than its due.

140

Chapter XI

OPHELIA IN SLACKS

JOHN SAT AS QUIET RECIPIENT for my despair as I wailed time and again, "I feel so full of misery."

He would answer softly, "You've got to face your unhappiness to be happy. You cannot rid yourself of the truth of the past."

I had been trying to deny my childhood. I had to accept it so I could stop living in the first years of my life.

"You have not really learned much since you were six," John said. "Unhappy adults live and die with the same feelings they had as unhappy children unless they face themselves."

If this be paradox, make the most of it, but I found I could not face fear until I felt safe, and I had to feel safe in order to know how frightened I was. It took a long time before I could know, "I am scared to death of life. How have I had the temerity to live on earth this long?"

I had been so frightened that not for a moment could I have known how deeply frightened or I might have been lost. It had always been less dangerous for me to assume I was not afraid and could lick the world than to admit my terror.

But it was only by knowing how frightened I was that I could become strong. I had to feel fear and then try to help my body, as well as spirit, grow stronger.

To play good golf I had to feel free enough to put my whole body into the swing if I wanted to hit a strong, true ball that would steer a powerful, direct course. Now I had to feel free enough to put my whole body into living. I had to live physically, spiritually and intellectually, not disproportionately in one sphere at the expense of others, but in all three harmoniously.

First, I had to stop trying so hard. "If you did not try so hard, you'd feel better," John told me.

"Me not try hard?" That was a laugh. All my life I had tried hard in the best of American tradition. Do or die. Get in there and win. Give it all you've got. Now or never.

But often the times I tried hardest I failed. Like on the golf course when I desperately wanted to show off for my father in front of a gallery of his golfing friends.

Nightmares still place me on the first tee of our golf club, often used for national tournaments as one of the most difficult courses in the East. The green of the first hole, a tricky par five, sits on a hill off to the right, encased in sand traps. Dear God, I would pray, as I staggered up to drive, please let me get through this first shot and I'll be a good girl for the rest of the week.

I would grit my teeth, tense my body and swing blindly at the ball. Usually I would either hook it into the rough at the left or top it, to watch it dribble disconsolately a few feet away.

"Poor father," I would moan. "Club champion, with a daughter who cannot hit to save her life. I've disgraced him again."

But he never scolded. He might make a face in jest, then show me what I did wrong. He seemed to enjoy my company on the course.

It had never occurred to me trying too hard might bring failure. I was too frightened to know those who feel no need to be first may really be the first. All my self-conscious strivings to beat others brought little satisfaction.

"Life is too hard," I complained to John.

"It doesn't have to be," he said gravely.

I looked at him as though he were crazy. Could life ever be easy for people?

"I must be awful dumb," I sighed.

"Not dumb, just confused," he kindly corrected me. "A lot of things are all mixed up in your life."

I felt better only with him. I could not even interpret a dream until I told it to him.

"What happens here that allows me to understand things I cannot understand any other place?" I asked.

"You are less afraid here."

"But I am afraid of you," I protested.

"But less than of yourself."

"You let me complain and get angry," I said. "No one ever did that. I'm very grateful."

"I want you to see what lies before your eyes," he said.

Literally I did not look. At times I would search in frenzy for my fountain pen. "Who the hell has taken it, now?" I would rage (blaming someone, anyone).

Then I would discover it on the desk. My fury had kept me from seeing what lay before my eyes.

I had to remember to try to observe what exploded inside me. Not inside U.S.A. or Inside Asia or inside others, but inside me.

"Look at Lucy, not at everyone else," John urged. "You have been running so you would not meet yourself."

After a week's absence from New York I raced from the train, snagged a taxi and headed for John's office.

I'm usually returning from a conference in some analyst-forsaken city, I thought. But this time a number of analysts came to the city to attend the annual convention of the American Psychiatric Association.

"Did you have a good time?" John asked as I rushed in.

"I had a fine time," I said heartily, lying through my trembling teeth but determined to prove I could enjoy myself with two thousand psychiatrists other than he.

I told him that one of the nation's most prominent psychiatrists took me to lunch, that I induced the retiring president, who said he did not know how, to dance with me at the annual ball, and that I was kissed good-bye by a third psychiatrist.

He said nothing.

I gave up and lit a cigarette. I stared at the picture facing me. Even flowers on the wall, I thought scornfully.

"I'm bushed," I sighed. "I can't sleep on those stupid trains." I had tossed away the night.

I added, hoping it would please him, "I guess I'll live, though." I knew he wanted me to lose my unconscious fear of dying.

He was silent, waiting for me to go on.

"What is there about a stinking train that upsets me so?" I demanded.

He kept quiet.

I guess he wants me to talk to myself, I thought. If he has anything to say, I suppose he will say it. ("Guesses" and "supposes" cluttered my mind, the apology of the unsure for being alive.)

"I suppose it's being closeted in a little space," I said, to say something. "It's certainly a desperate feeling. I feel as if any moment I'm going to scream."

John said quietly, "Can you hear yourself talk? Can you feel the drama in what you say and the way you exaggerate?"

Tears came to my eyes. "Do you have to criticize when you know I'm so beat?" I exclaimed. "You really are a bastard!"

Then I held my breath, waiting for the blow. I had never dared call anyone that. If I had tried it on my father, I'm sure he would have broken my audacious neck. If I had not felt so irritable from the sleepless night the word would not have escaped me. What would John say?

He merely commented in gentle voice, "Where else but here are you going to learn to know yourself?" by-passing my wrath as if it were a puff of smoke.

"I don't want to know myself," I said angrily. Then I thought, in alarm, I hope he knows I don't mean this.

I felt ashamed I cursed him. I apologized. "I don't want to get angry at you."

I wish I knew what I felt about him, I thought. He seemed different from all others I had met. He asked nothing of me except that I keep looking into myself. He wanted me to like myself, too—the strangest idea of all.

I would not believe him when he said he liked me. "You tell that to all your patients," I jibed.

"I wouldn't keep a patient I didn't like," he said. "I tried it once or twice but it didn't work out."

Hatred had no home with John. His seemed a room of peace and understanding. In it I could admit crazy dreams, stealing, murder. He would not strike me or tell me to shut up. Quite the contrary; he encouraged me to face feelings I had always been told were evil.

"I accept you as you are," he said. "That's what you've wanted all your life, isn't it? To be accepted uncritically, so you do not have to pretend."

144

We who are troubled want someone to take us as we are, I thought. We need someone to encourage us to take courage. Only an analyst will do this.

First and foremost I felt John was a friend. I said to him, "You're more friend than doctor."

"The doctor who is not a friend is not a very good doctor," he replied.

It was important I like John. If a patient does not like his analyst, I thought, he might just as well pitch his money off the Empire State Building and let the winds give it a good blow to sea.

Months flew by before I could allow myself to know what I felt about him. Part of me liked him but another part could not afford to trust him even though he was proving to be the most gentle person of my life.

I was still too frightened to accept him as doctor. I kept calling him John instead of "doctor" or "doc" as other patients did.

I wanted to please him as I wanted to please everyone. I felt I must humor and amuse him. He cannot want to hear my tale of misery even if he *is* being paid for it, I would think. (I paid more after the first year. I could afford $15 a session, following a raise.)

Sometimes I found myself challenging him. I would, in essence, sneer, "Help me if you dare." I wanted help from no one. It was difficult to believe people wanted to help, not hurt.

The part of me that could not trust kept using him as target for questions. I found out his father had been a schoolteacher. His mother, a religious woman, wanted him to be a minister (he chose a different way of helping people). He was one of thirteen children brought up on a farm in Canada. The family was poor so he worked his way through college and medical school.

As time went on I started to feel more deeply toward him. I found it hard to exist until the moment I could see him. I had to confess to myself my feelings for him were more personal than any woman had a right to feel for her doctor.

I desired him ardently. I wanted to be his slave, mistress, friend—anything to be with him. I dreamed we embraced warmly. I would wake filled with longing. It quickly turned to despair when I realized all was but a dream.

A slip of the tongue betrayed me, to my dismay. One morning I started to say I wanted to give up seeing a man because I felt the relationship was not happy.

"I've given up . . ." I began, intending to name the man. The name that burbled out was "John."

"What have I said?" I moaned. I said what I meant. Underneath I wanted John.

At first I was so ashamed I could not mention even the dreams. After the intensity of my feelings started to frighten me, I summoned courage to tell him at least of a dream.

I started out with a gulp. "I had a strange dream last night." Silence. More silence.

"It was about you." I was still caught in the feel of it, his arms tight around me.

"Tell me about it," he said evenly.

I wanted to cry out, can't you love me a little? Can't you see I'm perishing for want of you?

"Oh, I just dreamed we were making love," I said casually, tossing it off as if it were no different from eating ice cream together. (See later, what eating ice cream meant to me!)

"What you feel for me, you realize, is what you really feel for your father," he said quietly. "It's your father you have wanted all these years."

"It's *you* I want," I said stubbornly. He could not tell me for whom I yearned. "What I feel for you *isn't* what I feel for my father."

"You transfer to me the feelings you have for him," he went on, not heeding my opinion. "That is also what you have been doing with the other men in your life."

I would not believe him. I fought the idea with every defense in my body. It was repulsive, repugnant, indecent. I dismissed it completely each time he suggested it.

Dreams, again, helped point the way to truth. They were disturbing dreams, difficult to accept. But, as John reminded me and, as I could not deny, my dreams were me (a thousand times, sometimes, was not often enough reminder).

My father appeared in shadowy, desire-dreams. In one, I

146

snatched him away from the squalling family, rushed him out of the half-red, half-white house with its thousands of strangling trees.

"Where are we going?" he asked.

"You'll see," I reassured him.

I pulled him up a gangplank. We boarded an ocean liner.

"Where's the luggage?" he shouted.

"We don't need luggage," I muttered. We had each other.

The spacious liner stretched out for miles. I took my father by the hand, led him to a hushed dining room where we ate in splendor and solitude. No family, no homework, no baseball —just my father and me, forever on the water, an all-masculine crew to do our bidding (no women in *my* top dreams!).

My father asked, "Where's your brother?"

"Where's your brother, where's your brother?" echoed the nightmare voice of a dream.

"He fell overboard," I explained. Thus I rid myself of a chief rival.

In another dream my father and I strolled along the green fairway of a golf course. I wore navy slacks, as I often did in reality.

A group of women neared us, all young and pretty.

"Yoo hoo," they flirted, waving at my father.

He waved back at them, smiling. (This often happened on the golf course.)

Then, I acted in the dream as I had never done in reality (although I must have felt like it). I arched my back like a cat. I hissed at the women.

They paid no attention, kept waving at my father.

"It's no use," I thought. "The cats won't listen."

(*I* hissed, yet thought of *them* as cats.)

"Go away," I said to them. "Go away and leave my father to me."

Although I could not admit it consciously, the dream showed how I felt toward the world—"go away and leave my father to me."

But I could confess to John with passion, "If my father ever dies, I want to die, too." Ophelia-like, I wanted no part of life if my father were not around. Ophelia's feelings for Polonius must have been just as strong as Hamlet's for his mother, for Ophelia had to go mad and then kill herself after her father's death.

My affectionate father seemed my oasis. He loved me more than Mother did, I felt. He combed out my tangled hair mornings before I went to school, tied ribbons on it to hold it neat. He spent his leisure time with me. Mother had little leisure.

Many weekends he would drive my brother and me to Lake Placid or Williamstown or Manchester.

"Those were wonderful times," I recalled ecstatically. "Just eating, sleeping, playing golf." (And me the only woman with two men.)

My father's firm, capable hands steered the car expertly around mountain curves, past silent lake or plunging waterfall. He drove at proper speed, not too fast to endanger us yet not so slow I felt restrained.

On these trips I always became excited. The excitement made me want to go frequently to the bathroom.

"You just went!" Dad would exclaim as I asked anxiously if he expected soon to pull up at a garage.

He would point to the gas gauge. "When that's empty we'll stop."

But any time I made enough fuss, he would find a garage.

My brother aided and abetted me, pretending he had to go, too. Later he would whisper he really did not. I was so grateful I did not mind when he defeated me on the golf course. He would have risen to club champion like my father if his temper had not interfered. At crucial moments he would wallop a ball into the woods or add four strokes in a snide sand trap. After that he was lost to anger for the day.

My father knew how bitterly I resented college. To make it more bearable he asked if I would like to spend a few weeks of one winter period in Florida, living in a trailer which he had just bought. The New York Giants could not have held me North.

I wrote the family an ironic description of life in a trailer.

> Dear Folks:
> In case any of you may be so deluded you are thinking of living in a trailer some day, let me warn against it.

Every morning at dawn Dad crashes out of the bedroom as it is laughingly called and squints at the Army cot from which emerges my nose. The rest of me lies under ten blankets, for in this warm land the temperature drops fifty degrees when the owls come out.

He hauls the blankets away from my shivering shape, yells, "It's daylight!" I burrow into the sheets and murmur, "Go to hell."

"Get up, you lazy bum!" he shouts, knowing well the words I uttered (I yam my father's daughter). He kicks the Army cot out from under me. I must admit the floor feels softer.

"I'm going outside to fix the trailer and I expect you to have this place thoroughly cleaned and breakfast ready by the time I've finished," he announces. He exits, rocking the trailer so roughly that water spills out of the vase of red roses I placed atop Beard's *The Rise of American Civilization* (which I must read before I go back to college).

While the coffee percolates, I houseclean. I take each little rug (and the trailer is overrun with hundreds of lousy little rugs) by the corner and, holding my nose, heave it out the door with a vengeance. It is this vengeance that cleans. I sweep an unholy combination of fuzz from blankets, hairpins, face-powder and sand to the screen door where a gentle breeze wafts it back into the four filthy corners of the trailer. I would call the cleaning a success if I could ever beat the breeze, get one hairpin to clink outside. Then I beat the scatter rugs amid curses concerning the necessity of cleaning rugs to earn a B.A. degree.

Meanwhile Dad, with the aid of a neighbor whom he has awakened with his hammering, inserts a piece of wood under the trailer (heaven knows what he always finds to fix). The neighbor laughs in retributive glee for the awakening when the hammer slips.

I keep up a steady stream of calls for breakfast when I smell toast burning. Dad ignores them all. On my sixteenth yell he staggers into the trailer, dripping perspiration. In the meantime, of course, I have eaten all the breakfast (my appetite is ferocious after the housework). Dad sits down to drink cold coffee while I sullenly slap dishes in a pot filled with Florida water which smells as if it first ran through a sewer.

"You're the most impatient kid," he sighs. "Why can't you wait for me to eat?" Suddenly he screams, "Stop throwing the good china around!" This "good china" he has dug out of some dingy hardware store that has been using it to feed the cat.

"Stop screeching at me," I order. "You'll wake the whole camp."

He rises, knife in hand. I throw a piece of blackened toast at him and he uses the knife to butter it. He swigs the coffee, says, "I guess I'll get out the fishing tackle." He crawls under the breakfast table (the tackle is always underneath whatever article I am using). The rear end of his two hundred pounds sticks out in the air.

"Your law firm should see you now," I sneer, trying to get even with him for making me cook and houseclean. "You couldn't get a bum to give you a case."

He jabs himself with a fishing hook. I start to dash out the door with the breakfast garbage but don't quite make it. I trip over one of those darling little rugs, scattering garbage all over the trailer.

It is quite a vacation.

Love,

A Tired Trailerite

The letter was pathetic attempt to make fun of what I now know I felt as tragedy. Dad was thinking of remarrying, as he did several years later. I liked the woman he chose, for she was attractive and kindly to me. Unconsciously I wanted to pry him from Mother, yet I did not want another woman to have him. I could not afford to write seriously about these confused feelings which I would not face. I took out my anger by distorting the situation, as if by exaggerating some details, I minimized others.

I told John of this trip. I said, "Those were the good old days."

"Were they 'good' for you?" he asked.

Did not the nostalgia stem from recalling only the exciting moments, which had not brought real pleasure but only temporary relief from pain? The dangerous feelings (my anger at my father, envy of his women, hatred of myself) lay stored in the corners of my unconscious. They hid there, waiting for the day when, unless I faced them, they might grow intense enough to destroy me.

They were already strong enough to cause me to become sick with an illness that literally choked the breath out of me. They caused me to faint on the job, to lie quivering in fright at the darkness of night.

"What is it about the night that troubles you?" John asked. I often referred to its terror.

"I don't know. I just hate it!"

"What comes to you about the night?"

"I don't trust the lock on the door. Someone might break in. Someone might attack me." I repeated the word "attack." I added, "When I think of attack, I think of rape.

"Could it be I'm really afraid of rape?" I asked fearfully. I had thought it was burglary, but it seemed to be more than that.

"Possibly you also wish it," he suggested.

"Oh, no!" I exclaimed in horror. I accepted intellectually that the fear was also the wish, but I felt, in this case, I was not ready to take John's word. I was too willing to take his word for everything, I told myself, for that was how I got along in life. Never quarrel with the other fellow so you will avoid a fight (at the same time part of me never believed what anyone said about anything).

"Just who are you afraid is going to rape you?" John asked.

"A man," I said weakly. "He has no face or figure." My fear, though ever-present, was undefined.

"You do not fear an abstract," said John. "You fear the first man you knew."

Was he trying to make me believe the man I feared was my father? Preposterous. My father adored me and I adored him. I could never see enough of him. When I was with him I felt I did not need a firecracker to make me clap for joy; internal firecrackers exploded loudly and gaily.

"I'm not afraid of my father," I said scornfully. "My stomach quivers because I get so overjoyed when I'm with him."

"That's a sexual feeling," John said.

"Excitement is sex?" I was stunned.

"Although not localized, excessive excitement has sexual overtones," he said.

"But you've made me feel there is nothing wrong with sex," I said in surprise.

"There isn't, when kept in its appropriate place," he replied.

"My father loved me; he would never frighten me," I insisted.

"Was it a consistent love?" John asked.

Not always, I had to admit. I thought of one night at the dinner table. I liked our dining room better than any other in the house. Set in a corner opposite the parlor and sun porch, its six windows looked out on tall fir trees that cut off all view of street and neighbor. It was the one spot we gathered at least long enough to eat. (Our family possessed much of the spirit of *You Can't Take It With You,* each one going off in his own frenetic direction).

Meals were usually accompanied by the radio's full blast. Almost every room, except the bathrooms, boasted a radio. "What, no radio?" we exclaimed to my little sister when she became old enough to listen to her own type of programs, and we went out and bought her a small radio.

This was one of the many nights we tuned to Amos 'n Andy. Their complicated lives formed a far more important part of my childhood than the multiplication table.

I remember my voice rising over the Kingfish as I argued with my father. (I believe I was upholding the efficiency of the Communist method of government. I have since changed my mind about the value of efficiency if other qualities are missing.) I knew I should not antagonize my father. He worked hard all day, earning money so he could feed and clothe us. Also, he was famous for a quick temper which accompanied his red-blond hair. Usually calm, he might indulge in a sudden violent emotional storm, followed immediately by sunny smiles, a cajoling manner.

In spite of these excellent reasons to the contrary, I kept arguing.

Suddenly, "Don't talk back to me!"

Before I could stop it (somehow, too, I did not want to stop it) his hand cracked across my face. It was not a hard slap, but it felt like a sharp knife twisting away in my heart with bottomless hurt.

My brother stared at his plate, embarrassed for me. My youngest sister flashed a glance of approval; she could storm back at our parents with comparative ease. I stood up, tears flowing, raced from the table. I don't remember where Mother was (it has been easy for me to serve anger by blocking her out of the picture; I have a feeling she came to my rescue more times than I want to remember).

"How could he?" I sobbed as I ran upstairs.

I slammed the door of my room, wishing I could die. I stormed, "I hate him for humiliating me this way."

I sobbed now, in the analyst's office, loosing tears of betrayal carried through the years. I blew my nose several times.

I felt as though one of my psychic props had been knocked from under me. It pained me to remember Dad had slapped me at times. Oddly enough, part of me felt he was entitled to slap me if he wished, because, at bottom, he loved me and I loved him. (Mother had no right, but *he* might slap.)

"Shouldn't a child love a parent?" I asked sadly.

"It is all right to love but not to be in love with a parent," John said. "You sound as though you idolize your father. In idolatry there is fear."

Men who bow down before idols fear them, he said. Because of their dread of the wrath that these idols may show, they must keep reassuring the idols of their adoration. But all the while they resent such slavery.

"You get angry at your mother easily, but I am not aware of much anger for your father," John said.

"I'm not angry at him, that's why." The answer was obvious to me.

"I doubt that," he said. "You're angry at everyone. Your anger at your father is more deeply buried, and for that reason, more destructive to you."

Terror lurked in my deep attachment for my father, he meant, a terror more subtle than that I felt toward Mother. Worship contained its share of rage.

I realized while I had defied my father in intellectual arguments I never dared to go against his wishes or to express anger toward him personally. I felt almost paralyzed in his presence.

"My father seemed to need me," I protested to John. I always felt he needed me far more than Mother did.

"He needs support, not an idolatrous support, but a quiet support."

"I ain't quiet," I said sullenly.

"But you're getting quieter," he reassured me.

I'm sounding louder in my own ears, I thought. I would walk the street mumbling, "John's crazy as far as this Oedipus business goes. He may be right about everything else but not this." Freud was crazy, too, and Shakespeare.

I could look at fathers fondling small daughters and be aware of the subtle physical feelings between the two. But I was loath to admit such feelings once might have existed between my father and me. We were different. He was my life-line. (That some fathers might be a rope towing children to sea, rather than to shore and safety, never occurred to me.)

It is all right to hug your father, kiss him, get into bed with him on cold mornings and snuggle up to him, when you are a little girl. Except, when you are an unhappy little girl you want more and you cannot cope with the difference between right and wrong. You know only what you feel and what you feel is what you want.

But when you get a little older the feeling becomes more dangerous. There is a difference between fondling a six-year-old and an eleven-year-old, as parents know. Some parents cannot stop. One case stood out in my horror-stricken mind (and I had to ask myself why) the day I spent in Children's Court. Two weeping girls confessed their father had slept with them. The mother stood to one side screaming, "He's crazy, he's crazy! And my boy, if he hadn't gone to the Army, his father would have ruined him, too." Society's taboos had not held for these people, for they were too frightened to be able to reason.

"Why the taboo against incest?" I asked John (still seeking the "why" to relieve pain).

"Probably as protection to the survival of the human race," he said. "Incest would weaken the race."

Incest, one of the world's first taboos, echoing out from the darkest jungle, was a tough thing to face. John reassured me that everyone has incestuous feelings to some degree. If people did not feel like committing incest there would be no need for the taboo. Taboos and laws are based on what people may want to do but, for the good of society, are forbidden—incest, murder, stealing.

The Oedipus desire in moderation is natural, he said. But it becomes excessive, turning to hunger, when fear intensifies the feeling.

John could say to me, when he deemed the time right, "You cannot have your father. You are no longer a little girl."

You cannot have your father.

Those five words infuriated me more than all others. It was as though John attacked the only support I possessed.

I don't have to lie here and take this, I thought. I don't want my father the way he means. I haven't stayed at home and mourned because first Mother had him and now he is married to another woman. I have gone out with other men.

But I did feel I acted a part with others. Life sparkled as one long drama with me as heroine, only it never turned out like the movies. When a man tried to get close, I would want to escape. I felt revolted, ashamed of knowing him.

While out with other men sometimes I felt untrue to my father. In my child-mind trembled the fear that Daddy would not like it (the hope, too, that Daddy would not like it).

"Little girl, you're the one girl for me." That tune often spun through my head. Snatches of songs I remembered held meaning to me, I knew. Is that what I wanted my father to say?

And when I couldn't have him, I turned to my brother and when I couldn't have my brother, I turned to another and another. Everybody and nobody. Because the one I really wanted as a child I could not have. Society said so. John said so. You cannot have your father. You will never reach the promised land.

I really never had understood (the brain of me did, but

not the heart) why I could not have him. I was furious because he would not and could not belong to me.

Some girls get so angry they become promiscuous, refusing to settle for any one man, John said. Such girls want only one man—their father.

I asked about a friend's comment. She said, "If a woman wants a baby enough, she shouldn't care who the father is, she should just go ahead and have the baby."

"In such an instance, I would think the woman cared very much who the father was," John remarked. "Unconsciously she wants it to be her own father." Women who bear illegitimate babies unconsciously may be having their father's child, he added.

Real love may exist between parents and children if they will face feelings about each other, John said. It is more likely to develop between grandparents and grandchildren because of less guilt feelings—the incest factor is once removed. (My grandmother could hug and kiss me with less guilt than could my mother or father.)

Perhaps it was time to say to myself: Away with the frozen smile, the breathless gasp, the whispered words, not one of which you mean. Know the truth. Know why you flee a lasting relationship with one man.

I had to forsake fantasies of life with Father, know that dreams of sailing away with him no longer were appropriate.

As I understood I transferred my feelings for my father to John, I understood one of the important facts of life. I could not have John and I could not have my father. My father belonged to Mother or a reasonable facsimile thereof while John belonged to others.

The feeling established between John and me was part of the process known as "transference." To him I transferred all my conditioned reflexes of hate, hunger, prejudice, fear, shame, anger. I did this to a certain degree with everyone I knew. Most people, however, were not interested in what I felt except as it related to their own needs. But John asked me to pour out my soul so he could help me look at how I had lived or, rather, failed to live. As I could examine more how I felt toward him, I could know how I felt toward the world.

He, in turn, transferred to me the quality of peace and calmness. (Perhaps transference is not completely on the part of the patient, I thought. There may be a battle of transferences, with virtue, or the analyst, triumphant if the analysis is successful.)

My transference was profound because of the depth of my feeling for my father. (Other patients, including some of John's, have told me they did not feel so intense.) They even looked alike. Both had gray mustaches and expressive blue eyes that often held a twinkle.

I also had to address John by his first name, probably one of few patients to do this, just as I always called my father by his first name. It took several years of analysis before I could think of my father as "Father" or "Dad," just as it took years for me to think of John as a doctor who wanted me to face pain to free myself of deeper pain.

As with everything in the analysis, I accepted my feelings only when I felt ready. If they proved too dangerous I forgot them until the time I felt safer. I accepted only what I wanted to accept. John could not *make* me think or feel anything which I did not believe. The analyst cannot rush you if you will not be rushed—alas, poor analyst!

John knew I bestowed on him hunger I felt for my father. He knew that by wise use of aroused feelings, he might be able to instill enough trust in me so that eventually I would want to give up the feelings causing illness.

For John, whom I now thought I "loved" above all else, I would try "to do right"; reliving and relearning in the image of health just as once I learned for my parents in, perhaps, not so healthy a fashion.

Chapter XII

THE BRIDE WORE ORANGE BLOSSOMS

At long last I was able to get married.

The paper sent me to Dallas to cover an annual meeting of the American Association of University Women. On the third day of the convention we moved temporarily to Fort

Worth, the Dallas ladies generously permitting the rival sister city to act as hostess.

We returned to Dallas late that night, after barbecued spare ribs and carnival, to learn that two ships moored in Texas City, two hundred and eighty miles away, had burst into flames and exploded. The next morning I boarded a Navy plane flying plasma to the stricken city.

Roughly two hours later (and I mean roughly, for my stomach plummeted to earth ten minutes outside of Dallas) we landed on a small field near Texas City. We hitched a ride into the stunned little war-boom town. I talked to men bound in bloody bandages, numbed relatives of dead and missing, dazed owners of shattered stores. Then another reporter drove me to the Galveston Western Union Office, fourteen miles away. (Western Union office is home to tired reporters. All over the country I have found only courtesy and cheer on the part of managers and staff. This night in Galveston I marveled at the helpfulness and competence of employees who stood almost buried by the mound of press copy and telegrams, for everyone telegraphed because of a national telephone strike.)

Tired and sick at heart for the people of Texas City, I dashed off the story. Page by page, a clerk snatched it out of the typewriter so that it could be teletyped to New York in time for first edition.

I was lucky to locate a hotel room. I crawled into bed, emotionally and physically exhausted. I dozed, only to sit upright in bed at 3 A.M. An important fact suddenly registered in my feeble conscious.

I stumbled out of bed, groped for the carbon copy of the story I had filed. I moaned, "Oh, no!" I had written:

> Texas City, Tex., April 17. Terror-stricken Texas City today turned into a gray ghost town. House after house stood in splintered silence, deserted in destruction. In the shadow of the raging fires, a cow munched away at scrubby grass, no one around to milk him.

The "him" glared out like a bull in a china shop. I had insulted Mother Nature; even with cows my unconscious desire to ignore women prevailed. It was too late to phone a correction. The paper had hit the streets hours ago.

Dejectedly I crawled back to bed. I visualized *The New Yorker* quoting the sentence with the comment, "Isn't it about time city reporters learn the facts of life?"

(*The New Yorker* did cite the story a year later. It mentioned three stories by women reporters on our paper that won the annual New York Newspaper Women's Club awards. The first was this "on-the-spot report of the Texas City disaster," the second, an "eye-witness account of orphans and children in displaced persons camps" and the third, a column, "Cranberries for Dessert." *The New Yorker* called it "Anticlimax Departments." Perhaps *The New Yorker* should look to its unconscious needs, for is not food of prime importance to man?)

Somehow I slumbered. The next day held no time to worry about a mistake. I had to cover a mass memorial service on the football field at the town's edge for the five hundred who died.

I decided to walk to the field, first leisure in three tumultuous days. April in Texas felt like July in New York. I peeled off suit jacket, trudged along perspiring. My one suit reflected dirt, gore, coffee stains. I'm lucky it was black to begin with, I thought.

"You certainly don't look like a slick New York reporter," I told part of myself.

"You're not a reporter," said the other part.

"Oh, no? What am I?" asked the first.

"You're a woman," said the second.

The road curved. I faced a building that three days before served as a commercial garage. Now it held row after row of bodies, the identified and unidentified. Stretched out in death lay workmen of the piers, women and children who raced to the bay to watch the ship burn and were killed in the unexpected explosions; employes of the nearby chemical plant, trapped at work when it burst into the air.

A clump of pale pink flowers blossomed in the dusty road. I picked one and inhaled fragrance, trying to hold back tears.

One hour later 1,500 survivors stood on the field facing

159

the setting sun. They bowed heads beneath a sky black with billowing clouds of smoke. Two days after the disaster the pall still shadowed Texas City, pouring from flaming oil tanks set ablaze by the explosions.

Texans believe in keeping words to themselves. Each of seven speakers talked only a few minutes. One clergyman stood in silence, looking over the field, remembering, perhaps, that some who died had raced that field in pursuit of touchdowns.

The women wore slacks and cotton dresses. Some of the men had put on jackets for the first time in three days—they had been digging for bodies in their shirtsleeves.

Eyes which had seen only death, near-death and destruction now looked with wonder at a spectacular display of flowers. The wooden stadium flamed with the beauty of thousands of massed blossoms. Every town in Texas, through the Texas State Florists' Association, sent baskets, wreaths, plants. Almost every flower then in season in the United States bloomed in the brilliant banner that reached from goalpost to goalpost. Three large crosses flowered across the stadium, nailed to seats.

Until that moment I had not thought consciously of the risk taken by reporters. One or two received minor injuries. We all could have been caught if further explosions, which were expected, had occurred. We worried about danger after we wrote our stories, if we dared worry.

I prayed for those who died and those left behind. I also prayed for myself. "Please God, help these people who have lost their loved ones and bless those who have died. And please don't take life from me until I have shared it with someone I love."

The Lord seemed to answer the prayer immediately.

A young copy editor on the national news desk received my stories for editing and headlining when they reached New York. After I returned to the city room he walked over to my desk and shyly handed me some clippings.

"I thought you might not have seen all editions so I saved your stories for you," he said.

He added, "I also fixed the cow."

How nice of this young man to be so kind, I thought.

160

A few nights later I was playing bridge in the office. After supper, those of us with no assignment occasionally enjoyed bridge. A reporter might be typing out a story of a railroad strike or a gambling trial while several desks away a quiet bridge game progressed. Not so quiet, perhaps, when two prima donnas collided in erratic bidding.

I looked up from the game to see the young copy editor standing among the kibitzers. I stopped arranging cards to ask, "Would you like to take a hand?"

"No, thank you," he said.

"Pay attention to your cards," grumbled my partner. (Partners always wailed, "If you'd only concentrate, you'd make a good bridge player." If I could only concentrate, it would solve much, pard. That's me trouble.)

When I dared look up again, the young copy editor had disappeared. But he reappeared the same night the following week. (I learned later, one of his nights off). He waited until the bridge game ended.

"Would you like to go for a drink?" he asked.

"I'd love to," I said, thinking, He is tall, dark and handsome. This is just the way it happens in fairy tales.

We taxied to an East Side restaurant for drinks and late supper. We talked of the newspaper office, life outside it.

Several weeks and several dates later he asked me to marry him. I felt like Cinderella of the fourth estate.

I wanted to get married. No longer was I content to sell my birthright for a mess of anxiety.

I told John I felt free enough to try marriage. He rarely offered counsel, no matter how fervently I begged. He would reply, "How do *you* feel about it?"

But he suggested I delay decision on the marriage. "Why don't you wait a few months?" he said.

I abhorred the idea of waiting. I disliked living alone. The young editor seemed lonely, too. We appeared to be congenial. We shared in common the newspaper profession.

"I want to marry him right away," I insisted. "I cannot live without him."

Hunger, not love, but I could not know it yet.

"I guess marriage is more important to you than anything else," said John. He knew I was unable *not* to get married.

"Are you going to give me up if I get married?" I asked. Then I would not know what to do. I had heard that analysts do not allow patients while in analysis to take any serious step such as marriage or divorce.

"No," he said.

He is a peach, I thought. He is letting me have my cake and eat it, too. I will pay him back some day for being so understanding.

I wanted to elope. My fiancé asked I consider a wedding to which, at least, our families were invited. Part of me feared a large wedding. It would point up that I, the oldest, was the last of the four children to get married. Also, my mother and father, now divorced, had not spoken to each other in several years. I trembled at the thought of their meeting. On the other hand I knew they would probably be so proud I finally got married they would not object to entering the same room for the short ceremony.

But part of me wanted a large wedding to show the world I could get married. I now liked myself well enough to want to be star for a day. I thought, Even though I am the last, I am the only one to have a formal wedding. My brother eloped. Sally asked only the family and a few friends and Sue's ceremony was small, although the garden reception brought together a crowd.

I discussed with John the advantages of a formal wedding. He sensed I wanted one.

"Women who elope may feel sorry they didn't have a large wedding but women who have large weddings rarely feel sorry they did not elope," he said reassuringly.

Getting married meant facing another doctor for the blood test. I gritted my teeth, joked about it even though the needle prick threatened like a dagger wound.

"I probably won't pass and then the whole thing will be off," I said to Mother. She did not worry. She knew her daughter too well.

Mother shopped with me for wedding dress and trousseau. (In spite of my avowed independence, I wanted her with me at this crucial time. I felt I could not get through it without her.) She trudged with me from store to store until I finally found the kind of dress I wanted, princess style made of white satin.

We borrowed lace worn at her wedding from an aunt for whom I hold much affection. Using it for a halo headdress we bought a long, flowing veil to set it off. As I sat in the milliner's, fitting the cap, Mother suggested I also wear orange blossoms in my hair.

"That's too much," I said in disgust. How dreamy could a girl go?

"Please," she begged.

"No!" I was firm.

On my wedding day just before I dashed from the dressing room, Mother giggled and hauled out a few orange blossoms. She perched them behind my ear. I also wore others pinned to my slip, a gift from a friend who had worn them at her wedding. She had mailed them to me, knowing how much the marriage meant.

I had asked several childhood friends. One traveled all the way from Elizabethtown, New York, whose post office had received our steady exchange of letters for twenty years. Ginny came with her husband. "Don't get as drunk as I did at my wedding," she whispered. I recalled Ginny's marriage, at which I was a trembling maid of honor, when the champagne downed us all.

Mother poured some peppermint medicine down me to calm my nerves, she said. It had a soothing effect. As I left the dressing room, I felt quite possessed.

Possessed enough as I raced through the hall to whisper to a late arrival, one of our political reporters, "How are they doing?"

He knew what I meant. "It's all right—I can enjoy your wedding, now." he said. "The Dodgers won." That was the day of the famous Gionfriddo catch.

As I walked down the aisle on the arm of my father, I found an unexpected touch of comfort. A lovely four-year-old child named Sally, daughter of one of my copy-desk friends on the newspaper, jumped up in her seat as she saw me. She called out in delight, "Hello, Lucy!"

I thought, "She's glad to see me, bless her darling heart." I pulled in my stomach, remembered to stand straight.

I felt at ease before the rabbi, a friend of a friend who told me he would probably be in a hurry to get the ceremony over so he could play golf, for there were not many fall weekends left.

After the words were spoken, the young copy editor took me in his arms. We did not kiss—merely hugged each other tight. "Gee, you're a nice guy," I felt.

"It was a lovely wedding even if Mother and Father didn't say a word to each other," I said defiantly to John. I had been so busy accepting congratulations I had no time to watch them. My sisters told me later no words were exchanged.

I wanted my half-sister Alice, then eight, as flower girl, for I had promised her if I ever got married she might precede me down the aisle scattering rose petals. But I realized Mother might feel hurt. I trust Alice will forgive me and know my concern for Mother outweighed my own desire.

Alice, who truly is Alice in Wonderland, blond hair and quizzical manner, helped me conceive this book. When I told her I intended to write a book she asked, "What about?"

"Psychoanalysis," I answered.

"Phooey!" she retorted. "Write a murder mystery."

I started to think about that. Did I not feel my life held as much murder as the mystery books I hungrily devoured? If I were to write an honest book would it not have a little bit of murder in it?

"Thank you, Alice," I said. "You've given me an idea."

Alice enjoyed the wedding, flower girl or no, I am sure. She complained at not being allowed to drink more champagne but she said the food was excellent. My last glimpse of the guests in the Hotel Gotham reception room caught Alice eating a piece of wedding cake.

My husband allowed me to choose the destination of our honeymoon.

"New England," I said, without thinking. Associating, as usual.

164

Later, in telling this to John, I said in sudden alarm, "I think I know why I selected New England."

He waited.

"It's where my father usually took us on weekends," I muttered. "Unconsciously I still want to go away with Daddy—is that it?"

"If that's how you feel, that's it," he said.

The marriage did not last, for reasons that should be clear to anyone who has read this far. In getting married I was not fair to the young man or myself. I was not able to think clearly enough to avoid the error.

I rushed into marriage as I rushed into all else. "Please wait," friends and analyst begged, but I could not wait.

Many moments of misery culminated in two or three dramatic ones. One day my husband joined me in Atlantic City, where I was covering an American Hospital Association convention. (So many things seem to have happened in Atlantic City!) We were strolling along the boardwalk (as years before I strolled with my father and brother) when I said in high glee, "Let's have a chocolate soda!"

We had just consumed a large chop suey lunch but I had yet to file a story to New York. I needed the soda to give me energy to write, I rationalized.

"You're trying to lose weight, aren't you?" he asked.

"Ye--es," I agreed reluctantly. "But I feel like a soda."

"I don't think you should have one," he said. "We plan to eat a lobster dinner tonight at Hackney's and you've just eaten . . ."

"I know all that," I said sharply. "But I still feel like having an ice cream soda. A chocolate one, too." (Adding insult to injury).

"I don't think you should," he insisted.

If looks could kill, I would now be sitting in the electric chair. How could he do this to me, I stormed inside. My father never refused me a soda; he was always the one to suggest we stop. My brother bought me one any time I asked. And this—this *man*—possessed the effrontery to refuse me a slight but very important request (even though unreasonable).

He knew I was furious but did not give in. After I wrote

my story, he said humbly, "If you want a soda, we'll get one."

"Thank you, no." I would have died of thirst first.

We bought a new, five-room house in Westchester. I enjoyed furnishing it in modern style with streamlined chairs, sofas, lamps. We shopped for the latest in refrigerator and stove. Set in an acre of wooded land, the little house (half brick, half-wood, split, just like the house in which I grew up) looked comfortable and cheerful.

I even gained courage to purchase a plant for the parlor. I always envied those who dared grow plants inside a house. As a child I drew rage for every scrap of soil I tracked into the house. (Keep your muddy feet out of this house!)

But John grew luxurious plants of all sizes and colors in his apartment. I stared wistfully at the strawberry-shaped red fruit of the pepper plant; the exotic rose-centered leaves of the jungle plant; the shiny leaves of the rubber plant. Maybe I could try one small ivy plant, I thought.

Feeling adventurous one day, I drove to a florist and bought two ivy plants to hang on the wall.

My husband helped me nail them up. I watered them carefully every day in spite of his warnings I would kill them with watery kindness. They thrived on the water. Each one must have been as thirsty a plant as I was hungry a human. They flourished long and graceful, swept to the floor. I was proud of my achievement. I had helped something to grow.

One night I came home to find only a few short, ugly snouts in the pots.

"What happened to my plants?" I gasped to my husband. "Did you throw them out?"

"I cut them," he said. "They were too long."

He cut them, I thought in despair. He threw away the plants I guarded and cherished. If he cared for me he could not have killed the plants.

Love me, love my plant. Kill my plant, kill me. In my terror I could not know a plant was but a plant. No material thing should mean that much to anyone, and yet, if you feel you cannot love people, you must love some *thing*. Afraid of people, I placed love on objects. I saved scrapbooks and stamps as if they were part of me, to prove I really existed.

The plants never grew again. They turned brown, died.

I became more and more depressed. On days off I would sit staring out the large picture window into the woods beyond. Here I looked out at woods, as in childhood. I felt just as lost as when I was four.

My husband worked late and I would ride alone to Rye a few hours before he left. I hated to sit by myself in the house. It did not matter I owned a lovely home, an acre of land, a garden, a gnarled old apple tree. I wished I were dead. I owned things—I did not own myself.

I married to fill unconscious needs. That explained why I *had* to get married. If there had been choice, I could have waited.

I wanted to escape the growing awareness of my feelings for my father, for John, for Mother, for others close to me. The marriage was further flight.

Living with someone else proved too painful at that point. For one thing, I disliked facing anyone in the morning. I hated myself and the world when I tumbled out of bed to forsake dreams for the toughness of reality. Truly, I felt like murder in the morning.

To my unfortunate husband I transferred many childhood feelings of anger. Unconsciously I used him as target of the rage that belonged between my parents and me.

I was attracted to him in the first place because unconsciously he reminded me of my father and brother. He teased me as my father did, making me feel again (I thought) like a happy child. He was flippant and bright, like my brother.

But the minute he displayed characteristics of my father and brother that annoyed me, I grew furious. My father sometimes told in detail about an interesting legal case. Because of my anger I would not want to hear, but would listen resentfully. My husband liked to discuss his work in detail. I would interrupt, saying, "Can't you cut it short?" (My life was one of fleeing from details—his of collecting them. Our compulsions did not jibe.)

"Often women will hate their husbands for doing the very things their fathers did, only they never dared rage at their fathers," John said. "Instead, they will say, 'My husband is terrible,' and then sigh, 'Oh, if he were only like Father.' They are really angry because their fathers hurt them." By accusing husbands they can continue to maintain their little-girl idolatry toward their father and continue being unhappy, he said.

As I could look at the men I had chosen I realized they could bring me no happiness nor I them. I unconsciously chose men who would hurt me as I felt my father and brother hurt me, never daring to bestow love where it might bloom. I sought out men (and women, too) who would torture me in the same way I felt my parents did. My hunger sought hunger, not love.

Often I felt hurt without knowing I had sought to be hurt. I was looking for the familiar. The unknown—kindness and compassion—would have been foreign to me. I would have hurriedly brushed it away.

When a man from whom I wanted to hear neglected to telephone, I would moan, "How can he do this to me?" instead of asking, "Why am I doing this to myself?"

I "used" people to satisfy emotional yearnings, more interested in what they could give than what I might offer. No wonder such love never lasted. It was not the love of maturity, warm, soothing, radiant like the sunshine, but of a hungry child. I was asking the man to be everything, including understanding parent. That he could never be, because in turn he was seeking me as the good mother.

"The unconscious plays an important role in the choices made by unhappy people," said John.

Neurosis seeks its own level, he declared. Emotionally healthy people, able to love, attract other emotionally healthy people. Neurotic need recognizes neurotic need. If a man marries a woman who is cruel to him, he unconsciously needs cruelty because it is familiar to him.

While people who attract each other may seem different on the surface, fundamentally they are the same, John held. He quoted the rhyme, "Jack Spratt could eat no fat, his wife could eat no lean." He said that each Spratt was neurotic in his own fashion, but nature, striking for a balance, provided that between the two of them they "licked the platter clean."

I am glad I married even though I failed because I mar-

168

ried for the wrong reasons. For me to marry at all marked new courage even though I lacked the greater courage not to marry.

No longer could the family pity me as its lone spinster. Though they were kind enough never to do more than joke, I knew they felt sorry for me over the years because of my marriageless existence.

They tried to hide their concern. "You really don't have to get married because you've got so much else to make up for it," said Sue.

"Does she really think that?" I wondered. "Can't she see nothing makes up for lack of marriage as far as I'm concerned?"

But I was too frightened to succeed in making anyone happy. I lacked the strength to become wife or mother.

The job still meant too much. Not for one second had I been willing to relinquish it for home and family.

Chapter XIII

First Line of Defense

A JOB IS A JOB IS A JOB. But not for me.

As I could look at my supposedly admirable career, I glimpsed beneath the glamor a grimness of purpose that would have done credit to Sparta.

My life had become dedicated to obtaining facts about others. I fastened with fascination on the activities of the town, the city, the nation, the world. I fled from the facts of my own life. I started running in high school, accelerated speed in college, took on greater fury in newspaper work.

Eventually I had to run faster and faster, à la Alice in Wonderland, to keep up with my constantly increasing unhappiness.

I grabbed at words as life-savers almost the very day I could write, it appears from the scribblings I saved since childhood.

"What did you write about?" John asked.

"Does it matter what?" I was ashamed of most of it.

"I would think everything about your life was important if you are interested in living a less painful life," he said. (Every blasted word is important to an analyst, isn't it, I thought. Every blasted word was important to me, too.)

"Well, it just so happens that the other day I was going through a box filled with my original works," I said sarcastically. "One of my earliest opuses was the first act of a play." I stopped.

"As a matter of fact," I continued. "maybe you *would* be interested in it. It might tell you a lot about me."

"It might tell you a lot about you," he said gently.

"Yes, that's what I mean," I amended hastily.

At the age of ten I wrote a play set in a Grandly Furnished room, the parlor of Madame Duane. A little girl rang the doorbell. The maid was about to shut the door in the child's face when the little girl said she was one of the daughters of the woman who owned the house. The maid expressed surprise. She said she knew only the two girls who lived there.

As the maid conducted the girl upstairs, the two other daughters crept from behind chairs where they hid listening to the conversation. The following dialogue ensued:

> Rose: Oh, what a sister. She makes me sick. She probably doesn't know she has sisters or that we ever exist.
>
> Madge: (the other sister) Well, sister, anyhow the least we can do is to be aquainted.
>
> Rose: To be aquainted, why I suppose you are a diddle-daddly afraid cat and a dumb bell don't know anything

Madge explains to the new-found sister, that "when Mother got three children she thought three was too many so she sent you to Grandmother's to stay till you were older." She warns her, "Rose, my sister, does everything she can to hurt people so look out for her."

Obviously I was the sister Mother had sent way (feeling Mother disliked me, wishing, too, I might live with Granny). Madge is Sally, to whom I felt close; Rose is Sue, who, I felt, did not like me, for she would never lend me her clothes. Fantasy, but fairly direct at the age of ten.

"As I matured to the age of eleven, my writing also developed," I informed John facetiously.

In seventh grade I plotted the first chapter of a book, *Bare Facts*. (Facts were important even at that age. Also, the word "bare," come to think of it.) It began:

> William Durns, brother of the mayor of Amster, is found murdered in his office on Amster Avenue, in Amster on June 17, 1928. His head is severed off his neck, a horrible way of dying. However the authorities say that he was poisoned first and then his head blackjacked to make it look like murder, another way. No one can understand why this is. The murdered man is discovered by his secretary; the doctors saying about three hours after his death. There was no noise or any sign of struggle. No one had seen anyone enter his office that morning except a photographer who went in and came right out again. The secretary, not seeing Mr. Durns come out for lunch at 1:30, wants to enter but the sign "'Busy" on the door disturbs her because the boss's word is law.

Even at eleven I was busy with murder although I did not know I was a daughter murdering her father (not once, but twice, to make sure he was dead—sweet daughter, I). Thus in fantasy I took care of my father because I did not think he loved me.

"On the lighter side I dashed off love stories," I told John.

One, called *A Masquerader,* described the threatened kidnapping of "Marjorie Davis, the only child of Browne Davis, the famous millionaire, an innocent pretty girl with blond hair and dark blue eyes whose mother died when she was only ten and up to this time Miss Davis had been placed in a select school where no one dreamed she was the famous heiress, so when she arrived at school, the meeting was the same as if she was an ordinary child."

It ended: "Marge rushed into his arms. 'Margy, dear,' Jim murmured, 'I was so worried about those kidnappers, quick, say you'll marry me before anyone else takes you.' Marge replied, 'Yes.' " (I needed to write of romance to make up for its lack in my life.)

I also wrote about a hero in my life—Rudy Vallee (succeeded ten years later in my affection by Sinatra). My reverence for Rudy I contained fairly well within myself except for five pictures of him pinned on the green walls of my bedroom. I was generous enough to surround him with Clara Bow, Greta Garbo and Norma Talmadge. I wrote a message to him (never mailed) which started off: "This is not a jest or is it a sally, it's a poem written in distinction of my idol, Rudy Vallee."

Why did I like Rudy? My next lines (I abandoned poetry) explained: "Different from the rest, he tries to create an atmosphere of love, of violent longings, of untold and unfulfilled desires. His voice brings to each listener a feeling of comfort as if here was someone who would dare to express their ideals and wishes.

"His soft and persuasive voice lures woman's thoughts to higher things. Every woman imagines herself to be wooed and won by Rudy Vallee."

(If my father and brother scorned my love, where better to fasten it than on a man who would not scorn it because he would never know about it?)

At thirteen, bursting with excess emotion, I kept a secret diary. No one would listen, so I wrote. Down on the pages of a blue-lined notebook went such stirring stuff as:

Mar. 12: Today we had a fashion show in school and Mother said I stuck my stomach out and slouched. We're having ribbons in class for sports and stunts and I probably won't get any. I wonder which is better—love or being first in everything? Sometimes I think love is, but then I've been so disappointed. I wonder if somewhere there is a boy whom I could adore forever.

April 19. Am through with all members of the male sex. They're no good. If you could show me a boy who is unselfish, who is a gentleman and who does not cheat or lie—well, I might consider him. My father is a pretty good example of the three mentioned characteristics. [Contemporary note: Ah there, Oedipus.]

April 26: Gins came over and Bruce, that stuck-up boy,

fell in the sound where we watched him fish. [Note: I must have meant we watched him fish before he fell in.]

May 8: I saw my darling yesterday and oh, how pale he is. I hope that angel will soon be up. Everyone loves him. [Note again: this refers to my brother who had his appendix out.]

May 19: Gins and I acted on Granny's front porch and then Dad took us for tea at his golf club. Nothing much as usual on Sunday.

(A note on June 11 despairs because I think I have flunked my exams. But I am more worried by my failure to attract a boy who refuses to pay attention to me.)

June 25: Had graduation exercises this morning. Never so surprised in my life. I won four prizes, all there was to win and got the highest mark in everything. My regents average was the highest, our principal said, that anyone ever got in the school before. Arith—100, Spelling—98, English—94, Reading—100, Geog.—98, His.—96 and Writing—95. My secret boy friend was sitting right near. Why, oh why, doesn't he wake up?

Never did I feel I deserved the good marks. Our school principal, a disciplinarian but a kindly man, would sometimes look at me quizzically, amazed, I am certain, that such a boy-crazy, scatter-brain girl should be the one to raise the scholastic level of his school.

"I got high marks only because I had a good memory," I said to John, apologizing for them.

I crammed into my addled brain more facts about the world than I now dream ever existed. From an old notebook I see that once I knew that sensation travels one hundred feet a second; nerve fiber is one four-thousandth of an inch; Major Pierre Charles L'Enfant, a French engineer who fought in the Revolution, prepared the plans for the city of Washington, helped by George Washington himself; Anchises, the father of Aeneas, was crippled by Jupiter's thunderbolt, and pebbles are usually found at the mouth of a stream because the water has carried the small rocks from the source to the mouth and worn them away.

"As I grew older, I became more realistic in my writing," I said to John. "I edited the school year book and wrote short stories with 'social significance.' " (To my teachers I owe a debt, for they encouraged me to write, made me feel I was good at it.)

Our high school magazine printed one effort inspired by a peculiarly shaped rock. If looked at from a certain angle, it resembled the face of George Washington. I wrote about a "radical" from New York who visited the town to find himself staring into the face of George Washington, framed by the setting sun. Whereupon he gave up the Socialist Party and became an enrolled Democrat. (I was becoming more conscious of the world outside.)

In high school I became friends with a boy who covered school sports for a local newspaper. When too many events happened at once, he assigned me to write up a game. As I was official scorekeeper for our football, basketball and baseball teams, it was easy to translate the scores into a running account of the game. (If the boys no longer wanted me on their team, at least I could write about them.)

One day Ray asked if I would like to visit the newspaper on which he held the title of sports editor.

"I sure would." I was thrilled. I had never seen a newspaper office.

We stopped in front of an old wooden three-story building. Brown paint peeled from its slatted sides. A red chimney spouted from the roof.

Ray pointed to the chimney in pride. "You should see the smoke pour out on cold days when we light a fire!"

"Is this it?" I gasped. It looked like an ancestral home, not a modern newspaper office.

"It's a little different than most," he apologized. "But you'll like it. Come in and see."

We walked up porch steps, opened a creaky door. Ray led me through two large rooms, once parlor and dining hall. Desks, telephones and wastebaskets now cluttered them. I felt lace curtains should be draped at the windows and family portraits hung on the brown-papered walls.

"You can sit at my desk while I open the mail," Ray offered generously.

I glanced hungrily at the story of a football game lying on his desk. He caught my look.

"Say, why don't you try writing a story or two for us?" he suggested.

"I don't know how," I protested.

"You could do features," he said. "I'll help you if you get stuck.'

"Do you think your boss would let me?" I was overwhelmed by the idea.

"It's easy to find out," he said.

He marched into the next room. A few seconds later he came back saying, "He wants to see you."

A blond young man with an engaging smile greeted me as I walked in. He offered me a chair. He asked why I wanted to be a reporter.

"I—I really don't know," I said. "I just like to write."

"Do you drink?"

"Not very much." I blushed. I had managed to swallow some sweet wine at a New Year's party.

"Well, you'll have to learn if you want to be a reporter," he said with a laugh. He added in serious tone, "I guess we can't lose anything by trying you. I can't pay for stories but I'll give you a byline." (Ray later explained that meant the name of the reporter placed on top of the story as reward for a good job.)

"There's a poor old colored hermit who has been hiding for years in a shack in the woods on the outskirts of town," the editor said. "Go see what he has to say. I'll send a photographer with you."

He did not tell me this recluse had persistently refused to be interviewed by local reporters. He hoped, by sending the photographer, at least to get a picture.

I rushed back to Ray, told of my good luck. I wondered what kind of man this hermit could be. Why did he live alone? Was there some tragedy in his past that made him feel he could not face the world? The editor had described him as "poor." I would gain his confidence by bringing a gift to show somebody cared.

"I'll take him some candy," I told Ray.

"Candy!" Ray exploded. "He's probably starving to death. Bring him some meat."

Armed with pork chops and photographer I drove down the winding, wooded street on which the hermit lived. We parked the car, edged up to a small shack sheltered by trees. We knocked on a splintered door.

It opened a crack. A voice quavered, "What's 'at?"

At least this formed the ghost of a reception. I pleaded, "We want to speak to you. Will you come out?"

The door closed. The photographer and I looked helplessly at each other. I must not fail, I thought.

I recalled the pork chops. "I brought you something," I yelled.

The door opened. A tall, wrinkled, white-haired Negro stepped out slowly. He looked not at me but at the paper bag in my hand. I gave it to him. He tore it open, gazed ardently at the chops.

He walked to the side of the shack, stooped over and gathered up twigs. As he built a fire I asked questions, frightened, but more frightened not to ask. How long had he lived in the shack?

"Eighty years," he said.

Did he live alone?

"Ever since my mother died twenty years ago. She was a slave who escaped to the North during the Civil War." He sounded proud.

The photographer snapped a picture as the hermit stooped over the fire, pork chop in hand. He blinked in surprise as the bulb flashed, not knowing what happened, but said nothing.

Triumphant, we returned to the office. The photographer rushed off to develop his prints. I raced into the editor's small room.

"Back so soon?" he asked, looking up from editing copy.

"We saw him," I said, trying not to sound too jubilant.

"You did?" He was surprised. "Did he talk to you?"

"Yes, and we got a picture, too."

"Well, well." He seemed pleased.

"Shall I write it?" I asked eagerly.

176

"Of course," he said. Then asked suspiciously, "How did you get him to talk?"

"A couple of pork chops helped." I told him of the gift. He laughed.

The following week Ray brought a copy of the paper to me at school. A three-column picture of the hermit, complete with pork chops, graced the front page. Beside it, under my name, appeared the story I had written, not one word changed.

"The boss wants you to do other stories," Ray said. "He says come up and see him."

That summer, while waiting to go to college, I interviewed two golden anniversary couples, a heroic dog who saved children from drowning and the town's only Civil War veteran, a survivor of the second battle of Bull Run, Vicksburg and Gettysburg.

The veteran won my heart by announcing he had voted the straight Democratic ticket all his life (you might know it would take a Civil War veteran to be the only other Democrat in Westchester besides my father).

"Just once I gave it to the Republicans," he admitted.

"When was that?" I frowned.

"When I voted for William Howard Taft because I didn't like the way Teddy treated him," he said defiantly.

"Teddy?"

"Teddy Roosevelt," he explained.

"Oh," I said. That was a politician before my time.

The editor also permitted me to write humorous articles on sailing, golfing, tennis and skiing, sometimes printing them on the front page.

"You'll never be a newspaperwoman, though," he would say, shaking his head sadly.

"What's the matter?" I would ask worriedly. "Something wrong with the story?"

"You don't drink. How can you be a newspaperwoman if you don't drink?" (Alas, I have never learned. Recently I shocked a friend who pulled out of his liquor chest rare vintage Scotch. I swallowed some, choked, "It tastes like gasoline." He grabbed the glass from me indignantly, crying, "My best Scotch—gasoline!" and drank it himself.)

But to be a newspaperwoman I would consume gallons of whiskey daily if I must. (Luckily, I never had to.) The lure of my name in print above words written by me, to call the world's attention to my prowess, to win people's praise—there was nothing I would not do for more of that. (Then maybe my mother and father would pay attention to me!)

Then, too, I might achieve what I had written in the senior yearbook as my ambition—to travel.

"I sure got that!" I remarked to John. "Sometimes I wish I didn't travel so much."

"Perhaps we all get what we seek," he said thoughtfully.

"The catch is I'm finding out what I sought was not what I really wanted." I could now admit that.

What I really desired was a home and children, even though I failed at marriage. Instead, I drove myself to pursue a career with the same intensity with which I once stood at bat waiting for the pitch.

"Often, as I work, I feel as if I am standing at home plate, clutching the bat in panic, afraid I will strike out," I told John.

I said in surprise, "Just like the dream I had last week after I met someone at a meeting who had not seen me in years. He said, 'My, you look good.'"

I had felt pleased he thought I looked well. That night I dreamed once again I was running around the old baseball field down the block. In reality it had gone the way of many a vacant lot in Westchester. Several spacious houses now stood where once we yelled "out." I took it as personal insult the day the owner sold the property.

In my dream the houses disappeared. The field once more spread in unbroken splendor, edged by dandelions and daisies.

I stood at bat. A strange boy pitched one ball after another. I connected with every pitch, hitting long, clean drives smack out into center field. One, two, three—crack. One, two, three —crack. DiMaggio could have done no better.

Suddenly someone on the sidelines cried out in admiration, as, in reality, the man had done that day, "My, you look good!" I beamed.

In telling John the dream, I moaned, "See? That's what 'looking good' means to me. Only instead of hitting a three-bagger for approval, I must write a story. Isn't it disgusting?"

"Some girls play baseball in school, but later get married and have children," John said. "Perhaps it was the way you played baseball."

He means desperately, as though it were a matter of life and death, I thought. He is right.

"It's time you gave up wanting to play third base," he said. "You are not one of the boys. You are a woman."

"Do you mind if occasionally I go to the Polo Grounds to root for my hopeless Giants?" I asked sarcastically.

He ignored my sarcasm. "To be a woman you must understand why you fled from being a woman," he said.

I thought I had fled from women, not knowing I fled from one woman—myself.

I had always disliked girls. As early as fifth grade I would saunter to the playground of the sprawling red-brick school (through whose corridors I now chase in dreams, trying to find a lost classroom) in search of boys to play marbles. I looked with contempt on the girls who gathered at each other's homes after school to devour cookies and cocoa.

One afternoon I wandered to the playground to find it empty. I sat on a wooden bench to wait for masculine company. A tall, awkward youngster burst out of the building. He was the school's Peck's Bad Boy who endured perpetual punishment for making obscene remarks to the teacher and molesting the other children. The boys shunned him, as often children do to protect themselves from the weak; bullies stand among the weak. The girls were afraid to speak to him. He had stuffed too many wriggling worms down their backs.

He saw me, started off in the opposite direction. He changed his mind, shuffled over.

"Want to play marbles?" he asked hoarsely.

"Okay," I said, sliding off the bench. It was preferable to sitting alone.

He tugged at his back pocket, brought out a bag of marbles. I took mine out of my small purse. My grandfather had brought me some marble-marbles, not glass marbles, from Egypt, but these I hid in a bureau drawer. They were too beautiful to use.

The two of us kneeled in the dirt (that's why my stockings

were so black so often, Mother) and set out to beat each other in serious fashion.

Minutes raced by to the click of marbles. He trimmed me unmercifully. I lost the last marble as the sun set. I rose shamefaced but smiling (part of me wanted to lose to him).

"You really skunked me," I admitted.

He picked up the marbles, put them carefully in his bag. Then he held out the bag to me.

"I want you to have them," he said shyly.

"Oh, no!" I refused. He had won the marbles fairly. Besides, no boy had ever given me a present except my brother, and then I knew Mother paid for it.

"Take them," he insisted with such earnestness I dared not again say no. (Maybe I am interested in helping children labeled delinquents not only because I so often feel like one but because I remember how quickly the "worst" boy in school responded to a touch of companionship.)

Catch a girl doing that, I thought. Girls would have snatched up all the marbles, walked off with superior sneer.

Even though I wanted none of it I had to go to a girl's college to please my parents. I was miserable from the first moment I drove up the tree-lined entrance to the white buildings cresting the hill, until I drove away four years later, diploma desperately clasped in hand.

I felt despairing and like a dunce. Not only did I have to bear girls, but girls who knew much more than I. The public school I attended primarily prepared us to pass Regents examinations. Some of these girls, graduates of élite private schools, boasted long acquaintance with esoteric names such as T. S. Eliot, Gertrude Stein, Karl Marx. My knowledge of the National League players, the intricacies of the Lindy Hop and the plots of all Hollywood movies put out between 1930 and 1934 impressed no one. I kept quiet in the small classes so I would not show my ignorance of an intellectual aura of which I had never been aware.

I felt so unhappy that at the end of each year I tried to persuade the family to allow me to quit and go to work on a newspaper. I remained because my father wanted me to stay; he had chosen the college which stood a few miles from the one he attended. Also because my grandmother pleaded with me to finish. "The first time you give up on one thing, the easier it becomes to give up on many things," she said.

I buried my misery; took to the hills, figuratively speaking. I would stare for hours at the majestic mountains surrounding the small Vermont town. Suddenly I would slam down a book, sprint out of the dormitory, head my car into them.

Automobiles played an important part in my life. Both my brother and I would have had a hard time living without them. My father bought Eddie an Austin to drive around the roads of Granny's farm when he was thirteen. Eddie eagerly taught me to drive so I might rush for my license the day I hit sixteen (exactly what I did). Then I drove him on state roads, forbidden him until he was two years older.

I liked to whizz along the highway with the convertible's top down. The sun would warm my face, the wind toss off cares. I spun away the one hundred and eighty miles to college as often as I dared. Each time I would try to better my speed record.

"Gosh," I would groan, looking at my watch. "Last month I reached Great Barrington in two hours. I'm ten minutes over now. What's slowing up this Oldsmobile?"

Fastest time was three hours, ten minutes, set one day when I left home at 4 A.M. I sped sixty and seventy miles all the way. Those were lost, crazy days when the spell of madness had settled but slightly on my shoulders.

I drove through mountains day after day, especially in autumn when trees shielded them in purple and gold waves of glory. Sometimes I would head for the Mohawk Trail, entranced by its miles of vibrant foliage. Or I would guide the car up Greylock Mountain, up the narrow, dangerous curves, up, up to the top of the world. I would look off into the misty ranges that lofted over the green land, claiming allegiance from the valleys they sheltered.

Sometimes I would close my eyes against the agony of their beauty and endurance. These mountains watched the settlers of the sixteen-hundreds and they will watch those who follow long after I am dead, I would think.

I would joke about tossing myself off the highest mountain peak.

"You're teasing, of course," a friend said. "You're one of the happiest girls here." (How little she knew, too.)

If I could have been happy anywhere, it would have been at this college. Small and progressive, it gave more attention to the individual student than possibly any in the country. It cut out as much competition as it could, eliminating examinations, required courses, credits. It believed that facts alone were not enough for education; that learning, to be effective, must hold meaning.

Each student had her own counselor to whom she was entitled to tell troubles. A woman doctor trained in psychiatry was available to those who sought her.

"I should have been happy," I told John. "It was not the college's fault."

"You were not ready to accept independence," he said.

"I hated to leave home," I admitted. "I wonder how I ever had nerve, at the time."

The college offered no journalism course but suggested I major in social studies, acquire a background in history, government, economics, psychology, political science and sociology.

Each winter we left college for two months during which we were supposed to put into practical application the theory acquired during the other months. One year, instead of heading for the newspaper as I usually did, I worked as a volunteer in a settlement house in New York, my first contact with slums. For literature course credit I turned in an account of those months, calling it "the diary of a volunteer settlement worker":

Jan. 2—I am to work in the library, full of musty books, read and tell stories to the children. I shall do my best to overcome an inherent dislike for children and bring to the fore my superficial knowledge of child psychology and fairy tales, entertain them until I am hoarse with Goldilocks. I always thought of social workers as frustrated souls. My Lord! Why am I doing this? Well, I shall study up on fairy tales.

Jan. 3—I was given a class of fourteen children, average age eight, to amuse for an hour. After a few minutes I realized that the only way to hold their attention was to collect them in a circle. No trouble then except when they pulled my curls or fingered my scarf. I did not resent their boldness—only their inattention to my beautiful fairy story. I also cribbed from Twain and Dickens.

Jan. 13—Two of my class, Jo and Anna, invited me to their homes. Dad refused to let me go. "How do I know they haven't brothers who are gangsters?" he said. Parental opinion, as powerful as public, is against me.

Jan. 17—Jo brought me a valentine. This has got to stop. I told her that I didn't want her spending money on me. Several unruly boys in class fighting over the date of the writing of *The Star Spangled Banner*. I sent them to look it up in a history book, which didn't contain the information. The kindergarten teacher gave me a ride downtown. Having no children of her own, she can well place affection with these children—they need it.

Jan. 29—Anna asked me why she should believe in Santa Claus. She says she went up to one, pulled his hair, and his whiskers and face fell off. Moreover, she saw a white Santa, a red one and a chocolate one. I pointed out that Santa needed helpers and these were all just imitations of him. She and Jo walked blocks with me after class until I found a taxi.

Jan. 30—Found an aunt of mine here doing psychiatric work. She says poor environment, nervous nagging mothers, ignorant hot-tempered fathers, lack of social contacts, all help to make these children unhappy.

Feb. 5—Noticed a reticent little boy coming to class each day. Quick reactions, keen mind and polite manners. Gave him a three-block taxi ride on my way uptown. Was thrilled to death (both of us). I have never consciously gone out of my way to give a child pleasure. He had never had a taxi ride. He wrote a story for me and I'm encouraging him to write more. We writers must stick together.

Feb. 7—Huge class today. Grows each time. I missed my calling. Should have been a teacher. One young instructor here lost his temper when some fresh boys addressed him as "dearie" and "toots." Thirty children in class today, all as noisy as hades. My head has the habit of splitting after these sessions. But then, I think it can stand a few splits to air out the cracks.

Feb. 17—The instructor in charge of the settlement newspaper was telling today about the boy who wrote the news story on a lecturer who tried to make sex clearer to the youngsters. The boy's opening sentences read: "Dr. Blank lectured here last night on SEX! He explained the genital organs and the diseases we may get and how they affect us." Said the instructor, "I told the kid he should tone down his emphasis on the word 'sex,' that we did not have to put it in capital letters. I left the genitals part in because I wasn't sure what they were myself."

Feb. 18—This is my last day here. I have become attached to a small group of children to whom I have promised to write. I decidedly overcame some of my dislike for children. Was Jo responsible? I know not. But I don't mind being around children, now. I understand them a bit more clearly.

I wrote an aunt of my growing interest in social problems. She saved my letters, returned them to me before she died. In one I found portent of things to come:

We are studying hypnosis and the neuroses in abnormal psychology and have wandered a little into Freud's field. Psychoanalysis interests me greatly, but I realize the danger of a little knowledge and don't want to tackle it until I can really study it. In journalism, I am investigating the methods of propaganda in our country, especially the press. One hears so much about propaganda these days.

Several things turned me away from social work toward writing. After entering senior division, I had as counselor a young political scientist who once worked on a Texas newspaper. He inspired in me the belief that journalism was an honorable profession, in contrast to some faculty members who made me feel if I could not write like Melville I should dig potatoes.

Also, at this time, I took a literature course conducted by a warm, sensitive woman who encouraged me to write the satire I liked. For me, satire has been easiest; thus may I skim the surface, ignore the seriousness below.

To steel myself through lonely Saturday nights at college when I had no date and must sit with girls, I would return to my room and, instead of bursting into tears, write satirically of the scene I had left behind. I turned to wit that might amuse me and others (always the others must be amused), rationalizing that some day I would put it in a play.

I took time out for several romances and occasional weekends at Harvard, then attended by the Merlin of my youth. He had transferred his childhood ambition to be a magician to the study of chemistry, a modern Merlin. He offered weekends of dancing in Boston, which to me was "that city" at the end of the train ride winding past the famous Bridge of Flowers in Shelburne Falls. Even in winter when bare brown stalks jutted from the bridge I would think with delight of the blossoms that would burst forth as colorful cover in spring.

For my senior thesis I blithely decided to analyze the newspapers of this nation from the Revolutionary era to the present, wanting, again, to swallow the world in one gulp. A wise professor advised a smaller chew. He persuaded me such an ambitious survey might take more than a year. Regretfully I toned it down to the analysis of one paper during one year— the local Gazette in 1787.

I made the acquaintance, on paper only, of a gentleman named Anthony Haswell, who furthered my illusion of how romantic a newspaper career might be. In 1787 Vermont had not been accepted into the union, although she fought as desperately for independence from Great Britain as any one of the thirteen original states. Mr. Haswell, who came to town to start the state's first newspaper, spared no emotion in waging his cause for union with the other states. He threw his heart, as well as the type he set by hand, into the rag paper. In my mind I determined to be a feminine Haswell, fighting the evils of another century.

One day, gaining strength from an exotic-flavored sundae called chocolate malt, I marched into the town's contemporary newspaper office. I introduced myself to the publisher as a journalism student from college. He asked if I would write occasional feature stories for his paper. When I told him I had been digging into the life of Mr. Haswell, he also asked me to give a copy of the finished report to the town library.

"I was prouder of that than anything else that happened at

college," I told John. Someone wanted something I did to put to practical use.

As college ended I felt jubilant in one sense, unhappy in another. I wrote my Aunt Clare, trying to be optimistic, but knowing that trouble lay ahead:

> At this point I feel that I haven't obtained all I could from my four years, but I suppose I am lucky to have come away with something—the desire for further study. I recognize the distinction between preparing for a professional job and preparing for an intellectual life, and I am going to try to correlate the two. A difficult task, though, as I am a very lazy person—except when it comes to walking around a golf course or dancing all night.

I do not blame the college for my unhappiness. I am grateful to it for teaching me about much of the world outside, preparing me for a career. If both faculty member and student are wisely chosen, progressive education can soar to heights never before reached by any other system of education, I believe.

Some of our more kindly professors tried to help the unhappy students. One gentle man reassured us, "The capacity of the human race to endure suffering is vastly underestimated." He should know, for he had a cough that, at times, threatened to tear him apart.

But others, without meaning to do so, I trust, only frightened us further. One female faculty member spewed forth such sarcastic remarks she reduced some students to tears. She said fliply to me, "The trouble with you is that your attachment to your father is too deep." True enough, but she showed only cruelty by delving into my emotional problems without intending to help.

The woman doctor, though gruff, seemed kindly underneath. Yet she frightened one of my friends, a shy, repressed girl brought up in New England puritanism.

This girl returned from her final physical examination, a rather complete one, shaking in fear and anger. She beckoned me to close the door to hear in privacy what had disturbed her.

"Can you imagine?" she related in horror. "The doctor

186

wanted to know why I was still a virgin. She asked me what was the matter—didn't I like boys?" She recovered from her fear quickly though; she got married almost immediately after graduation.

I remembered with terror (remembering always the fearful) what we called "the inquisition." Each senior, before graduation, faced all the faculty members of her division for final quiz. I stuttered when by accident I met even one professor crossing the campus. As they gathered in one room to prepare to hurl questions at me, I wished I had flunked out my first year. Luckily, some were on my side, more than they had a right to be, probably.

As an American history major I was expected to discuss in detail the early struggles of our nation.

All I remember of that horrible hour is that one professor asked how some writers described this period.

That I knew. "As the critical period in American history," I flashed back.

"Why?" he asked.

"Because it was critical to us," I said. "We might have lost everything we gained from our fight for independence."

"Critical in what other sense?"

I could not think of any other sense. I looked wistfully at the ex-journalist who, I knew, would help if he could.

He raced to the rescue. He turned to the questioning professor. "What do *you* mean?" he asked.

"Critical to England, too," he explained. "She hoped this period would prove critical to America and she would get her colony back."

"I think Lucy's answer will do," said the other professor.

The quiet, gentle bachelor, he who observed "the capacity of the human race to endure suffering is vastly underestimated," sat reading a newspaper all through my inquisition, as though to say, Don't worry, this is just another minor tribulation which we all must endure.

My fear I never would receive a diploma still grips me. A recurring nightmare puts me back on campus for a fifth year, to face the cold stares of students, the barb of faculty wit. I wake depressed, finding it hard to believe I made the collegiate course in par.

"You can't imagine how wretched I felt in college," I told John. "And yet I feel I must have got something out of it."

It was then he upset one of my firmest beliefs. He asked, "What good did college do if you were unhappy there?"

"I had to go to college!" I exclaimed. "My parents wouldn't have forgiven me if I hadn't graduated." I thought, I am the only one of the four children to graduate, although the others also attended college.

John was silent. I felt his disapproval.

"I learned a lot at college," I assured him. "I wouldn't be in this room if I hadn't gone to college."

I thought of endless psychology tomes read in library quiet. Tiring of words, I would shift my eyes to windows that framed the serenity of mountains, as though hoping to find in them better answers to life than in pages of books. Then, with a sigh, back to the books, knowing mountains held no answer.

"You might have come here sooner if you hadn't gone to college," John said.

I protested, "I read books by famous authors like Proust and Joyce and Mann and . . ."

"Did it make you feel any better?"

"I got an education," I said sullenly.

"Did it make you any happier?" His voice was low, insistent.

"I guess not," I admitted. "I was just as unhappy when I graduated as when I first went there."

"Do you know why you were unhappy?" he asked.

"Living with girls!" I sounded contemptuous.

"Was it the other girls—or you?"

"I guess it was me," I admitted grudgingly. "The college tried hard enough to educate me but I needed a psychiatrist, not a professor."

"Before you could think, you needed to clear up emotional obstacles that blocked ability to think," he said.

"Don't you believe in education?" I asked, in wonder.

"I feel that sometimes education's goal is to prepare people to make a living, rather than to live," he said. "The accent is on competition rather than cooperation."

Education sometimes is visualized as apart from life, rather than as part of life, he felt. It continues to split the individual in two, separating even more emphatically emotions and intellect, rather than fusing them.

Educators may ignore the emotional problems of students because they are victims of these same problems, he held. Some may have become quite detached in their escape from reality. "In detachment there is no understanding," he declared.

"Would you want a world without art or science or literature?" I asked as though such a thought were obnoxious.

"They may be used wisely to advance the world's knowledge but man sometimes uses them to negate himself," he replied.

"Do you feel that talk of planning for a better world is also escape?"

"Man should not be too optimistic about himself as a social animal until he is more at peace within himself," he answered.

"Where would we be without the men who want to lead us into some kind of world peace?" I kept up this questioning session after session. Often, as John answered, I thought, I'm getting a far better education here than at college.

"Unfortunately, some are not our most capable, but our most eager, while those who may be the ablest feel no need to be heard. A look inside for some of our leaders might better help the course of mankind."

An unhappy person can bring no happiness to others, for he cannot give what he does not possess, and this applies to world statesmanship as well as to individuals, he believed.

He also said that research sometimes took men farther from the truth, for it was not research into their own hearts but in the opposite direction—into the realm of cold facts which could then be used as defense against the facts of the heart.

"What good did research do you?" he asked. "You had a high I.Q., on the opposite end of the intelligence scale from the feeble-minded, but you may have been as emotionally disturbed as some classified as feeble-minded."

"What do you mean?" This was a new idea to me.

"Some thought of as feeble-minded are capable of thinking but are so frightened and angry they won't think," he said.

189

Psychoanalytic treatment of some feeble-minded children has shown successful results, evidence these children needed only a safe, kindly atmosphere in which to dare to start to think. One institution classified as feeble-minded and gave up as hopeless a seven-year-old boy who refused to talk. A psychiatric social worker under the direction of a psychoanalyst treated the boy for several years, allowing him to know, for the first time, what friendliness meant. Reward came one day when the boy blurted out the sentence, "You won't beat me, like Daddy does?" He knew words. He had been too frightened to use them.

The college emphasized the scientific method in education with its aim of making students more objective and, thus, able to reason. At a community meeting a very religious student stood up to object to the stress on science. Where, she demanded, did spiritual values fit into the picture?

One of my favorite social studies professors rose slowly to his feet to reply to her charge. "Madam," he said dryly, "we can make no attempt to measure the cellular structure of the Holy Ghost."

How could I know what objectivity meant? I felt more at home with its opposite—subjectivity. This quality may be seen in the behavior of some of the very emotionally ill who are not successful in being objective. A tree to them is not a tree, but, seen as silhouette against sunset, an enemy advancing to destroy them. A cup is not a cup but one that contains poison meant alone for their lips. Everything becomes personalized and a threat to life because they feel so much in danger.

I could not be objective if torn to emotional shreds. As John asked, what was the good of all the books I read in college, if, while I read, I was confused by the feelings whirling inside me. What held meaning for me in all those pages as far as the resolution of my life was concerned? I could read Aristotle and learn that a man is a man insofar as he has developed his highest faculty—reason—but how would that help me to develop my reason if it stood blocked by fear?

The college did not aid in resolving my dilemma but rather intensified it by putting the stamp of approval on my attempts to carve out a career. It strengthened my defense, intellectuality, ignored the basic problem of emotional conflicts. But, perhaps, it is not within the province of higher education to cope with emotional chaos.

The college wanted me to observe the world around me. I was willing to look, but unable, because I could not observe myself. I could not look outside myself into the larger humanity.

If I had been able to see myself on graduation day I might have snared a clue to my unhappiness.

My mother and father drove up in separate cars, barely speaking to each other, for divorce brewed. The family was upset by news of my brother's secret marriage which filtered to us a year after his elopement. My grandmother, in spite of a violent automobile accident in which she was injured internally and fractured a leg, insisted on attending the ceremony on crutches.

As I walked up the steps leading to the auditorium where the president was to present the diplomas, I tripped over my long, black graduation gown.

"Now what's the matter?" hissed someone up front, turning to see who disturbed the line's continuity. By that time I had returned to formation, trembling but erect.

I cursed myself, wondering why I must always stumble at important moments. Looking back, I marvel I did not break my fool neck.

Chapter XIV

THE JACKPOT JOB

BEFORE I LEFT COLLEGE I read the grim words issued by Stanley Walker in his book, *City Editor*. He warned aspiring journalists against seeking work in New York:

"Even if Richard Harding Davis should come back and offer to work for fifteen dollars a week, he could not be squeezed into the already bloated staff."

But he did say the student who attended a school of journalism possessed little or no advantage over one with a rounded college course. At least I would get one-to-one odds against the specialist.

Afraid to steer straight for a metropolitan newspaper, I decided to break into the suburban field if I could. The weekly paper for which I first wrote features still could not afford to pay me. I tackled others only to hear "no opening."

As last resort I drove to one newspaper in the western part of the county, miles from where I lived. Here I met the publisher, former city editor of a New York tabloid who had achieved the desire of his life, to own a small newspaper.

Impressed, I guess, by my eagerness to learn about the profession which he obviously worshipped, he offered ten dollars a week, to me an exorbitant sum. No longer would I have to demand gasoline or food money from my father.

This sympathetic editor taught me the tools of the profession—editing, rewrite, headlining, proofreading, make-up. I learned everything from covering town board meetings to running the job shop's hand-press off which rolled wedding announcements and school programs.

Often I would wander into the back shop to breathe inky scent, nectar to my nostrils. I would watch the magic machine called linotype create cold type out of molten metal. I would fondle the different type fonts.

The newspaper stood close to the main line railroad tracks Each time a train thundered past the building quivered, except once a week when our heavy presses crashed into action. Then we shook the railroad tracks.

Although I liked this place something kept pushing me on, urging, get a bigger job, a better job. Do more, do more. After four months I became restless, wondered where to go.

One afternoon a friend telephoned. She was woman's editor on the newspaper in my home town. She informed me she planned to leave for Europe with her husband. Would I be interested in taking her job and, if so, would I please ride right over to be interviewed by her editor?

"In thirty minutes," I promised, elated. A daily paper offered more challenge than a weekly.

Work done for the day, I sped across the county, one eye on car mirror to make sure no policeman trailed. I dashed into the small newspaper office where Nancy worked, crossed the counter to the sacred side where reporters and editors made order of the hundreds of words flung at them daily by press wires and publicity chairmen.

Nancy introduced me to her editor, a soft-spoken, pleasant man.

"You know this town, don't you?" he asked.

"I grew up here," I said. "That is, ever since the age of six." I thought, I'd sure like to work here. I'd only have to drive half a mile instead of ten. Life would be easier as well as more exciting.

"I guess we won't count the first six years," he said.

Later he told me he accepted me only because no one else was available. I hope he half-joked.

I learned to admire him exceedingly. He was competent in his chosen craft, understanding of fellow-workers. Occasionally he tried to hide gentleness under mild barbs but deceived no one. He never criticized me or discouraged me from using my imagination.

"He gave me more confidence than anyone except you," I told John.

Now I see how much I owed to how many. This editor was another who helped me in my struggle to survive.

Struggle it was. The events I recalled revealed what disturbed me most. I felt I would go mad battling for accuracy in names.

I had to know the first name or two initials of a person in order to use it in the paper. People who brought in bridge lists or prize-winners in flower shows or guests at a tea often forgot to scribble down more than last names.

I said to John, "And sometimes even their best friends wouldn't tell me."

One morning I phoned a Mrs. Smith to plead the cause of first names. "Remember a Mrs. Jones who sat at the same bridge table with you yesterday?" I asked. "Do you know her first name?"

"Let me see," drawled the bridge-playing Mrs. Smith, not too happy I pulled her out of bed at eight o'clock to inquire about a rival. "She wore a green hat with blue plumes on the top. Her nails were painted that screaming-red shade. And she fired her maid the day before."

"Didn't anyone at the table call her anything?" I asked hopefully.

"As I remember," the voice recollected, "the woman on my left called her Snooky."

I sighed. "Didn't she have initials on a hand bag or a pin?"

"Just say they were J. R.," Mrs. Smith offered as contribution to the science of journalism. "She won't mind. She's really very sweet—and awfully lucky at bridge."

I groaned to John, "I felt when I greeted Satan or St. Peter, as the case may be, I would say, 'Your first name, please. Or two initials.'"

(I was screaming for accuracy because I felt my parents had never been accurate with me. At the same time I did not care enough to be accurate with others.)

To escape the monotony of flower shows, parent-teacher meetings and weddings, I wrote feature stories. They gave me a chance to indulge my fantasy. When I heard a celebrity such as Phyllis McGinley, poet, or Eddie Doherty, veteran journalist, lived in town, I would interview them. This made me feel important, gave me a kinship with the names of the world.

I left home for a nearby apartment house, first venture into freedom. My father had remarried and my brother moved to his own home. I did not want to live only with women.

My sisters visualized my independence with some alarm. To them I always seemed helpless. I pretended to be dumb about household problems to get help. I could not openly confess to fear; I must put on an act.

Mother stood by for emergency. One night I telephoned her, wailing, "There's a flame on the stove and I can't put it out though I've blown and blown. Do you think it's dangerous?"

"What kind of flame?" she asked.

"In the middle of the stove—a small, blue fire."

"That is the pilot light, dear," she said. "It's not supposed to go out."

I may have studied political science but no one bothered to tell me about pilot lights, nor had I troubled to observe.

194

"That is one of my brother's two favorite stories about me," I said ruefully to John.

I told him the other. I dashed out of the house to go to work one winter morning. I tried in vain to get the Oldsmobile to move. The engine purred evenly but the car would not budge from the garage.

I raced inside, grabbed my brother from the breakfast table. "My car's tires are frozen to the cement," I announced. "How do I unfreeze them so the car will move?"

He looked at me in horror. "You don't believe that?"

"What else?" It seemed the simplest explanation.

He investigated; found a broken clutch. I still prefer my explanation, unpractical but imaginative. (John would say these are excellent examples of how, as usual, I jumped to the wrong conclusions.)

My brave, new apartment held only studio couch, bureau and chair. But I reveled in possessing a place of my own; no one to tell me where to go, what not to do. I could soak in the bathtub as long as I wished; dance the Lindy in the hall with no reproof.

My youngest sister, Sally, always my main ally, offered to clean the one large room, knowing my funds were low. Eighteen dollars a week salary covered little more than meals and car expenses; my father paid the rent.

One day I found the following note:

> Dearest Lucy,
> This is the damndest rug to clean. I had to do it with the little brush, too. I couldn't use the vacuum as Mums doesn't like me to use electricity when I'm alone. I think I earned more than a measley 25 cents. I cleaned the big rug as much as possible. I hope everything is okay.
>
> Love,
>
> Sal

Right after that she quit as twelve-year-old slavey. I did not blame her. I struggled with my own housework (hating it, fit only for women). When the year's lease was up, I moved home, thinking, Let someone else arrange for meals, laundry and cleaning. I've had enough.

195

I wanted to hear the reassuring sound of voices. I wanted someone to sympathize when I made errors.

My biggest mistake occurred when I inadvertently married off the sister of a friend before her wedding. Often I wrote up weddings a few days in advance to prevent copy from overflowing the desk.

One hour after the paper was out I received a frantic call from the bride-to-be's mother. We had published the marriage, scheduled for the following day, as though already held. To make it more convincing, a two-column picture of the bride, clutching overpowering bouquet, accompanied my flowery account of the nuptials.

"What will the guests think?" wailed the stricken mother.

"What will my boss think?" I moaned inside. "I will probably get fired. How can I tell him?"

But I had to tell him. I stammered out the sad story. He did not seem too upset.

"Tell her we'll reprint the marriage tomorrow with an apology," he decided. "Those mistakes happen."

"Thank you," I said gratefully, holding back tears. Such understanding floored me. It is no wonder that for his faith I shall always hold for him a deep affection that neither time nor Republican party victory could dim.

He even gave me space for a weekly column of comment for which I dreamed up the title *Sociable Enough,* sarcastic reference to the innocuous news on the rest of the page.

In the stronghold of Republicanism that is Westchester there appeared in my column pleas for social reform and praise of books and plays that I felt stood for a humane approach to life and the platform of the Democratic party, northern variety. I was now starting to fight my inner battles with a typewriter, pounding away against injustice, not knowing I raged really against what I felt was injustice in my life. I also thought the college would be proud of me, for it stressed the importance of students acquiring and using "a social conscience."

Just before election under the title "Revenge," I wrote:

> Talking of politics we know a young man whose family voted against Roosevelt in the last election.

Last election day he was asked if he wouldn't like to serve the Republicans at the polls in some minor capacity.

"Sure," he answered.

He took the job and after collecting pay for his work walked into the booth and voted for Roosevelt.

Well, brother, things, we fear, are going to be evened up this year.

Under this item, titled *Just this Once?* I wrote:

Ye gods, we were supposed to keep politics out of this column!

We will, too, after Nov. 5.

The editor had hopefully suggested once or twice I limit the column to chatter and movie criticism. Yet he said not a word when I went political.

"Soon even the column started to bore me," I told John. "I wasn't satisfied, no matter what I did. At college I thought, Oh, if I could only work on a newspaper I'd be happy. I had landed on a newspaper but felt as unhappy as ever."

"You could not take the time to look at yourself," he said.

"I know that now," I admitted.

I received a phone call one Sunday morning. A feminine voice chirped, "Hope I didn't wake you. It's eight-thirty already, you know."

I recognized the voice as a friend of the family. "That's all right," I moaned. "I have to get up sometime." I had crawled into bed at 3 A.M. after an evening of dancing.

"My dear, I have a wonderful story for you," she gushed. "We have staying with us a young lady who just rode a horse down from Canada. The New York newspapers have heard about it and you don't want to be scooped, do you?"

"A horse?" I croaked in amazement. "Like what my voice is?"

"A real horse, my dear," she exclaimed. "She's leaving in an hour. You must come over right away."

I did not know whether I was supposed to interview the horse or the girl, but I slung into clothes, gulped orange juice and drove out. The lady of the house had gone to the store for cigarettes but her husband, who looked as though he, too, liked to be left alone Sunday morning, introduced me to the girl on the horse—minus the horse.

A timid, shy young woman with a slight English accent, she looked as though the horse would tell her where to go.

"Is it true you rode a horse from Montreal to New York?" I asked in surprise.

"Yes," she admitted with an embarrassed smile. "Riding is my hobby. Nothing like horseback if you want to see the country."

She rode down to study a plan to further American democracy on an international scale. She expressed excitement about potentialities for Canada.

Why had I selected this story to tell John? Why had I remembered the girl on the horse all through the years? Something important had jumped to mind as I drove away from her. I had thought, "Why haven't I nerve enough to ride a horse to work every morning?"

"Why didn't you?" John asked.

"People would have thought I was crazy!" I stormed. Inside I felt crazy but I couldn't afford to let anyone know it. I envied this shy girl. She did not care if people thought she was crazy. I felt like riding a horse off in all directions at once, but instead I had to choke back craziness, sit chained to a desk, write of the freedom of others to be as crazy as they wished.

I remembered, too, stories that brought pleasure. Chiefly about music which took me out of this world. Out of this world is a phrase I use again and again; I really must have wished to leave it. When the music ended I knew I must plunge back into a world I hated, but I thought it better to taste briefly of song than to live in a world minus music.

I told John wistfully of listening to some of the nation's top jazz musicians as they joined forces for a weekly swing session. The music seemed to dig deep into me, pull out my heart and twirl it around.

Peewee Russell started off by slanting his clarinet toward the ground. He played low, fooling around with a few notes as he wove a subtle pattern. Then he lifted the clarinet skyward, rounding out melody in sweetness and firmness.

Mel Powell, then a seventeen-year-old wonder, leaned so low over the piano he seemed to be using nose as well as fingers. Roy Eldridge, the trumpet's tyrant, twisted around some noble notes and Arthur Shapiro, bass player, swung the strings, keeping time by trucking his feet and shagging shoulders.

All the while Zutty Singleton, the man at the drums, beat out the rhythm. As he soloed, his rhythm took on provocation and tremendous power. It ended with bursting crescendo as Zutty shook his head violently in rhythmic trance.

But while Zutty beat peacetime rhythm, elsewhere on earth drums summoned soldiers to slaughter. For this was November, 1940.

I resented covering weddings and flower shows while the world prepared to explode (while I prepared to explode). It was time for me to get out of town, I thought.

I headed for New York City where I really wanted to work. A sympathetic assistant managing editor on the paper I considered the world's best told me, "Keep calling me occasionally and if there's an opening, I'll let you know." Here, too, I owe gratitude to a man who went out of his way to help me.

"I don't want to bother you," I muttered.

"You'll never get the job any other way," he warned.

Every month I would call him. "Nothing yet," he would say cheerfully. "Call again soon."

Month after month I phoned, even though I had given up hope. I became so discouraged I tried for a research job on a news magazine. It did not want me, either.

One night after a movie version of *The Philadelphia Story* at Radio City, I returned home. As I bid good-night to mother, who was reading in bed, she announced, "Your friend on that newspaper in New York telephoned."

"What did he say?" My voice rose in excitement.

"Shh-hh," she rebuked me. "You'll wake the others." Always the others, even on a night of glory.

"Wouldn't it be just my luck to be out the once he calls me?" I moaned. "Did you take the message?"

"He wants you to call back," Mother said.

"Right now?"

"I don't know. Why don't you try him?"

I grabbed the telephone. I gave the number and asked for the editor, not expecting him to be there as late as midnight. I was surprised to hear his familiar voice.

"You wanted me?" I asked breathlessly.

"There's an opening here now," he said. "Why don't you come down tomorrow and talk it over?"

That night I did not even try to sleep. New York. New York! New York. New York! The next day after work, I hurried to the city and "the" newspaper.

The editor, whom I had not seen since my first visit twelve months before, explained that the fashion editor needed an assistant. Fashion was becoming important newspaper copy. I would sit in the city room, available half time for fashion, half for general news.

"Do you know fashions?" he asked.

In college I edited a news sheet for a class in modern dress design, my concession to the existence of creative art within me. I served also as a member of the college fashion board of the magazine, *Mademoiselle*.

This experience evidently satisfied the editor. "You can start as reporter in two weeks," he said.

I would have been happy to scrub floors.

"That first day was seventh heaven," I told John.

I stood awed by the wondrous city room, whence sped the news of the world to the reader on the street. Reports from mysterious corners of the earth, culled by foreign correspondents, those word warriors of land, sea and air, whirled across the cable desk. The latest excitement from cities and hamlets of this country flashed across the national desk. Stories of New York and suburbs rolled over the city desk of which I would be part. I would write words that might find their way into print for hundreds of thousands to read. I would possess m own desk, typewriter, telephone and mailbox. This was, indeed, the Christmas of my life.

An affable young man sat next to me, writing of real estate news day after day. He showed me reportorial ropes, steering me to such essentials as morgue, reference library and dictionary stand.

I felt humble midst the royalty of the fourth estate whose

dignity at times gave way to play. The country's greatest feature writer, should the mood inspire him, would suddenly turn upside down in front of me as he plunged his long, lean body on his hands. Coins tinkled from his pockets to the floor as his trousers flew to his knees. Thus he exposed his exuberant spirits when he had no story into which to hurl them. Sometimes he would cup hands to his strong sensitive mouth, whistle like a train.

"Yet much as I loved this, I felt part of me really wasn't there," I told John.

"Perhaps you felt you didn't deserve to be there," he said.

I marveled he knew. "I couldn't believe such a wonderful thing could be happening," I admitted. "I was scared to death any minute I would wake up."

A newspaper office, composed chiefly of men, seemed a perfect hideout. Sometimes I would eat in our cafeteria, the lone woman at a table of seven or eight men. Just like the old days, I thought, but instead of a baseball field, it is a newspaper office.

I gave up living at home to share an apartment with a girl who had been a close friend during the last year of college. It was safer to live with a roommate than alone in a big city.

Mother let me go without a maternal murmur. She understood I wanted to live near the place I worked. She has always tried to make life physically easy for us, as though she knows it may be psychologically tough. She was not one of those parents who say to their children when they want to break away from home, "You're selfish, you think of no one but yourself." (May not such parents unconsciously be telling the child, "You can't leave me unprotected against the world—you're my shield and I need you?")

Fashion spun in a world weird with talk of silhouettes, trends and significant details. Our fashion editor, a generous tutor, hauled me with her three mornings a week to the heart of the country's fashion industry, the wholesale houses of the West Thirties. Models paraded before us wearing gowns for her judgment as high priestess of fashion. If a dress appealed to her she would summon the model closer, whisper to me, "Isn't this material lovely?"

No doubt it was, but I could not muster fervor about fabrics. I felt uncomfortable in this frothy fairyland.

I showed contempt for clothes in the way I dressed. I combined unmixable colors: navy skirt, red sweater, green coat, black shoes, brown bag and white pearl earrings—a caricature of a clothes horse.

A friend once halted me, gazing aghast at my combination of purple, red and green. "Some days, with all your flowers and feathers, you look like a woman of the streets. Today you've improved—you look like a tramp. Do you have to dress so horribly?"

"It suits me," I said sullenly.

Time came when supposedly I had learned enough to write about fashions intelligently even if I could not show intelligence in wearing them. Sent to report bush-league shows, I would slink out of the office like a prisoner bound for solitary, hoping the hem of my $10.95 dress had not escaped its stitching or my stockings were not too snagged from desk splinters.

I would grope my way into the Plaza's elegant Persian Room or the Waldorf's Jade where some department store was sponsoring a show. I would plop down at a press table reserved for sophisticated fashion critics dressed as superbly as the models who swayed through the room. Violins would mush out romantic music, usually *A Pretty Girl Is Like a Melody*, first, last and in the middle.

Between chews of fried chicken, I would seize a pencil and, with an agonized look at the model disappearing down the runway, try to decide whether the dress was green, aqua or sky-blue, whether the waist—no, the bodice—was pleated or tucked, whether the material was faille, silk or synthetic.

The minute the last model disappeared I would flee the chandeliered room as though pursued by Schiaparelli armed with perfumed pitchfork. She would have been justified, too, for the way I murdered fashions in print.

The city editor, sensing my unhappiness, nobly tossed in other assignments such as marigold shows and contests to find the healthiest child in the city. These unimportant news events I considered plums compared to the pinafore circuit.

I felt I became a reporter the day I achieved what no other

woman had accomplished—the dubious distinction of being permitted upstairs in the Mills, a hotel where, for fifty cents a night, the city's less fortunate men, economically speaking, could find shelter. Again, I took pride in being permitted to be with the men.

One of the more fortunate of the less fortunate had fallen heir to $6,500 left by a brother in Detroit whom he had not seen in twenty years. I was assigned to report his reactions.

"You can't come in here," wailed a distressed manager. "No women allowed!"

"I won't look at anything except this man," I promised. "Don't you want a story in the paper mentioning the hotel?"

That dented him. "Okay," he said. "But I'll bring the man to you. Don't move from this lobby."

"I must see what kind of room he's been living in," I insisted.

"You gotta?" His voice held a plea for pity, as if asking, "You want my blood, too?"

"I gotta," I answered heartlessly. Then compromised. "If you let me see his room for a minute, just to catch its feeling, I'll interview him in the lobby."

He agreed. He produced the heir, a gaunt, stooped old man, delighted with sudden fortune.

"Where do you plan to live, now you have inherited money?" I asked.

His answer floored me. "Right here."

"Here?" I exclaimed, picturing the tiny room upstairs.

"I like it here," he said reprovingly.

I thought to ask, "Where have you been living?"

He coughed. "Well, that's just it. I've been sleeping in the park most nights. When I could beg a nickel fare I rode the subway back and forth from Coney to the Bronx."

I understood why he wanted to stay at the Mills. To a man who called the subway's subterranean shelter home when he was lucky, the Mills was a palace.

"After that I raced furiously all over the city for months," I informed John, thinking to myself, yes, I was running away, but never knowing from what.

I got the chance to run, literally, when two star performers arrived in the city. The Duke and Duchess of Windsor made their first visit to New York after their earth-shattering marriage. Each paper assigned several reporters to keep a faithful record of the famous couple. The Duchess fell to me.

"We are going to lead you a merry chase," the Duke announced, grinning at reporters. He meant it. The metropolitan press took it on the chin trying to keep up. We trekked to war relief organizations, settlement houses and slum clearance projects, sometimes permitted inside with the Duke and Duchess, other times restrained to the street. Detectives and policemen, nerves sharpened by thrusting crowds demanding a look at royalty, occasionally turned on us in wrath.

While the Duke visited the sombreroed Mayor of New York and the brown-derbyed Mayor of the Empire State Building, the Duchess took steps to end clamor about her clothes, show how interested she could be in social problems.

She visited Inwood House to inspect the facilities offered destitute unwed mothers who not only lacked husbands but caught syphilis in the bargain. This was a problem in the Bahamas, she told the press.

She strolled through the four-story brick building, smiling graciously at unwed mothers. She paused to be photographed in the playground with cribbed infants as props.

She wore a dull black jersey dress of simple line, relieved only by a draped satin apron front; a tiny, veiled hat, diamond pin and matching earrings (my fashion training did come in for some use). Her chicness was cinched by sable scarf. I ended my story with the sentence that the ride from Inwood House to the Waldorf gave the duchess "a view of Klein's," more popularly known as Madame K's to bargain-hunting women. The copy desk cut out the store's name but substituted "Union Square." The point was made to those who knew the city.

One reporter, out to "do in" the Duchess, interviewed three of the women at Inwood House.

"What do you think of her?" she asked.

"She's swell," gushed the first.

"She's simply wonderful," gasped the second.

"She stinks," drawled the third.

Why did a number of women reporters feel so antagonistic toward the Duchess? Speaking for myself, pure envy of her poise and charm. Her deep blue eyes sometimes looked at us warmly. She acted as though she were accustomed to the luxuries of life and expected everyone to expect her to be.

The Duchess also visited the West Side Center of the Children's Aid Society to be greeted by tall, genial Newbold Morris, then president of the City Council. His grandmother had been a founder of the center.

Mr. Morris proved again, as one reporter so aptly described it, that he was "born with a silver foot in his mouth." He welcomed the Duchess, whose relationship with the country's First Lady did not appear too compatible, with these words:

"I'm so glad you're like Mrs. Roosevelt, in that you look where the shadows are as well as the sunshine."

The sophisticated Duchess merely smiled.

I told John about other kinds of newspaper stories I covered. By the time I completed analysis he had received a thorough course in journalism.

Most reporters at some time write about what one of them unsympathetically nicknamed "the drool circuit," stories of children who live in slums. Publicity people realize, many of them regretfully, there appears no better newspaper way of loosening pocketbooks for charitable causes than a soulful picture of a frail blond girl hugging a large teddy bear.

At first I felt sorry for what I considered exploitation of these children by settlement houses for publicity purposes. But at one of these affairs I started to feel sorrier for the fourth estate than the children.

I joined a group of reporters and photographers who were obviously not enjoying a Christmas party at a settlement house. A tall, slim photographer mumbled, "One more of these assignments and I'm going to poison every brat under ten."

"The kids can't help it," drawled a photographer with five children. "It's the organization that takes advantage of 'em." He felt as I did.

We walked into a gymnasium where red and green streamers festooned basketball nets. A Christmas tree sparkled in the center of the floor. In one corner huddled a group of youngsters holding plates overrunning with ice cream.

The photographers set up cameras, started to select children they considered photogenic. Several gathered around a little girl whose fluffy blond curls framed her delicate face. A pale blue dotted-swiss dress flared out from her tiny waist. She was daintily dabbing away at chocolate ice cream.

"Sit over here, sister," ordered the photographer who had threatened to exterminate all children under ten. He put his hand on her slight shoulders and pulled her up.

"Let go of me, you son of a bitch," said the tot. Drawing back her tiny fist she cracked him hard on the nose.

"Why, you little bas—" the photographer began, to find himself staring into the impassive eyes of the director of the settlement house.

"Can I help you, young man?" asked the director sternly.

"We were wondering if this—young lady—would pose for us?" he muttered.

"Of course she will, won't you, Kathy?" the director asked.

"Yes, sir," said Kathy submissively, "I always does." She smoothed her skirt into neatness.

"Over here," said the photographer, rubbing his reddening nose. This time he did not touch her.

Kathy sat where told. When one photographer asked her to turn a little more to the left she did so. When another suggested she smile, she asked, "Like this?" and flashed a winsome expression. Almost all the papers published her appealing picture the next day.

"I got an education other ways, too," I remarked to John. "I wrote a number of magazine stories which took me places I might have missed in the ordinary routine of reporting."

I spent hours in Children's Court, whose white stone structure bears the inscription, "For every child let truth spring from earth and justice and mercy look down from heaven."

At moments I felt justice and mercy must be busy with other planets. Sometimes stone walls sprung up between judge and child; this may occur when judicial appointments are made for political reasons alone, without concern for the humanity of a man.

I heard cases in Women's Court where policemen trapped prostitutes (as we set man against man to catch those who break the laws that many of us wish we could break).

"I felt much relieved to be able to write about Frank Sinatra," I said to John. "I jumped for joy when sent to interview him at the Paramount." Music, romance, love!

I added, in apology (I was always apologizing to John even though he kept saying I did not have to apologize for living), "I'm afraid I shall always be a spiritual bobby-soxer."

As Sinatra strode onto the stage, an ovation like that accorded the President greeted him. The spotlight shadowed his high cheekbones, threw dramatic shadows on the lean face, just this side of toughness.

In the first row, a girl reverently trained opera glasses on him. Another pitched a gardenia at his feet. Exuberant fans stood up, clicked cameras.

He sang *Night and Day* with poignant intensity. Each note, each word, seemed ripped from him, at the same time giving the feeling the torture was ecstatic. Love was wrapped in the lyrics; promise wrapped in Frankie's delivery.

As he reached the words, "You are the one . . ." a boisterous masculine voice from the audience boomed, "Says you!" Hecklers as well as admirers had paid admission.

Sinatra stopped. His wide mouth broke into a shy, one-sided grin.

"The customer is always right." He shrugged his shoulders.

"Attaboy, Frankie!" screamed the audience. Sinatra's humor is part of his charm, I thought.

He reached the middle of *I May Be Wrong* when someone hurled a penny at him. Again he stopped.

"Whoever threw that penny should have hung onto it. He needs it more than I do," he said. This time there is less humor in the Voice, I thought. I do not blame him, either.

In his dressing room (as, from the street below floated up the chant, "We want Frankie"), he tried to put his success into words.

"I see things the way the kids do," he explained in a tense, almost brash manner underneath which I caught a feeling of uncertainty. "They feel that any one of their crowd could do exactly what I've done. I could be from their neighborhood."

It is more than that, I thought. It is the suggestive voice that sends the girls into a twentieth century swoon. It is the sturdy stance and slim shoulders squared against a rough world. It is the way he clutches the microphone which the official newspaper of the Sighing Society of Sinatra Swooners describes as "that Sinatra-mike-that-makes-you-wish-it-were-you-grip."

But even music could not make me feel like living now. A war was being waged in Africa, Europe, Asia. At the beginning I kept busy enough to forget feelings. I worked not only for the daily newspaper but on assignment from drama and radio departments, book review and magazine section. I lost myself in a perpetual panic of activity.

The magazine asked for an article on women in war plants. I called the public relations director of a large factory who had helped on other stories. When I told him the assignment he advised, "Go work in a factory yourself for a few days; get the real McCoy."

"That's crazy," I retorted. I could not drive a tack without tearing open a thumb.

"After a day at our training school you'll be a full-fledged riveter," he promised.

The picture of me as riveter appealed to my sense of the absurd. I set off for Buffalo, which I will match against any place in the world for January coldness, Siberia excepted.

My notes at the end of the first day of training read: "Fingers cramped tight together from handling electric motor drill. Thumb red from hammer blows. Feet sore from standing all day. Back aches from bending over drilling. Arms shaking from vibration of rivet gun. Seem to hear a whirring in my head but it's only the instructor saying, 'Precision, precision, precision. That's the keynote of a good plane. A bad plane may mean the death knell for some pilot.'"

Once in the war plant where the aisles rang loud with the staccato smash of hammering, drilling and riveting, the labor pains of a plane, I ached from scalp to arch. Rivet guns beat at my forehead like a thousand woodpeckers (woodpeckers, again, to describe a sound of torture). All the old cavities throbbed; vibrations caught every tooth.

That week I found a thousand unknown muscles, each one holding unique hurt. Yet, I forgot physical pain in the thrill

208

of building weapons for fighting men. I could understand why women responded to the demand for their services, especially if they also happened to need money.

The foreman of our section (Panel Department, Nose 1, B, L & R. Tails, Outboard Skin, Nose Bulkheads, Match Angles, or the wing section of a P-40, the fighting Curtiss Warhawk) was one of the few who knew I was only temporary tribulation. He called me over the day I departed.

"Couldn't you stay here?" he pleaded. "We need women."

The country sure must be desperate if it could use machinists like me, I thought grimly. But I felt flattered that he wanted me to remain. To limbo flew backaches, fallen arches, broken fingernails and sore throat from trying to outshout the noise of machines.

I felt I was leaving an important job undone as I punched out for the last time, turned in my pass. Voices rang in my ears. The surprised tone of a mother who, after riveting all day, picked up her baby at the factory nursery: "How do you make Marvin eat cereal? He spits it up when I give it to him at home." The pride in the drawl of the tall Texas supervisor of the panel department: "I was the first one to put women in here and I'm proud of it."

And, making me feel less like a heel for going, the kindly, tired voice of the superintendent of the training school: "Stay where you are. We need the newspapers. How the hell else would we get the women away from their bridge tables?

"They won't stay in the jobs after the war," he added, "but they'll be better off for having worked in a plant. They'll know what it means then, when we say this is a free country."

I was prouder of this assignment than any other. I was helping in the war effort. I was doing the kind of work my father liked; he spent spare time puttering with tools, building radio sets, inventing gadgets. I also knew this was an important story and I could put my heart into the writing of it.

From factory to farm. Then I went to write about the feminine land army. Ladies also picked fruit and husked corn so the nation might eat.

Boarding a boat with twenty other women, I sailed up the Hudson River. We debarked at the city of Hudson where we were allocated to individual farmers. I was instructed to pick strawberries. I thought of Granny's garden where strawberry patch bordered rows of willowy asparagus.

My chosen farmer, bowlegged and energetic, greeted me eagerly. He insisted I see his farm before I pick one strawberry.

"Haven't got the time," I objected, wanting to get to work on berries and story.

"Plenty of time," he said, "you're in the country now."

I restrained myself from retorting, "There's a war on," and stumbled around after him, past cow barn, chicken coop and pig pen.

Suddenly he stopped in dismay. "The cows!" he exclaimed.

I stared at a group of cows that looked perfectly natural to me.

"They've broken out of the pasture!" he cried. "Will you hold them back while I open the gate?"

He pushed me in the direction of cows. I stood facing about eighty of them, each one weighing 1,500 pounds. Immobile, they measured me.

"Why aren't they chewing cud?" I thought frantically.

Four feet separated me from their front ranks. Suddenly one of them moved nearer. Then two, then three. Soft brown eyes took on determined looks.

"Help!" I screamed, running toward the farmer. "They're after me!"

He shouted back, "Yell at them. They're afraid of you."

"Not as much as I am of them," I wailed.

"Thought you told me you'd lived on a farm," he said aggrievedly, coming to my rescue.

"Our cows chewed cud quietly all day, right where they were supposed to be," I retorted. My grandmother's cows showed better bovine behavior.

After that, I was content to remain in the city, preferring to battle my own tendency to inaccuracy than probable charge by cows.

"It's strange I should land in a business where accuracy and time are so important when, in my own life, time and the need to be accurate drive me crazy," I muttered to John. (The unfortunate nature of compulsion, I found out; it fills one need, but never the real one.)

Luckily, I did not make too many mistakes. The most brazen occurred in a story for the radio section. I wrote that a singer appeared "on a nationwide television program." The next day I found a cheerful note from the kindly radio editor:

Is television here to stay?
While engineers give up the ghost
Our Lucy, handsome, blithe and gay
Calmly books it coast-to-coast.

I see by the papers that coast-to-coast television is about to become a reality. I was just premature.

As I worked, I grew more troubled. War casualties surfaced feelings of depression. I felt extremely guilty about the death or partial destruction of men in the armed forces.

The newspaper loaned me to the U.S. Treasury to write feature stories for two of the National War Loan drives. These trips to Washington helped ease my conscience until the day I faced the wounded in the Army's Walter Reed Hospital.

Only eight miles down the road from the center of Washington, the hospital seemed worlds away from the nation's bustling capital. Grass spread green and cool between brick buildings. A lieutenant, public relations man on the hospital staff, conducted me around.

"Ever been to an Army hospital before?" he asked. I shook my head no. I avoided hospitals if I could. I always felt I was fighting for my life, even though a visitor.

"The beauty of this place is that it doesn't smell at all," he said. "You'd never know you were in a hospital."

But there were other ways of knowing. In one large room thirty soldiers lounged in beds. Some listened to the radio with individual earphones. Others wrote letters. One group played poker. By the side of each man rested a pair of crutches. Either right or left leg was gone.

A husky blond lad sat alone on his bed. ("Bed, not cot," whispered the lieutenant.)

"Go on, talk to him," the lieutenant urged and walked away.

I looked at the blond boy from Malone, New York. I tried to concentrate on the curl of his hair, not the stump of his foot. I tried not to think of the thirty other boys in that room, each with stump for foot.

"Have a seat," the boy invited, gesturing to the foot of his bed. (I could not escape "foot.")

"How did it happen?" I asked. (The eternal, damnable question, "How did *it* happen?")

"We were about to launch an attack," he said, as if describing a jaunt to ice cream parlor. "I was walking back from breakfast and I just happened to step on a land mine." It blew off his right leg and hurled one hundred and fifty pieces of shrapnel into his body. He pulled up his trousers to show his remaining leg, punctured with scars left by shrapnel wounds. It was a sturdy leg, powerfully built like his shoulders.

"Several of the men have artificial limbs already," he said enviously. "I'll get mine soon."

Did the wounded resent reporters? I asked the lieutenant.

"They all want to talk," he assured me. "All but a few temperamental ones. Most of them will tell you anything."

Then he said, "Wouldn't you like to interview someone from Sicily? North Africa and the Southwest Pacific are old stuff now." Yes, Sicily casualties will make the best news, I thought bitterly. The world is already forgetting earlier battles.

We found a soldier who had just arrived from Sicily, a private who fought his way for fifteen days on foot across the island. He moved fast in those fifteen days—faster than he ever would again. His right calf had been shot off; he was also paralyzed from the waist down.

He and several other soldiers were being fed intravenously. He talked painfully. His throat held back his voice. Around him men breathed harshly. One threw up a tortured gasp each time he inhaled.

He told us, speaking slowly, that he was a thirty-year-old printer from Richmond, Virginia, where he lived with his wife before the Army slung a gun across his shoulders. He found himself in Sicilian hills, one of the heroes selected to wipe out the Germans. It took the enemy fifteen days to catch up with a man who set type for a living.

212

"We got clean across the island in those fifteen days," he said proudly. "Mostly we walked. Sometimes all night."

German artillery cracked into him on the home stretch. "We were going across the toe, outside of Palermo, when it happened," he said. "It was noon." (They all remember the exact time—noon, before breakfast, just after dark. They remember the moment they might have been killed.)

He was feeding ammunition to an 81 mm. mortar gun. Something sped toward him. "I think it was an eighty-eight," he said.

"I don't know what happened next," he apologized to us. "I kinda passed out." His voice trailed off in weakness.

"Get me out of here," I muttered to the lieutenant. When we reached the hallway I cursed to keep from crying. Then I apologized.

"That's all right," said the understanding lieutenant. "You get used to it after a while."

"I get used to it?" I gasped. "What about them?"

His face looked grim for the first time. He, too, had been thinking of legs that once jumped over fallen logs in Adirondack Mountains, of arms that once reached eagerly for football or girl's waist. He heard shells scream down in Sicily, watched pieces of these men fly into the air.

The hill in Palermo and the desert in Tunisia reached into every corner of the hospital. In order to bear the suffering, the lieutenant, like others who worked there, covered tears with jauntiness, as I had covered them with curses.

"I wish every civilian could walk down these halls," he said.

On those words we parted.

In my dreams I, too, fought at the front, hiding in Italian villages, scurrying from door to door trying to find shelter as bombs crashed down. Many a night I woke up screaming. It took long minutes to know I lay in the heart of New York, not in a coffin in Italy. It was only a dream because I was only a girl. Because I wore skirts, I did not have to face dying low in the mud or high in the air or deep in the sea.

Then peace silenced the guns but brought no silence to my life. Instead, the screams inside whined louder.

213

I felt even sicker when sent to report the angry rumble of resentment exploding at the Round Hill Community House in Greenwich. Elite rafters shook with the rage of property owners fighting the suggestion the area become permanent headquarters for United Nations.

One man rose to protest angrily, "When I was young, I heard all about Geneva. That was a flop. Let 'em go back!" The audience applauded. How blind can one be? I wondered.

The next day a small group of residents who wanted the UN site in Greenwich held a meeting. Said a speaker: "One woman told me she was afraid this would mean all kinds of people would come to Greenwich. I said, 'Didn't we fight this war with all kinds of people?' " I wanted to applaud even though reporters are supposed to be impartial.

Nothing in life held cheer, not even a day that should have proved joyous. The city editor assigned me to cover United Nations delegates as they momentarily forsook the clash of ideologies for the crack of bat against ball.

The Giants were to meet Philadelphia at the Polo Grounds to open the baseball season, April, 1946. I rode up with a photographer, also a Giant fan. I said to him exultantly, "Now I'll see Mel Ott."

That's what *I* thought. I forgot the nature of the assignment—a report on how the UN delegates reacted to the game, not how I did.

I was watching Trygve Lie, secretary general of the Security Council, who had confessed this was his first baseball game.

Suddenly there sounded a terrific clout. The crowds stood up and roared.

"What happened?" I asked the reporter next to me.

"Ott hit a homer!" he said excitedly.

"I waited nineteen years to see that," I wailed. I added sullenly, "At least I heard it."

I had to be content to watch Mr. Lie devour two hot dogs and Lieut. Col. W. R. Hodgson, Australian delegate, shell peanuts. I felt like beaning Colonel Hodgson when he mused after Ott's homer, "I've seen better cricket hits."

Conspicuous by absence was Andrei A. Gromyko, the Russian delegate, who evidently did not want to watch others take a walk—thirteen players trotted to first base, courtesy of pitcher.

Governor Dewey arrived, shook hands with Dr. Quo Tai-chi of China, serving his last day as president of the Security Council.

"You can talk freely now," joked the governor. "You won't have to be so polite any more."

The few chances I had to cover the United Nations pleased me, for I felt nearer to contributing in small way to the peace of the world, I told John.

Then I remembered I had refused the chance to become part of our United Nations bureau. What did I want?

I had thought working in New York would solve all my problems. New York was to be the gateway to psychic Paradise. The trumpets of titans blared a song of release, welcoming me to the city as I joined thousands who sought surcease in its detached, steel embrace.

But the city brought only sorrow. It could not answer questions; it could only help me run away. I could not destroy the past by throwing myself headlong into a whirlpool of anxiety so thick I could slice it.

I was still trying to find the answer outside myself. I could not know the city narrowed to one room and that room to one life and everything centered on that life when it was unhappy.

I lived in a twenty-fourth floor apartment on Riverside Drive where windows framed the slow-moving Hudson and the peaceful Palisades.

"You lucky girl," friends would say, staring out at the graceful George Washington bridge.

In spring luxuriant flowers bloomed in the parks below. Summer coaxed lazy sailboats to the river. Autumn turned trees to rainbow hues. Winter's snow, settling on river cliffs, flaked peace on that corner of the city.

I could not deny the beauty that stretched outside the windows, the skyscraper splendor spurting up from the wedge of rock that is Manhattan. I could only wonder why none existed in me. The apartment seemed a cell and I, a prisoner, confined for unknown crime.

Chapter XV

Why Words?

Bᴜᴛ ᴀᴛ ʟᴀsᴛ ɪ ᴄᴏᴜʟᴅ know why I felt like a criminal. I had been committing murder—with words.

Unconsciously I used work to keep from killing or being killed. I attacked the typewriter murderously, venting feelings of hatred on the silent, indefensible mechanism. Better that fingers wreak fury on keys than someone's throat.

I wrote desperately, as though hoping the white paper would absorb my misery as it absorbed ink. I wrote not out of conviction or thoughtfulness but out of compulsion and wrath. I wrote strictly from hunger, as the apt expression goes.

I was indignant when John first suggested, "Have you ever thought you might be using words as a safety device so you won't have to face your real feelings?"

How do I know what my real feelings are, I wondered.

"Perhaps the words you use are not honest because you must cover up what you feel," he went on.

"I don't cover up my feelings with words," I retorted angrily. "I choose my words carefully. Words are important to me."

"Words *are* important," he said. "They may be costly. But you must live words for them to be important. Do you live words or merely use them?"

Now I understood more of what he meant. Many of the big words I used did not count. The sparkling adjectives I tossed off for the columns of the paper describing the Easter Parade did not really count because I was too angry to care. The words that mattered I could not use—love, hate, fear, envy—the words by which I lived. The others were the ones behind which I hid.

It had been easy for me to mask feelings with words. Words poured out as one of my weapons against fear. I built strong barriers with words, to keep myself from myself and others.

I threw up a smokescreen of books, reading hundreds without understanding them.

I intellectualized to escape the pangs of more personal feelings. I tried to deny emotions that quivered directly under the surface of the words. When I argued heatedly about philosophy, politics or art, the passion in my voice betrayed me. I was arguing for things I could not dare admit.

I took refuge in intellectuality. I used my head for everything but living.

Children understand the simple words far better than some adults. I eavesdropped on two little girls in the ladies' room of a pullman train. The mother of the younger one was combing her daughter's hair. The little girl protested it hurt.

Said the mother, indicating the older girl, "I'll bet she doesn't mind when her mother combs her hair."

The seven-year-old replied frankly, "The heck I don't." She looked at the younger child. "Your mother paints your finger nails, doesn't she?" she said in open envy.

The tiny girl daintily spread her fingers apart showing off. "I'm dressing up to see my grandma. Why don't you get yours painted?"

"Because my mother doesn't think little girls should have their nails painted," the other apologized.

"But you're not a little girl," said the four-year-old in astonishment. "You're big!"

"Well—half-little, half-big," said the seven-year-old lamely.

The mother, smothering a smile, asked the older girl, "Where are you from?"

The young lady hesitated a moment, then said, "Either Detroit or Michigan. I always get them mixed up."

She could confess her confusion. I could only feel anger because I was confused.

I said to John rebelliously, "As far back as I can remember, Mother and Dad would talk and talk and sometimes they wouldn't keep their word or they would give me a reason that didn't make sense."

I added grimly, "They always had enough words to talk me out of anything."

"In a sense, you are protesting against their profligacy," he said. "They used words not caring whether you were hurt. It is as though you now say to them, 'Every word I use counts. *Words are important,* even if you, Mother and Father, didn't think so once.' "

"They would never listen to me," I said sullenly.

"So now you make sure they will," he said. "Now you talk to them through your writing."

I recalled, "It was my father who bought me a typewriter."

"Why did he give it to you?"

"I don't know." I could not remember any reason. "Maybe I asked for it."

"Maybe unconsciously he wanted you to be a writer," John suggested.

"Do you really think so?" I had never thought I wrote because my parents wished me to write.

"Children may fill the unconscious needs of parents as well as the conscious ones," John said. "They feel what the parent wants, as well as listening to what he says or watching what he does. Parents may impart to children what they wish they had been, and to get approval, children may carry out these wishes, unless they are too angry, in which case they may rebel and do just the opposite of what the parent wants."

Now that I thought of it, I realized my parents gave hearty approval to my writing from the moment I scrawled my first sentence. Crumbs of affection were tossed my way for high marks in school, gay English compositions, elaborate thank-you notes to relatives.

I mistook praise for love. Praise is part of love, but to me it became the whole of love. Eagerly I read, studied, wrote, so I would earn more praise, more love. (The body is dangerous, so concentrate on the neck up, like a good little girl, and we will love you.)

I went on to woo the world with words as others did with paintbrush or pocketbook.

It was not enough to live for the sake of living because I was not sure I wanted to live. I felt people saw through me, discovering my badness.

I felt unworthy of love but at the same time I thought I might work my way into the world's heart. The danger was

218

that, just as an alcoholic eventually must have drink to carry on, I began to depend on my career to live. I could not afford, emotionally, to give it up. I felt as though my life depended on words.

Words also represented my demand for attention.

"Need for attention is need for love," John said.

The greater the drive for the glory and the gravy, the deeper the feeling one is nobody and worth nobody's love, he felt. The person content to live and let live, demanding little from life and giving of himself in moderation, is the happy, emotionally healthy man. His achievement is a product of his self-liking and liking of others, not a way of earning that liking.

I had demanded much. I wanted to know all the answers. I wanted to know what everyone was thinking and doing. Reporting offered a way of carrying out these desires. The career had served many purposes, some constructive, some destructive.

But now I had to ask why I could not settle for love in a cottage? By the laws of nature I was a woman. Did it not occur to me there might be something wrong with a woman who was not content to assume a passive role, who must try to be like the men she envies?

Why was I competing with men, holding a job that obviously scared me? The answer was that while I was frightened of the job, I was more frightened not to work. I had deceived myself by thinking I had wanted to get married. Deep inside I feared marriage, as my failure at it showed.

I found some lines I wrote when twenty-one. Even a non-analyst could figure out from them what marriage meant to me:

> Each life is lush with a thousand dreams. And the most delicate of them disappear when one marries. They do not break—nothing so drastic. They crumble and crackle and corrupt. Slow death to dreams!

I had been fighting for my life with the best means at my command—words. I fought by automatically (unconsciously) choosing from my experience what I found would ease the pain —words. My barbed wire fence against the world was—words.

A certain amount of energy should be spent in every job but I poured into mine all the passion and devotion that many

219

women put into their home. I mistook anxiety for interest. I thought I found something I liked and stuck to it, not knowing I had found a defense against anxiety and was stuck with it.

I had been running away from my feelings so furiously it was a wonder my whole nose hadn't shaken off in protest, let alone merely becoming stopped up with sinus.

I raced through assignments, taking no time to enjoy them. My living lacked the quality of savoring the hours. I did not go along with time, I fought it—always a losing battle. I could not accept the clock as part of reality though I lived by it.

A friend called to complain her watch had stopped. "I thought maybe you'd tell me the time, if you have a clock," she said.

"Me *not* have a clock?" I retorted. "Do you want me to die?"

Time was enemy. I raced through life trying to escape it, the other extreme of those who show contempt for time by ignoring it. I fought the hours, the days, the months and the years, refusing to believe time one day for me would end. I would not accept the thought of death. I felt I had never really lived.

Life was a circle of rush. I never enjoyed where I was but worried only where I would go next. When I arrived I would think, where do I go from here? I never felt part of any one scene.

When no deadlines threatened, I manufactured some. When life seemed empty I sought excitement. I pursued false pleasure, based on things outside myself. "False pleasures bring genuine pain," warns the Bible. I ached with the pain genuine to all those who know no comfort in themselves.

The faster I ran, the faster fury built up within and the more determined I became to escape facing myself. Things must be put out of mind, I thought, not knowing I meant out of consciousness—in one case I forgot deliberately after I arrived at awareness, which happens with maturity, in the other, I buried hastily in order not to become aware.

In spite of so-called accomplishments, I wondered what I was achieving, why I was born. I considered life an overwhelming enigma, existence a giant question mark.

"Life was always a terribly serious matter," I told John.

"Perhaps because you felt no one took you seriously," he said.

But if I held an important job then people would take me seriously. If I became famous, people might like me.

I had, indeed, deceived myself about the reasons I worked. To John I had said defiantly, "My job is just work done for money earned. So I can eat and pay you!"

Early in life I aimed at financial independence. I held contempt for my parents' money. When I earned any of my own, I also had contempt for that. I threw money away playing the horses, making loans to irresponsible friends, overtipping.

When I bought shoes or dresses and they did not fit or I did not like them, I would not dream of exchanging them. To keep them was less terrifying than to persuade a clerk to take them back. The clerk might not like me then.

One part of me felt overpaid. "All this money for poor little me?" Another part, watching others who did less work receive more money, would rage, "Why don't they pay me more?" On the other hand I could not take from people because I wanted so much to take from them; on the other I wanted more than I was worth.

It was part of my tragedy that my weapon turned inward. Writing proved tortuous. When you feel loved the hardest chore dwindles into nothing but when you feel unloved the smallest effort looms difficult and unrewarding.

As I wrote I fumed because I could not listen to swing or go to the latest Astaire movie or, in summer, simmer in the sun. Utopia for me would be a long white beach on which I could feel the soft sand underneath my body, run it through toes and fingers, place cheek against its caressing warmth.

Organization in writing tore me apart. The feelings I wanted to convey became so intense I could not take time for thoughtful planning. I struggled for semblance to clear, orderly thinking.

I resented sketching in details. Just put down "big house" or "pretty dress," I thought. To hell with the details. (Just put down unhappy life, forget the details which made you angry.) It took all my strength merely to get the surplus emotion out of my system. I felt panic if called on to cope with extra details.

I hid behind the defense of the generalization, afraid to look at the specific—self. I wanted to believe I was at one with the rest of the world. (All women believe—people feel—everybody knows.) The specific infuriated me because the specific in my own life felt so sordid.

I liked feeling undefined—non-objective art, impressionistic writing, dissonant music—these seemed to speak to my unconscious as though some anger in the artist communicated harmoniously with my anger.

In painting I admired curved lines that led the eyes a dance over the canvas. Someone asked, looking at my copy of a Bauer abstraction of purple, green and orange bubbles in rhythmic formation, "What is it supposed to be?"

"Nothing. Just form and feeling. Can't you like it without knowing what it means?"

"People like explanations for everything," my questioner said.

I had never troubled to find explanation for my life. Why should I bother to find it for a painting?

Often as I sat alone, writing, sluggishness stole over me. I had to pull out the words painfully.

"Why is that?" I asked John.

"Perhaps because of unconscious suicidal impulses," he said.

Authors have been known to kill themselves, I thought Sometimes even after a book was written. Perhaps they staked all on the book and then, when it was completed, realized to their dismay, they were as unhappy as ever, John said. Their book may have solved few of their deep problems.

Though it pained, writing produced my only satisfaction. I had to work. I could not have stood myself without working. It was the way I compromised; knowing I was a girl, but wishing I were a boy.

I needed the work for many reasons. I did not trust the spoken word, for I felt too many spoken promises had been broken. If words were put on paper there was less likelihood of denial. This was part of my need for consistency in a life where I felt people too often changed their minds.

Writing was easier, too, than expressing myself vocally. I could not get words out when I was frightened, which was most of the time. I had to speak fast or be unable to speak. In my haste, often the words that tumbled out were not the ones I meant to use.

Writing also offered me a place to put my sexual feelings, sometimes so intense I despaired of handling them.

"When people are afraid of love they may put passion elsewhere so it does not destroy them," John said.

Passion that belonged only to love flowed into my typewriter. It was safer for me to be passionate about words than about another person. I did not dare risk love, so I joined those who spent their passion in the unfruitful meadows of conquest. power and ambition.

There may be sexual overtones to anything created out of man's anxiety, according to John. The speed of a plane, for instance, and the take-off with its burst of sudden, determined power symbolizes sex to me.

Also into my work I hurled disgust at bodily functions. Often I felt what I produced was no good, loathsome.

"I cannot bear to reread this stuff," I told a fellow reporter, gesturing toward a story I wrote.

"I know what you mean," he said. "It's like a dog returning to its vomit."

"Crap to me," I put it.

Another reason I worked proved difficult to pull out of the unconscious.

One morning I talked of a friend who had spent ten years in a mental hospital.

"She will never get better," I said sadly. "They've given her up as lost."

The last time I saw her, six years before, my father and I had taken her for a drive in the hills surrounding the hospital. I sat with her in the back seat, trying to communicate. Only gibberish flowed from her parched lips.

But she knew me, for she called me by name every so often. Then she would retreat into her world. I sat shocked, trying to understand her, then realized I could not.

She was a gentle, fragile woman whom I liked so much

I bought a copy of the popular painting, *Alice Blue Gown,* because it resembled her.

I started telling John about her. I choked on words. The tears began to roll.

"Are you afraid the same thing might happen to you?" he asked gently.

I burst into sobs of tornado force that made all the other tears I had shed look like a mere drizzle.

Madness is one of the things I've been afraid of all the years, I felt. One reason I write is to forget nothing makes sense so it must be I who am crazy.

I recalled the many times people asked why I worked and I replied vaguely, inanely, "To keep from going crazy."

I spoke the words as some crazy persons might, as though they bore no relation to me, because I felt so keenly they did relate to me.

I would often tell myself, "Don't do that, you idiot," or, "Haven't you got brains enough to know that?" In front of John I would refer to my "feeble mind."

One of the terrors of the unhappy person may be that he may go crazy, John said. But most people do not suddenly "go" insane, he believed. It may seem as though minds "snap," but fear has been building up over the years and holds millions of moments of fright and anger.

"Defenses may fall quickly but the signs of disintegration have been there for a long time," John said. "Perhaps no one has seen them. What is seen depends on who sees."

Some of us feel insanity is one of the worst fates to befall anyone. A leg lost is pathetic but a mind lost is the final tragedy. When we want to tell someone we dislike him we may say in disgust and anger, "Don't be crazy!" There is no greater insult, perhaps, except, "Drop dead."

During the analysis I found I wanted to change from reporting general news to welfare and psychiatry. I believed people could be helped with emotional troubles. I believed in welfare, if wisely given.

The other reporters thought I *was* crazy, giving up an exciting life that included an occasional suicide or court trial, for "that dull stuff."

"I'd rather understand why men need to murder, and perhaps help to prevent it, than cover the gory details of a murder," I explained. I believed reporting on the study of human behavior was far from dull stuff to those who tried to understand themselves and others.

A flood or fire renders thousands destitute and newspapers pour on the adjectives in describing the suffering victims. Or they conduct crusades for those who dwell in slums. These kinds of misery are easy to feel.

But what about the misery that gnaws away inside men? I thought. What about those who live in terror of their own thoughts or feelings? They are just as unhappy as those who have lost homes in a fire, but who does much for their eternally burning fire?

With the editor's consent, I started to cover mental health conferences and welfare news. I was much happier for many reasons. I was able to face more of what lay inside me. I felt safe enough to know my interest in writing about the mental health field was partial identification with the emotionally sick, as though, by saving them, in some way I also saved myself.

Sublimation is nature's way of protecting the human body from too much pain. The work was a fortunate outlet. I am thankful I found this means of fighting.

My mistake was in thinking I could forever escape inner fury by working so hard I had no time to think. The cauldron of my body would boil just so long before bubbling over with anger.

Chapter XVI

OTHER DEFENSES

WORK WAS NOT MY only defense. I found many ways to save my life; no sluggard, I, when it came to self-preservation.

Like the chameleon, I, too, possessed protective coloration. When faced with fear I summoned defenses full force. As I found myself less afraid, as with John, I could show more of my real feelings, let down the defenses.

Anger, appeasement, the question—these were some of my drugs against reality's pain. They were my fences, erected to hold back fear. They stood as obstructions between me and what I could not face.

John did not rush me into examining defenses. He knew if they fall too suddenly, as sometimes they do, reality must be completely abandoned because it becomes too threatening.

"If you remove too quickly the defenses of someone who is emotionally ill, he may become more seriously ill," he said.

When he first suggested I become aware of my defenses, I felt angry. What right has he to criticize me? I thought. I do the best I know how.

"Listen to the number of questions you ask," he said.

"I don't ask many," I retorted furiously.

He chuckled.

I chuckled. I knew I asked thousands. I could not allow myself one thought without checking first with him to see if he agreed.

I would describe a dream, then ask, "What do you think it means?" If I tried to interpret, I would wind up, "Is that right?"

For a while he allowed me to ask as many questions as I wished, knowing I was too frightened to hear myself asking. When he thought it time, he suggested I face what I did.

"Why do you think you ask so many questions?" asked he.

"I don't know," I muttered. Questions just seemed to come naturally. (As other things in life did not come naturally, I felt something should.)

Do I ask them, not for information, but for other reasons? I wondered. Was it one way of flattering people, of telling them I was interested in them and, at the same time, asking, please, wouldn't they be interested in me?

One day when John asked again why I thought I asked so many questions, I answered with the first thought that rushed to mind.

"So they won't touch me," I yelled. "Or vice-versa, so they will. I don't know. I'm all confused!"

I calmed down, thought of what I had said. I was telling him the question served as a way of preventing people from attacking me physically. Paradoxically, the part of me that screamed "or vice versa" wanted them to touch me.

"I suppose I've just told you I ask questions, in a sense, to be seduced and as seduction to keep from getting killed," I said sourly.

"Murders have been prevented by the victim's seduction of the murderer," he commented. "Sometimes seduction is used when no murder is contemplated."

I might use the question to ward off attack though no attack was imminent, he meant.

I also asked questions the minute I felt people were getting too close. Questions kept them at arm's length. At the same time I asked to make sure they would be interested enough to stay within reach.

Questions served other purposes. I recalled as a child I learned one way of forestalling anger was to ask a question. In the answering of it, my parents, or the teacher, forgot all else. I would not have to worry for the moment what they thought of me.

The question was a way of getting attention. If I talked, I could not be sure anyone listened. But if I asked a question, they would be forced to concentrate to answer.

Questions also kept others from prying into my unhappiness. Let anyone ask me one and I felt he stuck a psychic pin in my heart. I could not answer truthfully, so I did not want to answer at all. ("How are you?" "Fine, fine." When I felt lower than God's worms.)

By questioning John I was avoiding pain. Instead of pursuing a straight path, the shortest way to health, I detoured off on the question when I felt the road too rocky.

I might be talking of how I felt toward my father when suddenly I would turn to John, demand, "Do you really think this makes sense?" Or, as I spoke of how deeply I liked music, I would ask, "But you felt that way, too, didn't you?"

I could not stop searching the souls of others because mine felt so sordid.

"There really aren't any questions in life," John mused.

227

"What?" I screamed, mortally wounded. He was taking away my life, built on The Question.

"Your life is filled with 'why's' but never the one 'why' that is the root of it all."

"What might that be?" I sounded scornful.

"Why didn't my mother love me when I was a child?"

I was silent. I could not know, as yet, she loved me as much as she loved anyone, that it was not me she disliked but herself, just as I did not dislike others, but myself.

The question was also part of my need to appease, another defense. I bottled up anger with the cork of appeasement. Early in life, somehow, somewhere, many times, I found I received more approval, less wrath, when I appeased.

"In childhood, you tried to please people who never could be pleased, but that you did not know," John said.

I thought of "people who could never be pleased."

"You got a high mark in school? Next time get a higher one."

"You won a prize? Next time win them all."

"You have a boy friend? How nice. Who? Don't tell me you want to bring that dope to the house?"

"That's a pretty dress. But it makes you look fat."

"If you behave, I will . . ."

"If you get marks, I will . . ."

"If you, if you, if you . . ."

(Never, "I love you, darling, and I trust you no matter what you do.")

John said, "You lived with people who had the glint of anxiety in their eyes and promissory notes of love in their pockets. Those with the cold cash of love you passed by."

I had been too busy solidifying defenses to give much thought to love. My defenses had to be strong because fear of destruction was great. I was amazed when someone described me as defenseless.

"Why, I've got thousands of defenses," I complained to John.

"Those who need defenses are often thought of as defenseless," he said. "Those who are strong may need few defenses. Strength is the best defense in the world."

Any deviation from fixed habit alarmed me. I considered

228

change another threat. I lived in set ways, thinking always of what I should or should not do. I showed up at parties compulsively on time. I left compulsively shortly after. I went compulsively to the bathroom each morning (perhaps one of the original compulsions on which all others were based).

When John first brought up talk of toilet functions, I quickly steered off the subject.

"We've discussed this before," I would say.

"Just because you mention something once or twice does not mean you have faced your feelings about it."

"I know," I would reply, brusquely dropping the matter. Some things I did not want to think more about.

But I came to know I could not free myself of fear unless I could talk not only often but casually of things that upset me. I might mention a tabooed topic like auto-eroticism twenty times, but how I mentioned it, whether in fear or trembling, or calm acceptance, told me whether I was still frightened of it. I had to hack away at fear.

I could forever duck talk of toilet functions but not if I desired health. The way I felt about going to the bathroom was important because it showed how I was taught to feel about my body. My first toilet training shaped feelings about myself. ✓

"Emotional overtones of toilet training are carried into many things you do, revealing how you live," John said.

I finally confessed constipation was a perpetual fear in my life. At times I felt only dynamite could blast the badness out of me. I felt I *had* to go regularly every morning. If, by any chance, I could not, I slouched through the day, depressed and burdened. I needed the comfort of my own bathroom. It was agony to stay out overnight. I also had difficulty using the bathroom if anyone was near. Sometimes I would want to go at John's but would feel too ashamed to excuse myself. It isn't nice, I would think.

There was no reason, he assured me, to rage when I could not go to the bathroom regularly. "You do not have to go at any set time," he said. "That's advertising propaganda. Nature will take care of you."

I could not recall much about early toilet training; certainly not the spanking which my father gave me which kept me from wetting the bed after the age of two (and did he have to be so proud of it?). But I feel we children were hurried in and out of the bathroom because there were so many of us and that I resented the hurry. My whole life seemed hurry, hurry, hurry—get it over with.

As if in rebellion against the rush I now read magazines in the bathroom. I could not give them up even though John suggested it. One morning I entered his office triumphantly.

"I didn't read in the bathroom this morning!" I exclaimed.

"That's good," he said approvingly.

My face fell. "I cannot tell a half-truth. I didn't read—because I couldn't! I have such a hangover that I couldn't hold my head up to focus on the pages of a book." This was one of the few mornings of my life I owned a hangover and I felt proud of it.

He laughed. "You'll give up reading when you're ready."

I realized one reason I liked to remain in the bathroom so long was because of sensuous pleasure that came from successful bowel movements. Because I felt bad, that no one loved me, I would love myself. Nature made it pleasurable, to a certain degree, to go to the bathroom, but she did not intend this pleasure to be abused as I was doing.

I dreamed I entered a bathroom, found it overflowing with blood. I started to tell John, "I dreamed I walked into the . . ." I nearly said "john," popular word for bathroom. I hastily substituted "toilet." (My anger at him must have been at a minimum that day or I would have used "john.")

I also ate compulsively. "If I could only lose weight," I would complain. Yet I hungered for each meal. I consumed every one as if it were, indeed, the last supper.

I craved chocolate in any form, ice cream, fudge, cocoa. Once I returned from a convention, face beaming. "Did you have a good time?" asked John.

"I sure did. I discovered chocolate whipped cream!"

When I despaired over failure to lose weight, he said, "Perhaps you cannot lose because of the way you eat. No secure person craves food. He may like or dislike certain foods, but he has no obsession about them."

I might crave food because of what it meant as bodily pleasure when I was a child, he said. Children live for bodily pleasures, especially unhappy children.

I added a reason of my own. "If I finished all the food on my plate, Mother looked pleased. When I left any, she seemed angry. Perhaps I continually eat to reassure myself I am a good little girl."

I moved compulsively; quick to open a door, quick to undress, quick to jump into bed and turn off the light—everything quick except sleep. That came slowly as though to punish me for showing such speed all day. In the morning I dashed out of bed at alarm's sound.

Why, I even wake up running, I thought.

Underneath, it was as though I knew unless I moved fast I might not move at all. If I stopped to think about what I felt I would be lost. I would die of lethargy.

The defense often hides the directly opposite characteristic. It is as though to protect what we feel is inner weakness, we strive to be opposite on the surface, he said. ✓

"Watch out for masks," he warned. "Those who appear soft outside may be hard as nails underneath. The tough guys may really be softies. Neither is firm, gentle or mature."

Some drunkards feel, underneath, it is wicked to drink; they have such strong consciences they cannot bear life unless they do drink, John held. On the other hand, those who cannot drink may know, if once they start, they will give in to dangerous feelings, so they fear to drink.

Both extremes, excessiveness and prohibitiveness, may be seen in the same person, he said. An individual outwardly pious may feel full of inner wickedness. Somerset Maugham caught this expertly, I thought, in the story of Sadie Thompson where the missionary and the prostitute end by reversing feelings when masks are torn off.

There may be a world of difference between a person's outer life, which seems prim and proper, and his inner life of chaos, John said. Those who demand a life of perfect outer order may often be those whose inner lives feel disorderly.

"You mean people who are compulsive about cleanliness and must wash their hands twenty times a day underneath feel very dirty?" I asked.

"They feel so 'bad' that their unconscious has to receive the excess of 'dirty' feelings to protect them. The conscious makes up for the inner feeling of 'badness' by an outer show of cleanliness or 'goodness.'"

"I always have to leave a room in perfect order," I muttered. No ashes must mar the serenity of ashtrays, no clothes disturb the perfect folds of the bed. A high point in my life occurred, when, during analysis, one night after a party I returned to my apartment, kicked my shoes high in the air and left them where they fell. (Mother's voice sometimes held high anger when I did not put things away. Although she no longer stood within striking distance, I could still hear her anger.)

John had shown no alarm at my expressions of savagery. He expected this turnabout from sweet humility to darkest rage as part of analysis. This often happens, he said, as the patient drops defenses and reveals fear. If the analysis is successful, the patient then swings back to the middle, settling for temperance where nature meant him to live.

When excessive fear is present in a person, nature will seek to balance it by overcompensation. Nature will never be defeated; she always tries to find a balance. This was John's philosophy.

I had never thought much about nature. To me, it was something mysterious associated with walking in the woods and catching poison ivy. Camp life attracted only fools, I thought.

John's feeling for nature bordered on reverence. When I asked him what he meant by nature, he said, "Nature is growth or God or whatever you want to call it."

Man, he felt, was only part of nature, and sometimes a very destructive part. Man, like the dinosaur, might even become extinct because he was getting too big for his own good, John believed. Nature was interested in life, of which man was only part.

At first I did not understand his respect for nature. I told him with scorn I did not want to exist like a placid cow in a pasture.

"There is magic in a cow which chews green grass that turns

into milk that feeds babies who grow into men and women," he said quietly.

I admitted grudgingly, "I accept the theory of evolution. I realize I'm probably related to the nearest gorilla."

"Gorilla?" he exclaimed, as though I were the highest of snobs. "You mean the first protozoon that oozed its way out of the slime."

I did not know whether to feel proud or indignant. I thought, Maybe it is patronizing to believe we can go nature one better. For all our vaunted progress, perhaps the truly civilized man is the one humble enough to accept his kinship with the animal kingdom.

"Man should bow to nature," John said. "She is far more powerful than he."

He asked me to accept that I was only one of her creatures, to learn from her instead of fearing her and transferring my hatred of self and parents to some of her smaller animals.

"You have such faith in nature," I marveled.

"What else is there?" he asked. "Even doctors are dependent on nature. They can put metal plates in a man's skull but what good is it if the tissues around the plate fail to heal? A doctor can try to help nature. He can set a bone straight instead of crooked so nature's work will be easier. But he should ask, 'How can I help nature?' not, 'How can nature help me?' It is the life force, or nature, that mends."

As a doctor, John was helping nature to mend psychological wounds. Within all of us, natural processes of growth take place. People grow, just as do trees and flowers. If emotional nourishment is lacking, they will grow stunted or twisted.

Fear can be so great and anger so intense they warp development. One may grow up psychologically crooked, the logic of his psyche distorted. John was helping me "to straighten up and fly right."

"Can you really cure neurosis?" I asked. "What about 'as the twig bends so the tree inclineth'?"

"A skillful tree doctor can straighten the tree," he answered. "But slowly, otherwise it may break."

"Some sort of crutch is needed, isn't it?"

"Analysis is a kind of crutch at first. But, as with the tree, you will gain enough strength so you will be able to stand straighter by yourself."

He was trying to help me get strength. He was asking me to peer beneath the protective layer of defenses into the fear, to know that no longer was the fear valid.

But because I was so afraid, I could not understand, for a while, what he tried to do. It seemed he was tearing down everything I had created (as he was, but for my own good; for my mind's buildings stood rotted, parasitic, tottering).

"You must remember what you felt like at the age of six and eight and ten," he reminded me. "Don't forget what a tomboy you were."

"You remember so much," I accused him.

"You forget so much," he said with a laugh.

I had forgotten plenty. I had forgotten how I always felt that as oldest, I was entitled to ride in the front seat of our car with my father, never giving the other children a chance. I had forgotten jealousy of my brother who always seemed to be getting away with murder, while my murder slowly corrupted me.

There was much of Othello in me. When John first suggested I might be jealous of others I laughed. "I'm not the jealous type," I told him.

"You are so jealous you have to hide it under the guise of loving everyone," he said.

He added reassuringly, "Jealousy is fear of not being loved."

How can he accuse me of such a thing? I wondered. Then I remembered telling him a dream in which he preferred one of his other patients. When he kept me waiting I felt slow fury rise against the other person, especially the buxom blond woman. I was jealous of John's other patients.

My whole life sputtered with jealousy of shining blond (brother) or red hair (sisters). I had always felt the outcast, the duck-ugly in a family of beauty. Mother had dark luxuriant hair and large, blue eyes, in a face sometimes haunted by worry, but which still held much of the loveliness she possessed as a young woman.

My father had sensitive, finely drawn features. As a boy, he owned shoulder-length golden hair. A picture of him at the age of seven with long curls framing his face, the rest of him clad in the velvet and frilled cuffs of a Little Lord Fauntleroy suit, hung in the hall in our house. I wish I knew a boy with long, golden curls, I would think, looking wistfully at the picture.

My blond brother with his high forehead, intense blue eyes and wide, firm lips was handsome enough to be a movie star. Tall and lanky, he moved with casualness. He would drape himself over the hall railing, bend over to answer the telephone, and look graceful. (I tried this once but the mirror next to it showed my rear stuck out so far that forever after I walked down the three steps and sat at the telephone table.)

My sister Sue, four years younger than I, was a pretty, willowy red-haired maiden, who looked stunning in clothes. She could wear a burlap bag and it would become her.

Sally was piquant and fragile as well as red-haired. She was the only one of us with brown eyes; a family joke centered on mother and the iceman, when it came to Sally.

This was stiff competition for a brunette inclined to be plump. Or, did I grow plump out of despair, feeling that the odds were against me so why try? Anyhow, I had always wanted, above all else, to be considered "pretty." Instead, I was the one to whom something ugly usually happened—acne, poor posture, stomachaches, sinus.

"You were probably a pretty child," John said. My baby pictures were cute, I thought, but I have changed much since then. Unhappiness distorts faces.

"How could any little girl wearing braces on her teeth, a harness on her back to improve posture, steel plates in her shoes to strengthen fallen arches and lotion plastered on her face to remove pimples, look pretty?" I asked sarcastically.

"That was you?" John sounded duly sympathetic.

"That *is* me," I shot back. "Braces, harness, steel plates and lotion all gone from sight but still in mind."

"Perhaps some of your defects were psychological," he said.

"There's nothing psychological about crooked teeth," I retorted.

"Feelings of unhappiness may have something to do with the

way a child develops physically as well as psychologically," he said.

"If only I had been born with red hair!" I sighed.

"I like dark-haired women better," he said.

"How could you?" I expressed the horror of disbelief. "Red hair is much prettier."

"I don't think so," he said. "Some men don't."

"Then they're crazy," I retorted.

I remembered being jealous of my brother when he caught the flu at the same time my father did during the epidemic that followed World War I. I used to pass the open door of the darkened room which I was forbidden to enter, see my father and brother lying in bed side by side. I thought, "Why couldn't I have caught the flu, instead of Eddie? Then I could be with my father." In high school, when I came down with scarlet fever, it was again my brother who caught it several days later. The rest of the family packed off for a hurried vacation, leaving Eddie and me in the care of a trained nurse. Poor brother—he would always catch anything anyone would give him.

I had many feelings about my brother I had never faced.

"My parents seemed to like my brother better than me," I told John.

"So you thought, 'Maybe they do not like girls and maybe they'd like me more if I were a boy,'" John said. "That was the only other thing you could be."

"Why, yes," I agreed in sudden wonder. Then I added, "But he was luckier than I.'

"Why?"

"Because Mother let him do anything he wanted. He could even stay up late at night." I always thought I should be allowed the later hour. It made no difference that he was a boy and, as a girl, I supposedly needed to be protected.

"Maybe he also had something else you wanted," John said.

"What?"

"What do little boys have that little girls don't?"

I was shocked. "You're mistaken. I never even saw my brother naked."

"You mean you don't remember," he said gently.

He told me what he thought an amusing, perceptive remark made by a little girl watching her mother bathe her baby brother. She asked her mother wistfully, "How can you like me when I'm so plain and he's so fancy?"

I dismissed such an idea as preposterous when John suggested it. I might want to be a boy as far as playing baseball was concerned but no farther! Unconsciously, the struggle as to which sex we are may torment us, not so intensely as one recent instance in which a boy, after an operation, became a girl, but in milder degree.

I confessed to John a terrible, unreasoning fear that someone would cut off my feet while I slept. This, he said, represented fear of castration.

The emotionally disturbed person may hold both feelings, penis envy and castration fear, he said. He referred to a dream in which I endowed an amputee with a leg, another in which Mother accidentally cut off my thumb.

Perhaps, he suggested, unconsciously I felt Mother had deprived me of something that rightfully belonged to me, thus making me different from my brother.

"I'm different from him all right that way," I muttered, changing the subject, "but we're a lot alike in other ways."

Eddie moved as swiftly as I did, never at rest with himself. He and I in one room gave a good imitation of human perpetual motion. I remembered him as a sweet, quiet little boy, wondered what drove him into flight.

A little animal helped me to accept the envy in my heart. John acquired a small, dark dog named Eve, of mixed and unknown parentage. She greeted me eagerly at the door each visit, often joining our sessions. She would snuggle up on the couch beside me and, if I did not make too much noise, occasionally would fall asleep.

"Eve's the therapist, not you," I jeered at John.

"She gets along well with the older patients but she snaps at the children," he observed. "She's jealous of them."

Eve, jealous? Yes, a little dog could be jealous, and if she were, she could not hide it. She would growl and show her teeth and everyone would know what was wrong. But if a little girl were jealous she would be taught it is not civilized and she is bad. She would have to bury her jealousy, hide the knowledge that it simmered inside.

I felt as if Eve understood my troubles. Her big, brown eyes would look into mine sadly and knowingly, or so I thought, until John told me I was reading things into Eve. She was only another dog, and, as a dog, quite ordinary, he said. My feelings for her were exaggerated as they were toward Midas, the fourth soul of our little group. This was a gray she-he cat of distinguished ancestry, as full of credentials as Eve was minus them. But Midas' ancestry cut no ice with me. I detested her as a slinky, sly, stealthy animal.

"How can you stand that cat?" I demanded. At that moment, Midas was trying to devour the leaves of a plant and John had risen to shoo her away. He had moved to a larger apartment where he was able to grow even more plants. I liked the new place which overlooked midtown New York, except I missed the piano. John had space enough now to set aside a separate room as office.

"I like Midas," said John. "Midas isn't my mother."

He was telling me I transferred to the cat (feline, feminine) hatred and jealousy of mother. In my world even a cat took on meaning beyond its nine lives.

My jealousy of mother and of brother and sisters had pushed me to excessive competition in school. To get attention, I set forth to win all the honors. I *had* to be the best; there was no other means of survival. Competition was a good defense against fear—beat out someone else and, for the moment, I lost helplessness. Except that medals are little solace to those who seek love.

At the same time, I won sportsmanship cups to prove I was a good sport so that no one would suspect underneath I was really the world's worst. If I had really been a good sport I would have wanted others to share the honors. Friendship and affection would have been enough reward for living.

But as a child I was not capable of considering anyone else. I could not care for people because I was too frightened to trust them. (We all trust, once, as children, and if that trust is turned against us, it is difficult to trust again.) In turn I could not believe anyone would trust me because I did not trust my-

238

self. No matter how many people told me how good I was, I would not believe them. A thousand, a million, are never enough to reassure those who possess no faith in themselves.

I felt different from everyone else. I wanted to be like others, yet something inside made me different.

"I felt like a god-damned freak!" I raged to John.

"And so you had to keep reassuring yourself you were the same as everyone else," he said. "That is the tendency of many unhappy people—to judge everyone else by themselves so they will not feel quite so different."

"I felt there wasn't anyone in the world as lonely as I—and hoped there was not," I said.

As I lay on the couch I captured once again the haunting feeling of loneliness. My furious flight was to escape knowing I felt lonely. (I must never know how forsaken I feel or I shall truly be gone!)

Because I felt so alone I had to make sure I never was alone. (Always be with people, always be doing something, so you have no time to remember how lonely you are.)

Intellectually I knew I was lonely but it took a dream to show me deeper roots. In it gangsters broke down the door of my apartment and hurled me into the hallway.

"Where shall I live now?" I sobbed.

"What do we care?" they snarled and closed the door in my face. I wandered the city from hotel to hotel trying to find a room. The lobbies were deserted even of clerks. Wearing a mink coat over a golden evening dress, I sat down in a chair in a lobby.

"I am dressed beautifully," I thought, "but I have no home."

To John's familiar question, "What comes to mind?" I answered, "I really seem to be spending my life in hotels, just like in the dream. I wander from city to city, hotel to hotel, covering convention after convention, calling no place home. I've been thrown out of my home. A gangster threw me out. Just like I felt thrown out when my father left home. Mother did not want me and my father had a new home of his own and so no one wanted me. I have all the beautiful clothes I want but I have no home."

Tears of self-pity started as, for the first time since my teens,

239

I recalled how abandoned I felt when my parents got divorced. I do not believe divorce in itself is bad. But parents likely to become divorced are likely to be those who have trouble making children happy, and the act of divorce to the unhappy child becomes a crisis out of all proportion to its real meaning. It is moot question, I guess, as to whether the child would be any happier if there were no divorce. In my own case I believe the divorce was all to the good. I had to stop some of my fantasies about Father (now he really *was* lost to me) and my mother outwardly seemed happier.

Nothing held greater terror than the loneliness of my room. It was a cheerful room, filled with the books I liked (*Alice in Wonderland, The Great Gatsby, What Makes Sammy Run, The Grapes of Wrath*), and pictures I liked, a large Waugh seascape, several Von Gogh prints of fields and trees, and a dramatic photograph I once took of the ramp at the World's Fair leading up to the Futurama exhibit, hoping, as I snapped it, there would be a future.

Yet, I fled the room as though devils dwelled with me. I sought movies, bridge parties, dancing dates—anything to keep on the move. Even when I read, I read quickly and furiously as though I must not stop to think what the words meant. Reading added nothing to my understanding of myself or others.

Out of my loneliness I did some desperate things, for in their loneliness men commit desperate acts. Loneliness eats away at body and soul, a perpetual parasite, and sometimes a man may destroy himself and others because he cannot stand his lonely self.

Loneliness was of my suffering and my emptiness and I could not ask another man to take over my terror. It is the lonely who demand the most from others, John said, and at the same time they cannot accept from anyone else. Only faith in self, he warned, could appease the insatiable hunger of loneliness.

As I recognized loneliness I grew to know its cloak, self-pity, in whose deceptive comfort I had snuggled for years. It was difficult to give it up, for it seemed the only warmth I had known.

240

When people lack love, they will turn to self-pity as a substitute, John said, for it is better than nothing at all.

I had skulked into John's office that first day, timid and shy, not in true humbleness but in Uriah Heepian humility. This poor-little-me attitude was but another face of the coin called conceit.

When trust was offered to me by John, it took months before I could touch even a tiny share of it, months filled with the pattern of my life; seeking and obsequiousness. I was truly the split soul, hungering for affection on one hand, repulsing it on the other.

I did not have the strength to do for others. I was strong-willed but that was not strength, although sometimes mistaken for it. A strong will is stubborn and inflexible; strength has flexibility and gentleness, as well as firmness.

I was too frightened to tackle anything without consent of elders. I lacked spine and structure, oozed like the jellyfish past which I would shudderingly swim each fall. I never admitted openly I felt sorry for myself, but sniveled and sniffed and got sinus and thought, poor me, nobody cares.

"The happy person wants love—the unhappy person wants love plus sympathy," John said.

"And why am I so unhappy?" I asked. I was still asking that, four years to the day when I first asked. Who says facing yourself is easy?

"Because you don't like yourself—because you felt you were not loved in childhood," he said patiently, as though I had never asked before.

"Is that all?"

"That's enough for anyone," he replied.

Chapter XVII

A Better Way Than Anger

From whisper my voice changed to snarl. I felt I had been given permission to experiment with anger. The psychic pendulum now swung far over to the other side.

The fury that for years had congealed in hardness began to melt, breaking through the surface sweetness I had carefully stacked over it.

Originally I insisted my childhood was heavenly. Now I declaimed it as totally miserable. Sure, my parents fed and clothed me, gave me a good education, but they hated me, too, and the hell with them.

"Your parents are more generous to you than you are to them," John said.

"It's easier to do unto people who haven't done unto you," I retorted. I wanted to bite the hands that fed me. I felt angry because I felt hurt.

I blazed with fury. I understood how anger might drive a man to kill thirteen innocent persons as Howard Unruh did last year in Camden, New Jersey. Confined to a state hospital as psychotic, he mystifies psychiatrists who hold that his is a "special" type of insanity. I wondered if there were anything "special" except the amount of anger in him which caused him to destroy others and himself. I thought Hitler's need to destroy could have destroyed the world.

We excuse more readily murder by the person judged "temporarily insane," as opposed to the person who kills when he is supposedly sane. Unconscious needs drive both. Both types suffer emotional illness and society needs to be protected from them. But society could, perhaps, prevent more murders if it dared to understand that men murder, whether they are "insane" or not, because no one has ever cared for them and so they cannot care enough about themselves or anyone else to observe society's rules.

Anger whipped into everything in my life, including the one thing more important than all else—my work.

"I hate the job," I told John. "I'm going to quit."

"What *do* you like?" he asked.

Nothing, I had to admit. I spent a vacation in Florida, felt just as miserable lazing away the sunny days on the beach as fighting copy in the city room. John wanted me to be sure I had a known quantity before I gave up what little I possessed.

I said to him wistfully, "I guess you are the only one in the world I love."

"You don't love me," he said.

No, not your kind of love, I thought. It does not make sense that I call you a bastard one moment and protest I love you the next. That is not love.

"I don't want to love anyone," I said sullenly.

"You're too angry to love," he said.

He doesn't have to tell me, I thought.

I said to him accusingly, "You hate me, don't you?"

"No, I don't hate you. Why should I hate you?"

I knew he was truthful. He did not hate me even though I might feel he did. It was I who hated.

How many more persons are there like me, I wondered, holding what society calls important jobs, but choked with fury? They hate, but they always accuse the other fellow of hating, just as I accused John of hating me.

I had believed I either loved or loathed, not knowing this kind of loving also held loathing. I had heard much about love and hate spinning close as part of the same feeling— "where there is love, there is hate." But if I were happy, I would not need to hate anyone. I might dislike someone for realistic reasons but I did not have to indulge in the extreme emotion of hate.

"I'll try to learn not to hate," I muttered.

"You do not come here to learn," he said. "You come here to feel better."

The words "learn," "understand" and "know" confused me at first. I used them interchangeably. Then, "learn" and "understand" took on meaning as of the mind alone, and "know" became the word that stood for awareness in both mind and body, in all my senses, as it were.

The more I could know that I was not in analysis to learn, the better I would feel.

Once in a while as I lay talking, John would write the hours of appointments in a small black book (the only writing he did). This infuriated me though I said nothing about what I considered his rudeness.

But one morning I could stand it no longer. I said accusingly, "Do you have to keep writing in that blasted book while I'm talking?"

"Why are you angry?" he asked.

"I don't know," I muttered. But I did know. I wanted his undivided attention.

I apologized. "I shouldn't get mad at you."

"It isn't a question of should or shouldn't but of what is," he said. "Try to look at what is in your life. If you feel angry, you must acknowledge it and stop deceiving yourself. The deceit has helped make you ill."

I had been too angry to know I was angry. Anger seemed natural. I was angry when I got up in the morning. If I bumped into a chair or dropped an orange on the floor, I would curse the chair for standing in my confused way or the orange for slipping from my frantic fingers. Anger boiled within, waiting only slim spark to set it off.

Moving into a new apartment, I hurriedly unpacked a suitcase into which I had thrown a few essentials. I plunged my hand into one of the compartments, drew it out covered with blood. A razor blade I tossed in for underarm shaving had sliced into it.

I gazed at the blood as it gushed out, thinking, razors make wicked cuts. I wrapped the reddening finger in a handkerchief, raced downstairs. Next door stood a bar and grill.

Bartenders can cope with any emergency, I thought. I tore in. A stocky man in white apron stopped mopping the bar to give me a "What's-the-matter-now?" look.

"Can you help me?" I begged. I held up the finger. "I've just moved in next door and cut myself and have nothing to stop the blood."

He looked at the cut, yawned.

"Not too bad." He hauled a bottle of iodine from behind the counter, dabbed some on the finger, then bandaged it. "Good as new," he announced.

"Thank you," I said gratefully. The apron now spread behind him into white wings.

"I know I cut myself because I was so angry," I told John. "If I moved in less fury, I would have been aware of what I was doing. I would have looked before I plunged my hand into the suitcase."

244

"If you cared a little more about yourself you might not have put in a loose razor blade," he said.

For years I had envied actresses. Now I knew why. They could storm and rage and get paid for it. I had to hide anger behind dry, factual reporting of a world I thought crazy and hope the war rumbling inside would not break out in the open.

Before I started analysis, I once had to leave a meeting because I feared I would make a fool of myself and get fired. I was huddled over the press table in the grand ballroom of the Waldorf-Astoria, a mammoth cave of a room, listening to a speaker beg passionately for aid to China. Several reporters scribbled away, notebooks set on the green flannel used sometimes to cover press as well as billiard tables.

Anger closed in as I sat hating myself, hating the speaker, hating the audience.

Suddenly I felt the urge to stand up and scream. "Talk, talk, talk," I thought. "I cannot stand any more talk. I must scream." I had better leave for a few minutes, I thought. If anyone asks, I will say I'm just going to the ladies' room.

The short walk calmed me. I returned to take notes with the other reporters.

As I could loose my anger with John I found less need for it on the job. Meetings held less torture.

John allowed me to indulge in orgies of rage and self-pity. At the same time, he tried to show me there was a better way of life than anger.

"Anger is no solution to unhappiness," he said.

"It's such a wonderful feeling to be able to get angry," I sighed. "It's better than buying a new car."

"You still think of being able to fight as magnificent, don't you?" he said. "But how much more magnificent is lack of a need to fight."

He can say that, I thought. I was the one who cringed through childhood, cringed through college, cringed through career. Now the lid was off. I was feeling my oats of fury.

No longer did I have to envy those who could fight. How jealous I had been when Sally talked back to Mother or Eddie wisecracked to Father. Always I had to be up front with ap-

245

peasement, offering the sweet smile. Now, down with appeasement!

But the angry were not the happy, either, John said. He gave as example four patients in a mental hospital—one who sits in silence saying nothing; the second who sits quietly, tears streaming down his face; the third who smiles foolishly, agreeing with everyone; and the fourth who screams in anger at everyone. He said they all share as fundamental, fear.

I certainly felt something in common with all four, especially the one who shed tears. Mine coursed all over the couch.

If nothing else I was finding what John called "a natural release of fear." I dissolved into tears at the drop of a thought.

"People will think you beat me," I joked.

I felt I literally cried my heart out. "There cannot be another tear left in me," I would groan. Ten minutes later I would weep again.

"Isn't this harmful?" I asked worriedly, thinking of my overworked tear ducts, thinking also, some day I must send him a truckload of tissue to replace the thousands dissolved by my tears.

"The need to cry is more harmful than the tears," he said. "If you feel the need, it's better to get tears out."

(The need to cry, the need to express anger choked back for thirty years, the need to release screams stifled inside, hidden from a world that would lock me up for screaming.)

Tears also stood for something else. One day I cried again because I had lost my grandmother. Two minutes later I was calmly discussing her philosophy of life.

"Doesn't it occur to you as strange you regain composure so quickly?" John asked.

"You mean my tears are a kind of temper tantrum," I said angrily. I knew Granny's loss made me feel forsaken; I felt angry because now no one loved me.

"I want you to observe everything about yourself—both your fear and the way you meet it with anger," he said.

"Perhaps you should have been spanked for throwing temper tantrums when you were little," he added.

What is he saying, I asked myself in bewilderment. I thought

246

he felt sorry for me. Now he thinks I should have been spanked. Why the reversal?

"Lives there a man who has not some hostility to his parents?" I defended myself angrily. "They were the ones who started it."

"Degree, degree," he cautioned.

Always a matter of degree!

"Besides two wrongs don't make a right," John added.

What a different world this would be if people acted on this basis, I thought. But too many like me are too angry.

"I should turn the other cheek!" I snapped. "My one cheek still hurts too much."

I did not want more pain, not even from John who suddenly appeared to be dishing it out.

I wonder if his change in attitude is due to the new hour, I thought. I had switched from late to early morning.

"You're too sharp at this hour," I muttered. "Later, you're too beat up from seeing patients to be critical. Now you insist I look at myself even though it hurts."

"I should think you'd prefer that," he said.

"Me prefer pain?" Never.

"When I go to the dentist I'd rather he'd do a good job even if it is painful."

In the long run the dentist would be sparing him pain, he meant. The argument was academic to me, for dentists, unlike doctors, did not stand for pain.

In my whole life I had gone to only one dentist. For twenty-three years at various intervals I tramped up the steps of the side of his house which held his office. In spring I would sit in the chair and look out at cherry blossoms as he cleaned my teeth.

Not once did he hurt, even when drilling out the inside of a tooth. He used no drugs. He possessed a light, easy touch, never striking a nerve.

He must like people because, like John, he is so gentle with them, I thought, as he recently worked over a dying tooth, saving it for a few more years of use.

There was no doubt, though, John was turning stricter.

Trying to impress him I said, "There's a line from a song

summarizing how unhappy people feel. It goes, 'The world owes me a loving.' " I expected him to say, "That's very perceptive of you."

Instead he remarked, "That's not realistic. You're grown up now. The world owes you nothing.

"Not all people feel the world owes them something," he went on. "Some are lucky enough to have had happy childhoods. Others are not that lucky. A cockroach is born a cockroach. A caterpiller turns into a butterfly."

He's calling me a cockroach, now, I thought bitterly. Well, maybe he's right. I've always felt lower than a cockroach, jealous of butterflies.

What about his reference to luck? Would I have to accept the place of luck in the scheme of life? Did my need to insist everything was a matter of free will (my free will) arise from not having been allowed as a child to do much of my own free will? I thought I had ploughed full steam ahead in a direction which I was certain I had charted. In reality, I knew no more where I headed than a ship without compass in a night of black fog.

Maybe luck had something to do with who we were and where we landed. Perhaps I might have been luckier as a child but perhaps I was lucky to be in analysis, to have found an analyst like John.

I felt he must be an exceptionally good analyst. He possessed sensitivity, imagination and the capacity to sympathize with me yet remain aloof enough from my unhappiness so he could help. He showed compassion for those who suffered but was practical enough to know you cannot fight nature and win, that the strong survive, the weak perish. As a doctor he was helping the weak grow stronger so they would not perish.

He derived satisfaction not from power or prestige but from watching sick persons grow healthier. Because emotional health develops slowly, some psychiatrists may find this kind of satisfaction difficult to achieve and turn to shorter means of therapy where the results appear more dramatic but may not be as enduring, I thought.

I admired his highly developed observation and perception. He seemed able to strip the sheen off civilization and watch people, naked and afraid, trying their best to live in spite of terror. He looked at the frantic scurry of men, ant-busy amid television sets, stock market tickers, automobiles and planes, felt sorry for their need to live so much outside themselves. At the same time he knew they could do nothing else; they were doing what they had to do.

Perhaps I have overrated his patience. There may have been moments when he wished to slash my stubborn throat, though I doubt it, for he seemed to possess no need to murder. In terms of my fear he showed deep understanding. Often as I lay terrified on the couch, he would bring comfort with a reassuring remark. From other patients I heard he was much less active in their analyses, at times not saying a word the entire session. He honored my fear until he felt I was strong enough to look at it.

He must think I am getting strong enough to stand criticism, I thought. Up to now he has been so kind. He understood I felt I had never done anything right (at the same time feeling I had always been right).

I could not understand why he now blamed me for my unhappiness.

"What have I got to do with it?" I asked him.

"You were the one throwing the temper tantrums," he said. "They happened inside you, not inside your brother or sisters. If you saw a little girl screaming at her mother, wouldn't you think she had something to do with it?"

"Maybe," I said grudgingly.

"Think, Lucy," he urged. "Use reason."

Reason was a word I tossed off thousands of times in conversation. It was what I was supposed to develop in college. Use your head, use reason, people were always saying.

"I do think," I retorted.

"You intellectualize," he corrected.

"You're always debunking the intellect," I said angrily.

"That's because all your life you stressed it as so important. If you had ignored the intellect and concentrated on the emotions, I would stress the intellect."

"They won't *let* me think for myself," I said, without thinking. The thought just seemed to come to mind.

"Who's they?"

"Teachers. And my mother and father! Do this! Do that! Don't answer me back!"

"But you're grown up now," he said. "You *can* think for yourself."

He added, "Think in all directions, like a cobweb."

"That's chaos," I said in scorn.

"A cobweb is a finely organized pattern with purpose to it," he said. "The one-track mind, never daring to explore, is the narrow one."

I had never explored. I had never dared enter the territory of emotional health. I lacked courage to break through the border that stands between good emotional health and illness, a thin line but one possessing the firmness of steel.

As the analysis progressed, occasionally I edged into health. But shortly after, I would plunge back into moodiness. I could know the difference but still be unable to maintain the feeling.

"How can I hold on?" I asked John.

"By bringing thinking and feeling together so the touches of calm may gain consistency in your life," John said.

"Also by steeling yourself to observe yourself," he suggested.

It is not easy, I would think ruefully, to observe in myself such feelings as murder, incest, homosexuality.

I would try and fail, again and again. I was so bemused, I could not reason. I was too angry to reason. No chip sat on my shoulder—just constant, slow-burning fury that never seemed to dim.

I kept careful notes all during analysis, humorous reversal of the usual procedure in which the analyst is supposed to do the writing. A sheet of paper, dated November 18, 1948, reads:

> For the first time today, two years and seven months after I started analysis, I realize what John meant when he told me I did not think. It happened on a train, traveling from New York to Milwaukee. For the first time in my eight years of covering conventions out of town, I felt good. I wasn't frightened as I usually am. Frightened of what, I don't know. Just frightened. I thought: there's nothing for me to fear except inner fears.
>
> I remember how mad I was last week when John told

me, "The trouble with you is not the way you think but that you don't think." He said it politely but I burst into tears. All that night I had a headache. The next day I said to him accusingly, "You told me I couldn't think and I don't think that was very nice."

"I told you you *didn't* think, not *couldn't* think," he said.

I had no answer. But now I know what he meant. If I used my brain instead of my terrified nerve centers—thoughts instead of associations—I could live without so much agony.

I know I am fighting the past. (Go fight Tammany Hall, go fight City Hall, go fight the past.) But I should be capable of judging for myself, not always feeling I am being judged each moment as though by a stern parent.

Someone said this is a society of suspicion. But my life need not be one of suspicion. I am not a criminal although at times I felt I had committed a crime.

But now for the first time I know what the words mean "to be in possession of oneself." I never felt as if I possessed myself but always as though something unknown and fearful possessed me. I also feel we really cannot expect to "possesss" anyone else. Maybe it is enough that each man possess himself.

There the pencilled notes ended. Evidently we had reached Milwaukee or I had fallen asleep.

One thing that helped me realize how little I used reason was when I could feel the nature of prejudice. It appalled me how often I had repeated as true, prejudices held by my parents, without thinking for myself.

I might meet a person I thought interesting. I would rush home and describe him excitedly to the family.

"I know him," Dad might say. "He's a fool."

"Yeah, I guess I made a mistake," I would agree, not daring to possess my own opinion.

I came to know that those who hold prejudice against a person or a group are not grown up enough to dare to question the bias of parents. They are still "doing what Daddy and Mommy think right," out of fear. Prejudice is part of infantile fantasy, as John put it.

I complained to him one morning of the fanatic manner in which some disliked Catholics or Jews. He said, "You aren't tolerant of intolerance, are you?"

"What do you mean?" I asked, puzzled.

"Can you put yourself in the place of parents who beat a little girl? Can you put yourself in the place of a Nazi or a Japanese? Have you ever thought about people who are intolerant?"

"You mean what causes their intolerance?"

"Do you know it is fear that breeds intolerance?"

"People are intolerant because they're afraid?" I was amazed at this idea.

"Intolerance is another defense."

"What a nasty one," I remarked.

"Usually the things you dislike in a person are his defenses against fear," he commented.

"But some people in their defenses are so unpleasant," I sighed.

"And some are magnificent in their anxiety."

"It's better that way," I said, thinking of the magnificent ones —many of our artists, musicians, writers, entertainers.

"Both types are unhappy because they are engaged in self-deception," he said.

"Then the important thing in life is to be honest?"

"Yes, but not to use honesty to hurt others. Use it to help them."

I knew some who made a virtue of being honest, handling honesty as a weapon. They were brutally (and that is the word) honest with others.

My intolerance showed on another basis. I felt it did not matter whether one was Jewish, Catholic or Protestant, Indonesian, Chinese or Lithuanian, but only whether he kept me waiting or was supercilious or disagreed with me violently on politics.

The idea that there is conflict between psychoanalysis and religion (at least the psychoanalysis I have known) is fantastic to me. Analysis gave me what feeling I possess for religion.

"Spiritual—it's a lovely word," I said to John one day. "Funny, it never meant anything to me before I came here."

I had been too busy fighting inner devils to give much thought to the reality of spirituality.

I began to read the Bible. I started to think about why I had ignored religion. When first I mentioned it to John I said, "Religion has never been a problem to me."

"It has been with most of my Jewish patients," he observed.

"Well, my case is different," I said blithely. "My parents always accepted it casually."

Then I wondered, was I really different from other Jewish patients? I did not like that. My grandmother would not have liked it, either, I thought. She wanted me to share my kinship with Jews, be proud of our heritage.

"The Jews have a wonderful tradition," I remember her saying, gray eyes sparkling with pride. "Don't ever let anyone make you ashamed you are Jewish."

Formal religion did not play much part in our lives as children. We observed important holidays such as Passover, which we looked on as feast rather than religious service. We went to synagogues only for funerals.

One winter our parents sent us to Sunday School. Mother and Dad were surprised at how much I enjoyed it.

"You like Sunday School, don't you?" Mother asked, beaming.

"I sure do," I said fervently. I displayed five mystery books I had borrowed from its library. The school's generous supply would sustain even my fast readership for months.

Mother seemed more religious than Father. She always observed the Day of Atonement, starving herself into irritability, whereas Dad ate if hunger hurt him. He believed in the religion inside a man rather than organized religion.

But religion concerned him, for my diary, April 12, 1930, reads: "Have just had a lovely talk on religion by Dad and it's done me good. He's so darn sensible."

At the public schools I attended, the Christian children never taunted me for being a Jew, as they do in some schools. In college, religion, if anything, was de-emphasized. The college possessed no chapel; students drove to town for church. As I had mixed with all religious sects in high school, so did I in college. Sometimes I would attend services in an old Vermont church, drawn there by respect for the historic quality of the building rather than by the sermon.

Religion occupied but a small share of our bull sessions. We were interested more in what would become of us after college —would we choose home or career? Or, if we were to select a man, which would we take—brains or brawn? Or, who was the most disliked faculty member?

I raged momentarily when some acquaintance would confess confidentially, "Some of my best friends are Jews." But I quickly fled from that insult as I quickly fled from all danger, too frightened to admit fury.

When I went to work in New York I learned many Jews felt persecuted not only by Christians but by some of their own. Internecine warfare existed between some of the "snobbish" German and English Jews and those supposedly unfortunate enough to be born in Poland, Hungary or Russia. Westchester insulation had prevented such quarrels from reaching my naïve ears. I grew up in a community that accepted Jews, except for membership in exclusive clubs, if they possessed a fair amount of money.

"If anything, I'm guilty of anti-Semitism," I told John. "I probably identified more with the Christians who allowed us to live in their midst than with Jews who, because of discrimination in other places, clung to their own."

One set of grandparents came from England, the other from Germany, so I fell in the category of favored Jews, if I chose to think of it as such. When one must sit with the snobs, one belongs with the frightened.

Now I find growing pride in being a Jew, a result of liking myself better as a whole. As long as I disliked almost everything else about myself, probably I also disliked being Jewish. But my desperation found other depths.

I could not take criticism about my writing. An attack on it was like an attack on my life, since it was my life.

At college I overheard one professor say to another, nodding in my direction, "She is not much of a writer."

I crumpled inside. Why can't he wait until I am out of earshot, I moaned. Doesn't he know how much writing means to me?

254

"Maybe it will harm my writing if I learn how to think," I rationalized to John.

"The best writers are the ones who both think and feel," he said.

"Like D. H. Lawrence," I mused, for he was one of my favorites.

"I don't think of him as a writer."

"You don't?" I was astounded.

"He's too full of emotion."

"You believe in the heart and head combined, don't you?" I said in wonder.

"I believe in using your feet *and* your head," John replied. "You have feet to walk with and, as you walk, use your head."

I had been running furiously, little more composed than the proverbial chicken minus its head. Often I "lost my head," so enraged I could not think.

"Your favorite pastime is jumping to conclusions," John told me.

I jumped to conclusions like the irate reader who called up our crossword puzzle editor. The telephone sputtered wrath as he fumed, "You have the definition for forty-five across as the manager of the Globe Theater. I've just called the Globe Theater. There are two managers and neither name fits into the space of eleven letters. The person who made up that puzzle is crazy!"

The editor explained, "The Globe Theater referred to is not the one in this city in the twentieth century but the one in London in the sixteenth century. The manager was a man named Shakespeare and he has eleven letters in his name."

"Oh," said the reader sullenly and hung up.

John asked me to start considering possibilities, to use reason.

"Give me an example of reason," I demanded.

"Reason would enable you to solve a problem such as, What number is four times larger than another and ten times as much as the number next to it?" he said.

"My God!" Although I got high mathematics marks I had never been able to do a problem since. I memorized, I did not think.

"I couldn't answer a question like that if my life depended on it," I groaned.

"Your life does depend on it," he said quietly.

Upon the use of reason would depend whether I could live without terror, he meant. I would have to keep assembling the unknown factors in my life into a logical equation. This, for me, would be reason.

"I wouldn't know how to begin," I muttered.

"I would try even though I never found the answer," he said. "Maybe it isn't so important you get the correct answer as that you try."

Not only did I fear I would not get the correct answer, but I did not want to take time to try. If I could not get the answer in a hurry, I would not try at all.

My inability to use reason created trouble in many ways, some not so serious as others. I traveled the country almost as frequently as any reporter with headquarters in New York, yet I never cared to acquire a concept of the shape of the U.S.A. I let the train whiz me through lonely plain, past smoky city, knowing only I headed west or north.

On one trip I arranged to meet a friend in Chicago. We are still waiting to see each other. Chicago did not lie, as I thought it did, on my path homeward from Detroit.

I told a high Army official who came from Lincoln that once I went through Nebraska on my way to Seattle.

"Just before we hit Butte, Montana," I explained.

He informed me gently that Nebraska did not lie on that particular route west. I apologized. I had mixed it up with North Dakota, of course, or South Dakota.

One day the editor assigned me to a conference in Memphis starting the following day. "You'd better phone right away for a plane reservation," he suggested.

"Plane?" I exclaimed in alarm. "I'll take a sleeper."

"You won't get there by tomorrow morning," he said worriedly.

"Memphis is just a little south of Cleveland," I protested.

I learned Memphis lay a lot south of Cleveland, and a lot west, too. I raced for the plane; found misery's company in the woman next to me as we held off nausea.

256

She kept moaning, "How do they stand it? How do they stand it?"

Finally I moaned back, "How does 'who' stand it?"

"My sons," she said. "I have three and they're all pilots and they make fun of me if I don't travel in a plane. So I fly and hate every minute of it." She looked envious as I climbed out in Memphis; she had to endure agony until San Antonio.

One state I do not believe exists, for I cannot seem to find it no matter which train I board. Where is Idaho? To me it is still but a potato. I believe our map-makers have created a myth.

I did not learn geography because I did not care where I was going—only that I moved, and moved fast. I did not take time to look carefully at life around me because of the anxiety in my own.

But if I could think without anxiety, that would be use of reason. Then I could see the truth. And the whole truth, not just a part of it. Often I seized a kernel of truth and claimed it as the whole, not knowing a little of truth may be a dangerous thing, as John meant when he advised me against jumping to conclusions.

"If you were a doctor, I certainly wouldn't send any patients to you," he chuckled. "They might die because you operated on sudden impulse without examining them thoroughly."

He suggested I count to ten the next time I felt anxiety stealing over me.

"Ten!" I exclaimed. "I'll never get further than two."

Then I asked, "Do you mean that literally?"

"Is there any other way?"

Yes, for me. I did not want to want to be literal about anything.

Some people stand on the sidelines and observe life; others plunge into the sea of sensation, rarely to leave it, John said. The one risks the danger of not living; the other, of living too intensely and, in that living, enduring torment on torment, I thought. The wise man will dip into the sea every now and then as he chooses, also spending time in the solitude of the shore.

Fear prevents some people from reaching the happy combination of feeling and thinking that makes them "human" be-ings, John believed. Fear has two faces. It may keep some from being able to think because feelings are so intense and it may keep others from being able to feel because their thoughts are so intense. In each case fear keeps them from being able to reason.

Here, again, John warned, it was neither black nor white. Some could think about some things, but perhaps not about the things that stood for danger. A mathematical genius might be able to think about abstruse problems but not about his feelings for his mother or father. On the other hand, some could feel intensely about the starving Armenians or the Republican party but not know what they felt for their parents.

I had felt deeply but only about the unimportant. I never dared know my feelings about the important. I could think glibly at surface level but found it painful to reach the more dangerous feelings. I would be talking about the house in which we lived, when I would think of the carved wooden chest Father brought home one day which stood on the outside porch and into which we hurled rubbers and galoshes. "That makes no sense," I would think. "I will not tell John because it does not fit in with the rest."

It fit in too well, perhaps, with the part of my life I wanted to bury. Later, when I could talk of the chest I found I had felt resentful all the years because Mother had used such a beautiful gift from Father for storage of dirty rubbers. I thought, If this were my house, I would not use my father's present in such sordid fashion. If I were mistress here . . .

My body sizzled with so much feeling that no rest or quiet existed in which thought might take root. I had never used my head except to store away useless facts. It was dangerous for me to think because feelings were so intense that, had I thought about them, they might have destroyed me. If I had stopped to feel self-pity, I might have killed myself. If I had stopped to feel anger, I might have killed my mother. Instead, I fled.

My life resembled a raging river of emotionalism without direction. In my climate of conditioning, emotions reigned supreme. I associated; I did not think. I let my emotions think for me.

I had been afraid to think about myself or for myself, to know what I truly felt. I had accepted things verbally and intellectually but never emotionally.

I had never stopped long enough to ask myself, "What do I feel?" or, "What do I really think?" I had been too afraid to question myself or anyone else about the important things. I dared not question as the Germans dared not question Hitler and the Russians dare not question Stalin. No wonder the Russians forbid psychoanalysis, I thought, for it would free people to question the value of tyranny. Economic or emotional— tyranny is tyranny. A parent's tyranny over child or state's tyranny over subject differs not from feudal lord's over serf. Tyranny under any name, whether labor union, church or government, is unhealthy because the individual, to be free, must learn to think for himself. The tyranny of dependency cripples a man, keeping him a child emotionally.

Those who act on feeling alone, like me, cannot bring happiness to themselves or anyone else, for they are thoughtless and impulsive. People who cannot feel, who use only the mind, are like rocks, lacking the quality of warmth.

"Many of our so-called 'psychopaths,'" said John, "cannot feel for themselves or others. They cannot care for anyone because they are so afraid."

Almost everyone could think and feel in proper proportion if emotions were not tampered with in childhood, John believed. When someone interferes with the early emotional life, people may become neurotic or psychotic.

I had thought of the emotions as separate from the rest of me, instead of vital to mind and body. One reason there may be confused thinking about emotional illness is because we speak of people as "mentally" disturbed rather than "emotionally" disturbed. "Mental" means mind. Some still believe that persons become psychotic because of something affecting the mind. This is only partially true. Some psychotics possess excellent minds; it may be emotional confusion that keeps them from using reason.

When we think, our bodies feel. When our bodies feel, our

minds automatically register a reaction. We fuse feeling and thought, mind and body. We ask, "How are *you?*" not, "How is your mind?" or, "How is your body?" We answer, "I feel fine," or, "I feel lousy," not, "My mind feels good," or, "My body feels lousy."

Nature designed our thinking apparatus as well as our body to protect us, equipping most of us faultlessly for life if we were but able to use her gifts to the fullest, unhampered by fear, John believed.

Perhaps we are starting to use this wonderful weapon—the human mind—and, perhaps, some day we will use it to solve injustice and inequity, I thought. Ape to man may be one step in evolution, savagery to civilization in man, another.

The line between genius and madness is sometimes thought thin. Perhaps this is because both may be full of intensity in feeling or thought. Some geniuses may feel a little mad, some madmen a little like geniuses. Both may feel unique, different. But genius has the strength to use these feelings in productive ways, caring more about self.

Some day, when the world has more time and faith, the very sick in mental hospitals may be helped, John believed, just as the less ill are being helped today by psychoanalysis. The very ill need much patience.

He held there is no "cure" for a very emotionally ill person except one that takes place inside him, one in which he actively shares. Man must struggle, as though climbing hand over hand up a mountain, I thought. God helps those who help themselves. The emotionally weak need extra help but not the kind that ends their struggle, depriving them of the right to fight.

We might learn much about ourselves from the very sick in the mental hospitals if we would but know the lesson they teach, I thought. They are the frightened who possess such an unbearable amount of inner guilt they must flee the pain of reality.

We are all born with the same potential feelings, John said. In the happy person they are temperate, well balanced, well used. Because of the fear in his life, the neurotic or, to a greater degree, the psychotic, finds it difficult to cope with these feelings.

I sometimes used the expression, "I feel lower than a snake's belly." While visiting a mental hospital recently I saw a young man brought in because he had crawled over the floor in his home screaming he was a snake. What was the difference between us? I often felt as he felt, only, *because I was less frightened* I could accept more of reality, know I was not a snake. (When you add or subtract a quantity of fear, many things in a person change, John explained.)

I was shocked, and a little relieved, to discover I was not the schizophrenic type. I had been sure I would be classified as such if ever I went crazy. I told John of my fear.

"You're more like the manic-depressive," he said.

"You're kidding, of course," I declared in disbelief. "I'm withdrawn and I have a split personality and . . ."

"Your flight has been into reality, not away from it. Your life has been one of ups and downs."

So I was the manic type, seeking escape from reality by allowing excess emotion to flow out of the safety valve of my unconscious. Why, then, had I believed I was schizophrenic?

"Perhaps you identified with them because you envied them," John said.

I recalled how jealous I had been of one girl at college who could sit quietly in a room and detach herself from the collegiate bedlam. She would appear relaxed, not listening, not caring.

"If only I could achieve such peace," I would wish.

When I told John of my jealousy, he asked, "Did you think she was happy?"

"How did I know what happiness was?" I retorted. "All I thought was that everyone who was different from me must be happy." Only *I* was vile.

Defending my now-found category, I said bravely, "Oh, well, I'll take the misery of the manic-depressive with constantly changing moods as against the unfeelingness of the schizophrenic. It would be horrible not to be able to feel."

"You won't have to worry about that," he chuckled.

We all possess in moderation the qualities of the manic-depressive and the schizophrenic, he held. They merely become more pronounced in the very ill.

For instance, I believed everything happened to me, that misfortune sought me out personally to deliver her vicious blows.

"I *always* expect the worst, always feel people are out to get me," I told John.

"There's a word for that, in its most extreme form," he said.

"What?"

"Paranoia."

I stiffened in shock. Paranoids had to be locked up because they screamed that enemies pursued them, that bugs climbed all over them (my bugs and everyone else's bugs, too; do we not refer to some as "bugs" and talk of "the bughouse"?). But with less intensity, were those not my feelings?

Fearfully I asked, "Is there a lot of the paranoid in me?"

"Quite a bit."

He doesn't have to be so cheerful about it, I thought.

Then with a private chuckle, I recalled, I do sometimes feel like the man whose car breaks down with a flat tire on a lonely road. In the distance he sees a house with a light in the window. He thinks, I will go there and a friendly farmer will lend me a monkey wrench so I can fix the tire. As he walks along he thinks, But maybe this farmer will not like being disturbed and he will resent my knocking on his door, and he will yell, "What's the big idea waking me up at this hour?" As he walks along, the man grows furious at the thought that the farmer may refuse to give him the monkey wrench. He finally knocks on the door, and as it opens, he screams in wrath, "I didn't want your old monkey wrench in the first place!"

Expecting the worst to happen was part of the drama that was my defense, drama which caused me sometimes to distort the simple truth which never seemed enough for my hungry heart. I would rush into John's room, throw myself on the couch and exclaim, "I've never felt so miserable!"

"Never?" John would ask quietly.

In the words of the captain of the Pinafore I would reply, "Well, hardly ever." Then admit to myself, "Maybe even sometimes often."

"Drama is a form of lying to yourself," John said. "You distort the truth to serve your anger."

Nature meant us all to be in her image—natural, he said. Drama in living was unnatural, caused by fear.

He asked me to listen to the drama in my voice.

I've got more important things to do than hear myself talk, I grumbled to myself. I had to find out how to reach Worth Street where the Commissioner of Hospitals was to give me a story on the latest plans for dealing with the tragic tuberculosis situation. Men lay in hospital corridors, cots jammed to walls and elevators because there were not enough . . .

"As you listen to yourself speak, try to hear the anger in your voice," John was saying.

"I'm self-conscious enough without listening to myself," I retorted.

"The way to lose self-consciousness is to look at the self," he said.

"You're lucky you can hear me at all," I grumbled. "When I first came here I whispered."

"You're doing better," he said. "But you can do better still if you will listen to yourself."

His voice was low, yet firm. So many are so wrong in such loud voices, I thought. Truth is spoken softly but firmly. No shrieks, no insistence, accompany it. It needs no drama, for the truth is dramatic enough.

John's voice also held a slight quality of seduction in it, but purposeful, necessary seduction. Perhaps, as part of the music that charms us toward health every good analyst needs this, I thought. A small amount of seduction, like a small amount of everything else, is good and proper.

The tone and pace of a voice may indicate a person's happiness, John said. Some express fear as they speak—or fail to speak. They may talk too loudly or whisper; too rapidly, or slow and haltingly, perhaps with a stammer. A calm, easy, gentle voice bespeaks happiness.

"What about actors?" I asked.

Actors control their voices as they portray feelings of pleasure or pain, he said. But we amateurs betray our feelings unconsciously by tone and tempo.

263

Some use their voice as a weapon, to whip others. Some use it as a concealed weapon. I thought of one smooth, appeasing voice that conveyed the feeling, "I wouldn't hurt you for the world, you bastard."

I used my voice as a receptacle for anger. The words I chose and the way I hurled them at the world showed my wrath.

I defended my need to dramatize. I told John reporting was a dramatic profession.

"It doesn't have to be," he said.

Doesn't have to be? What does he mean? I asked myself. Those words spun like psychic pinwheels. Doesn't *have* to be. I don't *have* to rush through life. Nothing *has* to be a matter of life or death.

"It is not what you do, but how you do it," he said.

I had never thought that might hold true for the whole of living. It was not, then, the act performed but the manner in which it was done that held meaning. I could lift a spade of dirt proudly, feeling I engaged in noble work, seeing in the dirt nature's life-giving qualities, or I could lift the shovel as if I were ashamed of such menial labor, as though the earth were filthy and disgusting.

Thus also might I write or paint a picture or make love—thoughtfully, carefully, with choice, or frantically, furiously, driven to it.

It was not what I did, but how I did it. And with this went another point that John made: it was not what I did, but what I was. Which tied in with how I did things.

I had said to him, "If I had my life to live over, I would choose to be a dancer. Don't you think I would be happier?"

It was then he said, "More important than what you do is what you are."

Whether I was a kind, thoughtful human being counted more than my accomplishments. That was quite a revolutionary thought for me.

I had believed what I did counted above all else. No one ever sat down with me in silence, made me feel that what I was mattered far more than the medals, diplomas, by-lines I sought out of fear.

Because of fear I worried lest the "what" diminish me in the eyes of others, rather than whether I lived in reason and harmony.

Some of what society does reflects the same philosophy, John said. Even to help the poor, for instance, legislation is sometimes passed for political reasons that play on the guilt of the collective conscience rather than out of a real concern for people, he pointed out.

"You mean the means must justify the end," I quipped.

"We should do things for the right reasons," he said. "If we are going to help people, we should help them because we care for them. We should give them what they seek. Some ask for food but they really are saying, 'We know we have failed in life; help us to know why.'"

He added, "Perhaps some day we will help people because we want them to become emotionally strong so they may survive by their own strength."

This will happen as more men use reason, I thought.

Those who argue there is no use trying to help man because his savage impulses make him "instinctively" wicked are throwing reason out the window. We all are born with a certain measure of savage instincts—children have to be taught to be civilized (clean, polite, courteous). If they are taught with love and wisdom they do not object to controlling instincts and using reason. But if they are brought up in fear, forced to acquire the veneer of civilization without coming also to care for themselves or other humans in it, they will not want to control their instincts. They will be too busy setting up strong defenses against fear to take time to reason.

If my life depended on the use of reason, as John said, maybe I had better try to use it, I thought. Maybe if the world tried harder, it, too, might exist with less agony.

Reason was difficult for me to achieve. I did not know where to start. One day, walking along Broadway in the sunshine, I thought, Start anywhere, just start.

Don't you know by now there are no big things but just little things added one to the other, as John keeps telling you? And if you do not use reason about the little things, it will not exist for what you think of as the big things. You cannot be reasonable about the international situation if you fly into tantrums because the toothpaste is squeezed out of shape.

To me the little things had never counted. I had brushed them away in anger. But as anger abated, I saw they counted very deeply, indeed. The fact that waiting for someone nearly drove me crazy showed how important it was I not be kept waiting. I was betrayed into showing how childish I was by the way I met minor emergencies.

Thus, just as if I could take care of pennies the dollars would take care of themselves, so in emotional health, if I took care of reasoning out the small things, the large ones would develop naturally (cents, sense, the same).

By the use of reason I might cut through my defenses, face the excessive fear that was so unhealthy. Reason would allow me to acquire faith in myself. If I lacked this faith I would spend my life beating myself over the head with physical sickness, frantic rush, depression—choosing my own path of punishment.

"How will I get reason?" I moaned to John.

"You will acquire it in time," he said.

I haven't got the time, I felt like mumbling. There is no time now for all I want to do.

But John seems to have time, I thought. He can sit there and say the same thing over and over until it finally sinks into my thick skull. How does he do it?

"Don't you get tired of repeating?" I asked him.

"You've heard other things many times during your life," he said. I had learned as a child by hearing the same things over and over until they became part of me.

"But it will take so long at this rate," I wailed.

"Time is my ally," he said.

"Am I getting better?" I asked worriedly.

"You are doing much better," he said.

"Was I ill when I first came here?"

"You were ill."

By now I knew. I was not afraid to take stock of myself. I felt flattered that he could be honest with me, for it was a measure of his faith in my progress. I knew he would never frighten me.

266

"You were running so fast you could not listen," he said.

He told of one patient who *could* listen. This man would think over what John said and then, a week later, perhaps, show by some remark that he had absorbed the knowledge into awareness. But with me, John was forced to repeat, repeat, repeat.

"I must wait until you are ready to accept," he said, with a smile.

"I'm sorry," I apologized, not knowing what to do about it.

"I don't mind waiting," he said, "as long as you feel better."

I thought of Milton's line: "They also serve who only stand and wait."

Chapter XVIII

THE PHANTOM BATTLE

REASON WOULD LEAD TO TRUTH.

Reason would set me free, give me the chance to answer Dostoevski's question: "Do you know who you are?"

It had always mystified me that I possessed two sets of feelings, one for the workaday world, the other uncovered at night in dreams. But I could never stop to solve the puzzle of my life.

Now I saw I lived in two worlds. One was the world of reality—city streets, newspaper office, restaurants. The other was the world of fantasy in which I lay dreaming.

In the world of fantasy my unconscious was king. I could hate, murder, order things to happen as I willed. It was a wonderful world of glitter and glamor. It was a world of the past. I drooled away in dreamland, thinking of what might have been. I made unreasonable demands on what I considered an unreasonable world, using the good old days as an excuse for not facing up to the responsibilities of days that were here.

It was a world in which I could escape the torture of what I felt lay around me. The only trouble was—it was a world that led straight to illness.

We all have a right to enjoy fantasy. Nature gave us the

power to call it in so that life might be fuller and richer. A little fantasy is a healthy thing; without it there would be no art, writing or invention.

But I had moved too far in to the world of imagination. I sought to live in it more completely than in the world of reality. The sicker I became, the more I lived chiefly in my inner world, trying to force the outer one to conform to it.

The real world often seemed to me fantastic. It was as though the two worlds almost changed places in my life, fact turning to fantasy, and fantasy fact.

Facts had been so important because I feared my fantasies. Only as I faced fantasies could I relegate facts to their proper place.

In analysis I gradually talked less about the outer world on which I blamed my unhappiness and more of the world inside me, the one that really troubled me. As I felt happier, the two worlds fused, becoming more of one world.

When I started analysis, friends argued, "Why are you going to a psychiatrist? There's nothing wrong with your mind."

They were right. There was nothing wrong with my mind. But they did not observe there was something wrong with me.

I lived as though dazed by emotional lightning. What good was a bright mind if I had to hide hate behind a smokescreen of sweetness and sentimentality?

I had lived a lie. I had deceived myself to make life bearable. But I could not expect to get away with it. Not with nature standing by, waiting for me to grow up and be a woman. Nature wanted the species to continue and I had been refusing to meet the old gal on her grounds. So, instead of rewarding me, she was socking me on the nose, but literally!

What was the truth?

The truth lay in the emptiness of my life, an emptiness I tried to hide by seeking excitement.

No sweet Cinderella, I. John had given me permission to tear off the mask and reveal the face underneath. It was a face of quite opposite countenance, a face distorted in rage. A face that felt unloved, unwanted. A face in search of its body.

The starry girl-reporter-makes-good dream was but an illusion. The chin-up careerist hid a lonely child who never dared express the anger in her soul.

I had visualized myself as dashing romantically from assignment to assignment, a feminine Richard Halliburton swimming the Hellespont of prejudice-against-women-in-careers. My dazzling reportorial life was but vain attempt to make up for loneliness inside. I thought outer sheen could compensate for hollow center.

I had pictured myself as a combination career girl—Cinderella waiting breathlessly for the arrival of the fairy prince. While waiting I indulged in occasional romances but the young men never seemed to measure up to my ideal of prince with golden slipper.

Breathlessly I kept the vigil, deceiving myself with false hope and half-truth. I presented a smiling face, curved in cheer, to everyone I knew. If I felt they were knowing me too well and glimpsing the horror underneath, I fled them.

I looked like an adult, I acted outwardly like an adult, but an unfulfilled part of me colored the whole, making it impossible for me to grow up. Now I understood what John meant by a neurotic—one who matures intellectually and physically but not emotionally.

Emotionally I was still an unhappy child, and until I understood that unhappy child, I could not grow up.

I had to live through my temper tantrums with Mother and Father, live through my rebellion against being a girl, live through jealousy of my brother and sisters. *For I had never changed inside.*

My demands on life were still those of a four-year-old and an unhappy four-year-old at that. I wanted life to be easy; I became annoyed at the slightest frustration, just like a child. The only difference was the child might grow red in the face with rage and scream, while I suffered stomachaches and sinusitis and insomnia—all symptoms of a rage unrevealed. The tantrums had never disappeared. They merely became disguised into illnesses that symbolized self-pity for a lonely life.

But no longer did I have to live a lie. I could admit savage impulses, know only as I faced them would I stand a chance of becoming civilized. The horror of them had been in the hid-

ing. As I could expose the feelings and understand them, the horror would disappear.

Yet part of me was stubbornly refusing to give up my warped childhood. Change was too painful.

"I cannot change," I insisted to John.

"Perhaps you won't," he said.

"I would if I could but I can't so I won't. That's how I feel," I retorted. I can't, I can't, *I can't.*

"Can't?" he would ask gently.

"Well, maybe won't," I would sullenly agree.

Slowly, persistently, quietly, John asked me to know that "I can't" contained a large share of "I won't."

He is criticizing me again, I thought, when he first accused me of uncooperativeness. Then I wondered, can this be truth, not criticism? He has never criticized to destroy. He wants me to face truth so I may build. He believes people can change if they care enough about themselves to want to change. He believes if a man is a coward he becomes strong only by knowing he is a coward, then, because he does not like being a coward, determines to become brave.

Can't—won't. Cannot. Will not. Had it not always been a little of both but had not I always seized only "can't," ignored the "won't"?

My powerful "can't-won't" axis was held together by anger. Because of anger, I would not face the facts. I would not take any responsibility but kept blaming others for what happened to me. Even the asking of questions represented a "won't"—unwillingness to think for myself. "What do you think I should do?" Ask the other fellow and if the answer is wrong, then it is his fault and no one can blame me, for I merely follow his suggestion.

Did I think I stood without blame in my unhappiness? Could I not see that I also held responsibility for the misery of my life?

When I was a child, Mother occasionally turned on me in wrath as I raced through the upstairs hall upsetting laundry she was busy sorting.

I said angrily, "She shouldn't have yelled at me!"

"You shouldn't have **run across** the laundry," John remarked. "Why did you do that when your mother had work to do?"

I was silent. I knew how Mother hated to put together laundry (dirty, soiled laundry). Why did I irritate her further?

John went on, "You *had* to make her mad. You wanted to antagonize her."

He is right, again, I thought. Something drove me to see how furious I could make her. I disliked rage, yet I had to create it.

I would also have to antagonize my father. I knew nothing made him angrier than to have his judgment questioned. He took pride in how well he knew Westchester roads. Yet, I always had to put in my tormenting two cents.

Once as we were driving I turned into a side street.

"Why didn't you go straight ahead?" he asked.

All I could think of to justify turning off was to reply fliply, "That road doesn't go anywhere."

"What do you mean it doesn't go anywhere?" he asked, his voice rising. "I know where it goes."

"It doesn't go anywhere," I repeated stubbornly.

I did not know where it went. But I would not take my father's word. I had to show him I knew better.

He got furious. I moaned to myself, "Oh, God, now what have I done?" knowing, though, that I could not have done otherwise. It was as if I *must* infuriate him.

Often had I thus provoked my parents to anger. Anxiety was comfortable to me because it was familiar. If none existed, unconsciously I stirred it up to destroy the unfamiliarity of calm.

Because of fear I had not been able to acknowledge my part in the unconscious conspiracy against peace in our home. Because of fear, I had blamed my parents, holding myself blameless.

Often had I taken advantage of them. Mother would ask us not to eat candy or cake before supper because it would spoil our appetites. If I felt like it, I would eat all I wanted, not heeding her advice. I did not see she was trying to help me, that she had always tried, but that I would not let her. If I had my stubborn way I probably would have eaten only sweets.

When I wanted something from Mother and she refused, I

would race to demand it of my father as soon as he came home and had put down his briefcase. If he refused a request, I would wait until he left the house, then ask Mother, telling her, just incidentally, that he would not let me do it.

I knew the angles, all right. At the time our parents were pitted against each other in unhappiness, all of us children played one parent against the other for our own selfish ends.

My mother might storm at me for five minutes, then try to make me comfortable and happy the rest of the day, but I had remembered only those five minutes because they served my anger.

With my father I had remembered primarily the exciting, glorious moments, forgotten the times when he raged at me.

No, I could not hold myself up as a shining example of the good, the true and the beautiful.

I did not know the whole of myself either. I believed myself a dreadful little girl who could never do anything right. I did not see there were nice things about me, as there are about almost every child.

My first piano teacher, from whom I had not heard in nineteen years, wrote, when she read of my engagement, that she was delighted to learn of the marriage because I had been such an adorable child. That cannot have been I, I thought sadly. I never felt like a sweet little girl.

I had not seen the whole, but merely the part that frightened me, interpreting that as the whole. I had lived with terrifying symbols, the parts standing for and blocking out the more tolerable whole.

"Why did I do that?" I asked John in wonder, when I could understand more of my contribution to the disaster in my life.

"So it could serve your anger," he said. "Your anger was your means of protecting your life. Self-protection comes first."

Busy protecting myself, I could never stop to consider the details, the extenuating circumstances. I had blocked out many of them. No wonder I refused to deal with details in writing; not only did they remind me of the sordid ones I wanted to forget, but of others that, should I remember them, would lessen the cause of anger.

I told John I could not recall much of early childhood. It

was not that I could not remember but that I *would* not remember. I remembered only the frightening, black outlines. I forgot the details which gave the picture warm coloring.

But if I could now use reason I would know these details. If I could ride herd on my anger, I could see the whole instead of the part.

Reason would enable me to know that all the feelings of terror—murder, self-hatred, jealousy, sexual hunger—were exaggerated. I had blown them up out of all proportion to reality because of my fear.

But that is emotional illness.

If I had not been an unhappy child I would not have seen life as threatening, with ants looming as goats, goats as elephants, and elephants, giants beyond comprehension. Fear dramatized each feeling. It turned a woodpecker's tapping into an enemy out to kill me.

I had distorted my parents' feelings toward me and mine toward them, *but until I was able to accept my fear, I could not know distortion.*

My feelings toward my family, intense to begin with, became even more intense the faster I ran away. I reacted like a dog who, treated thoughtlessly as a puppy, snarls at everyone, expecting no kindness. The older he grows the louder he snarls, his anger inappropriate to the threat of the present and greater than the past ever warranted.

It all took place in my mind. Those who dismiss emotional illness by saying, "It's all in the mind," do not know their own hearts well. What can be more important than illness in the mind? Is that not where wars begin?

There had been war inside me, the kind of war the Bible tells us creates the larger ones. "From whence come wars and fighting among you? Come they not ever of your own passions which struggle within you?"

I was only one person but persons make nations. Some nations, like frightened people, want what belongs to others. Nations, like people, must realize they cannot have what belongs to someone else. (I might want to possess my parents but I could not have them.)

Like those who would like to murder but cannot, I yelled

273

high murder about everything else. "People did not understand me." "People were cruel." "People were selfish." I could not admit that the trouble existed between me and my parents. I had forgotten it was my parents before whom I cowered. I hit out at the wrong enemies because I was too intimidated to look inside to find the real ones. I had been too full of fear of my parents, fear that kept me silent when they were present but which often broke out in rage against others.

The child who is angry at his parents, when he grows up may attack other men even though they may never have spoken one word to him, because he feels his life so threatened. When a man murders a wife or daughter or another woman who may be a stranger, in his unconscious way he may be killing his own mother whom he dares not kill because he is too terrified of her. Some experiments with sodium amytal have shown that, as murderers unconsciously relive the act of killing, it is not the actual victim they murder but others in their lives.

I wondered if men in those nations that wage aggressive war might not fear and hate their parents and envy their brothers and sisters to such terrifying degree they must transfer hate to strangers? If man had no fear of family, he would have no fear to transfer elsewhere and nationalism would be a thing of quiet pride. Man, perhaps, would not fight no matter how violently leaders commanded if he did not unconsciously want to fight. But then, if man did not want to fight, perhaps he would not choose leaders who stand for battle. Reason would tell him there should be better ways than war to solve problems.

But reason is the hard way. It is easier to fight. I could understand how difficult is must be for some men not to fight. Had not my inner war kept me from using reason? At one point I told John I felt guilty taking money from Mother to help pay for clothes.

"It's not ethical to take money from people you want to murder," I muttered.

"It's not ethical to want to murder," he chuckled. My inner war had fed my prejudice.

Everything I felt everyone else also felt in lesser or greater degree. The feelings were natural if they but lacked the dramatic quality. If someone pointed a gun at me I should get

274

angry in order to try to save my life. But I should not feel when someone pointed a finger at me it was a gun.

John was trying to rescue me from this world of delusion. He wanted me to know that excessive fear and anger were illness, that I was ill, and that I would not feel better until I could face just how emotionally ill I was.

He wanted me to be able to tolerate myself as one of God's angry creatures. He wanted me to stop crying for a childhood I never knew. No matter how loudly I screamed, the world would not turn backward. No one could give me what I demanded—an infancy in which I was cherished.

I could cry forever to the moon in outraged grief for my unlovely self but I would not receive love, since I had none to offer. I could give only what lay stored inside me—anger, self-pity, envy—and who, in his right mind, would accept such gifts? I had to replace these feelings with more pleasant ones if I desired a happier life.

Ever slowly, in subtle snatches, I started to know I destroyed only self by anger. The anger was invariably followed by guilt, which only made me feel more unworthy. Anger is no solution; it is like shoveling manure in your own face and the faces of others.

Formerly I had been powerless to stop the self-destruction, for I was so angry I could not use reason. It took all my energy merely to loose furies before they consumed me. I let them fall where they would.

But what did it profit me to keep on raging? "What profiteth it a man if he gains the whole world but loses his soul?"

I had achieved the goals in life I sought. I wanted prestige as a reporter, I wanted people to like me. But my goals had been sick ones, for I had covered up real desires to scream in rage, to kill myself, to hurt others.

I had always wanted one explanation, "the" answer. That, too, was seeing only part of the picture. I could not accept the grays, the fact that many things went into the making of the whole.

Life is not one truth but many truths. There was no one truth about me but ten or twenty or one hundred.

"How on earth will I ever put all the pieces together?" I demanded of John.

"They all fit," he said.

Painfully, as though my fingers turned thumbs, I started to piece together some of the parts. It was the hardest work I ever had been called upon to do.

The old childhood rhyme, with some new words substituted, kept running through my mind. "Row, row, row the boat, the truth shall set ye free. Merrily, merrily, merrily, the truth shall set ye free."

Only it was not so merrily. It was often exhausting. It reminded me of the days when I hunched over, shoulders rounded, stomach stuck out (ashamed of girlish curves for I wanted to be a boy).

"Stand up straight—don't let your stomach sag," well-meaning relatives and doctors ordered.

I would try. The muscles were not accustomed to the straighter posture. They would slip back as soon as I forgot to remember. I would forget soon, for I did not care enough to want to stand straight. Through the years I let stomach muscles sag, showing everyone I did not care.

But if I wanted to use reason, that judicious combination of thought and feeling that makes a man wise, I had to remember muscles do not move by themselves without first receiving instructions from the brain.

I had to change my conditioned reflexes. In high school I had studied the power of the conditioned reflex in dogs, little dreaming my bones also bent to its beckoning.

I must remember all the time, every minute of the day, to try to use reason, not to give in to feeling—to stand up straight, as it were, in my mind. For my reasoning muscles were flabby from never having been disciplined.

Don't let your psyche sag, I must keep reminding myself.

This for me was the start of responsibility, the snaring of the hope that I would be able to stand on my own feet, give up demanding what had been denied me and start to care for myself and others.

I began to realize the world of reality should possess enough enchantment so I no longer needed to spin a web of illusion around it to veil its truth.

Reason would tell me it was not the fears of today but the fears of yesterday that troubled me. Terror lurked not in what happened at the moment or might happen but what had happened. I might have long forgotten the events but the memory of fear would linger on until the day I died if I could not gain strength to cast it away.

Reason would tell me I was no longer five years old, living in a world peopled by grinning giants who could slash off my head at their slightest whim. No one wished to murder me even though I felt I moved in a mist pursued by armies, pursuing me not as in dreams, with hatchet, gun and dagger, but with words and looks. (Sticks and stones would break my bones but words and looks could kill me.)

Reason would enable me to know I was waging war against enemies of my own making, invincible, wavering ghosts of childhood. It was a battle I stood in danger of losing before the analysis. It is the battle lost by all who give up the fight, body and soul, because it is too fierce, who must dwell in the darkness of fantasy all their lives.

Reason would have me realize no longer was I a child. The only threat to life was death itself, not the shadow but the reality of death. All other threats that, in my uncertain mind stood for death, were created out of inner terror.

Reason would have me know all through the years I had been fighting a phantom battle.

Chapter XIX

Understanding Why Is Never Enough

The analysis sometimes dragged agonizingly slow, measured in hours and days. But not slow, perhaps, if I could remember the days of distortion in my life.

The anxiety of years felt so driven into my bones nothing would dent it. John would remind me of a truth ("You need be frightened of no one") and though I knew life would be happier if I could remember it, I would forget immediately.

I could only hope he would repeat and, like a child on a merry-go-round straining for the ring, I would get another chance to seize a bit of truth. I had missed because I did not try hard enough. Next time round I might be able to exert myself to capture a brass ring of truth.

I sang the neurotic blues. "This is so slow," I moaned. "Will nothing hurry it?"

If I could not get better fast, I wanted none of it. As I demanded all else, I demanded emotional health.

But only as I recognized I would inch along at infinitesimal rate would I know I was making progress.

"I feel *much* better," I announced breathlessly to John one morning.

"I could believe you if you said you felt a little better," he replied.

It is sickness to think in terms of sudden drastic change, I thought. I cannot hurry health. Nature, which John respects so deeply, does not operate like man—blindly, frantically. She moves slowly, with ease. It is I who wail, "There is no time!" There is always time, John would say. Urgency is of man's making.

Better change your theme song, sister, from *All or Nothing at All* to *Little by Little,* if you know what's good for you, I thought.

Sometimes I deliberately kept the pace sluggish, holding back thoughts, fearing what John would think. I did not want him to be ashamed of me as so often I felt certain my parents had been. It took time to bring terror into the open. I could not quickly expose naked feelings to anyone, no matter how many medical degrees he possessed.

I could hurry only as fast as I could use reason. At the rate I was going that would take ten light-years, I figured. I seemed to be able to use reason only as I cleared some of the fury out of my body.

I would enter John's office in the usual rush, fling myself on the couch and start to spill out words. At first I could but whisper the important things. Then words began to pour out in torrents. I wanted to tell him so much I could take hold of no one idea. I would whirl from job to mother to brother to friend, never daring to follow through on a thought.

Sometimes he suggested I speak slower. As I could slow up I found it easier to think about feelings. I might remember how abandoned I had felt as a child, be able to storm at my loneliness. Then I could use reason. I could know I felt that way because I was an unhappy, angry child. But no longer was I a child. No one abandoned me now, unless it be myself. There was no reason why I should not have faith in myself.

But after I left John's, I would once again be caught up in chaos. I would sink into depression, wonder wildly what life was all about.

Why cannot I think, I would rage. What the hell is the matter with me? I know I am destroying myself by anger, yet I cannot halt it.

I understand that no longer must I fear my parents, yet the sound of Mother's voice on the telephone sometimes shoves me into a tailspin of submission. I understand physical hunger is part of fear, yet I cannot halt it. I understand I should not feel like murder when someone keeps me waiting. I understand I cannot bear the slightest opposition without feeling it is aimed directly at my obliteration because of my unconscious fear of death.

I understand all this. Why cannot I help myself more?

It took a long time for me to know that *understanding is never enough*. If it were, the books I read about psychoanalysis would have solved all my problems. Instead, I grew steadily more ill emotionally.

If words were enough I would have needed only a few weeks of analysis, for the words could all have been spoken by then.

If words were enough I could have followed the advice of well-meaning souls who kept urging, "Slow up," "Relax," "Take it easy." Instead, these suggestions only infuriated me. I knew what I should do but I stood powerless to change. If I needed advice on matters important to my life, I needed more than advice—I needed a new feeling about myself.

"This will be my epitaph," I thought ironically. "Here lies poor Lucy! She never understood that understanding why was not enough; that, in addition to knowledge, one must feel free enough to do what one knows one should do."

It is one thing to understand; another to be able to do. Some of the sickest understand all the words, yet writhe in unhappiness. Others, who may never have read a book on psychology, who, perhaps, cannot read, instinctively know what makes for happiness and health.

Words never cured anyone of emotional illness. The intellect alone would not help me live. I could use it only as a tool.

Some things are written in this book ten times but not written once in my heart because I still do not possess the courage to accept them any deeper than the intellect. But I keep trying.

Words did not halt my flight. Analysis was not primarily intellectual. It held far more profundity than that. What slowed me down, enabling me to try to use reason, was the slowly acquired feeling someone believed in me and wanted me to believe in myself.

Analysis was like being wrapped in a protective cocoon of gentleness, permitted to find a safety I never knew. It was an experience through which I lived, comparable to growing up again. It was like receiving painless injections of love and trust which gave me the strength to accept myself.

First I had to trust someone enough to lean on him for a while. The weak learn strength by leaning on the strong. Thus I developed a dependency that was good, in contrast to a childhood dependency which at times was unknowingly damaging. The new dependency enabled me to strive for independence.

Unconsciously I had always been seeking a reliving of childhood with someone I trusted. Until I could achieve that, I would never gain enough confidence so I could love unselfishly.

John became a substitute parent, but one trying to guide me to maturity without exacting the demands that some parents make of children. In return, I gave him affection and promise of growth. I changed not through exhortation or pleading but because I wanted to please him as once I had walked and talked to please my parents. I changed after many tries, failures, half-hearted gestures. But change there was.

While covering a convention I bought a rose taffeta evening dress for the banquet because I had taken only a dark suit.

"I didn't want to disgrace you," I told John. Some of his friends attended the banquet.

"Don't you want to look nice for yourself?" he asked.

"No!" I was still too angry at myself.

But because he trusted me, I eventually started to trust my-myself. He treated me like an equal, an adult. I tried to become one.

I expected his disapproval one day when I told him I had been going out with a married man.

He merely said, "I hope you've learned something from that experience."

"Aren't you going to bawl me out?" I asked in wonder.

"You're grown up," he said. "You have a right to make your own decisions."

Next time I would do better, I promised myself. I would try to behave in a responsible manner instead of like a selfish child. Next time I did not, nor the time after. I would continue foolish deeds.

When I shamefacedly told him, he said, "That's something you have to live through."

He occasionally made this remark when he did not entirely approve of my actions, yet considered them improvement over former behavior. If I exploded in wrath where formerly I dared not express wrath, he would approve, yet, at the same time, give me the feeling there existed a way in which less wrath was needed.

"How can I stop this damned anger?" I asked.

"Keep trying to use reason," he said. "Practice makes perfect." Another adage that has lived through the centuries because it holds meaning for many men, I thought. Adages contain words that are livable for those not too frightened to use them.

I had never cared enough to practice anything, even golf. If I drove far or putted accurately, I felt elated. If I missed an easy putt, I silently cursed myself into the ground.

"Your swing is so easy and effortless," people would tell me. Not easy, but careless.

Part of the struggle against use of reason was that unconsciously I did not want to give up my misery because, for me, it had been the only way to avoid death. All my defenses—my haste, my anger, my refusal to face details, my illness—these were the ways I fought, body and soul, against the unconscious threat of death. I could not afford to relinquish my weapons until I stood certain what I received would arm me better.

"Do you like being sick?" John asked.

Who likes being sick? I thought. Then I recalled how I often felt sick when I felt depressed, bad. Sickness offered a way of feeling sorry for myself and, perhaps, getting sympathy from someone else, in the bargain.

Sometimes I was sick when I feared I might fail on a job. It was as though the sickness would serve as excuse if I did fail. But in spite of headache or stomachache I would crawl through assignment, never daring to give up. I merely made life more terrifying.

It requires much energy in analysis merely to halt the emotional illness which has gathered momentum through the years, like a snowball plunging downhill. First, I had to decide to put on the brakes and come to a stop. After that, I started off again, slowly and unsurely, in the other direction, the one leading to health. Analysis seemed to fall into two parts: the first, knowing what created the unhappiness (the halting), the second, becoming healthier (being able to change direction). Neither step was easy because of the large amount of anger I had stored up.

I felt as though I had climbed out of the sea after almost drowning. At the beginning I pulled myself up desperately for fresh air to fill my waterlogged lungs. Then the force of the sea dragged me down to drown. Once again, I strained to the surface, to remain a little longer, gulp a few more breaths of sweet air. Again unknown terror sucked me down. But this time I fought to rise and when I succeeded I started to splash around. I knew only an awkward stroke, but it kept me afloat. I learned slowly to move arms and legs with less desperation. I could even take time to paddle in the water, enjoy the feel of it, look at the surroundings.

It came as a shock to realize the analysis had to end. I had not been aware of the extent to which I depended on it to relieve the pain of living. I had become fond of the comfort gained from John.

I, poor fool, brought up the idea. I remarked, "I've got to stop these tears sometime. I can't keep coming here all my life, I suppose."

The suggestion did come from me and of that I am proud. Part of me must have wanted to get well—the wisp of strength that first fought fear as opposed to the rest of me that lay dying on he couch.

"I've been meaning to talk to you about that," said John. "You should be thinking of ending."

I felt fear and anger begin their familiar creep through my body. He wants to get rid of me, I thought. It had been all right for me to suggest ending, but not for him to take me up on it so quickly.

This is the final, ultimate rejection, I felt. Now nobody cares. I was crazy enough to think maybe John did, but I was wrong because he is throwing me out.

If that's the way he feels about it, I'll quit right now. A few months, hell! When I walk out of his office today, I'll never come back.

But I said, voice tearful, "You know best. I've got to trust you." And that was more tribute than I could have paid anyone before analysis.

When I stalked from his office that day, fury fed on me. Knowing I deliberately indulged in melodrama, I thought humorously, I will kill myself to disgrace him in the eyes of the world and to make him feel sorry for having cast me off. Which river shall it be? The East River, of course. It is the one nearest his home. But I knew I would never kill myself, because now I wanted to live.

Much of the misery and despair of the past surged up again. Nightmares tormented me. I started to catch a cold. I realized I wallowed in self-pity. I would not, as yet, accept independence.

When I returned to his office, I made an effort to look haggard and harried. I threw myself on the couch, nervously lit a cigarette, hoping he would see my hand quiver. I announced, "I've got the jitters. I haven't slept in days. I feel as if you've thrown me out the window."

I added defiantly, "I didn't even want to come back here or, if I did, I wasn't going to tell you how I felt. Then I thought, the least I have learned here in four years is to tell you what I feel."

All he said was, "Maybe you're not doing as well as I thought you were." He showed sympathy and, at the same time, told me I was not living up to expectations.

He has since admitted he felt if I could think of the analysis as eventually ending, a fact I blithely ignored, I might progress faster. I continued to see him for another year after this episode. Whether by then I felt stronger or whether, in self-preservation, knowing I would soon be on my own, I put more effort into facing myself, the results showed John to be right. As this book comes out, I am about to end the analysis.

During the first year I could feel anxiety ease for an hour after each session. The second year I felt good for a few hours. The third year I could usually endure a whole day before anything would upset me. The fourth year I could go through an evening, too, before terror once again set in.

When we first discussed ending the analysis, I thought, This is not enough! I will never be able to get along without John.

I felt furious even when he took a summer vacation. I knew he was entitled to one and a good long vacation at that, if other patients were like me, yet I felt he forsook me in my need as my parents had forsaken me when I needed them.

Then I reasoned, John does not go away to hurt me. It is paranoid to feel others want to harm me. I must grow up, act my chronological age.

What if growing up at the age of thirty-three is more difficult than at ten or twelve? Does that justify my wanting to perpetuate childish dependence on someone else all my life? It is illness not to be able to take responsibility. Do I want to remain ill forever? (At least I now asked questions of myself, not others.)

Also, one difference existed between my life then and four

284

years before. I knew the nature of the enemy. That was half the battle won.

But part of me did not want to settle for half a battle. I wanted the whole battle to be over. Little did I realize the rest of it would last my whole life.

"You spend your life getting over an unhappy childhood," John said. "But as you feel better the effort becomes less."

He assured me what I experienced in analysis would continue to be part of life, helping me to live more happily.

"Do most people have this much trouble growing up?" I groaned.

"The more starved the childhood, the more difficult it is to grow up. The person with a healthy childhood accepts growing up as part of reality. He does not fight it."

I discussed the possibility of ending with a friend, also in analysis.

"I feel as if my father and mother threw me out in the snow without a penny," I complained.

"That's just what you get—a penny," she retorted.

"Fortunes can be built on a penny," I said weakly, wanting to believe it.

John pointed out, in addition to gaining strength from them, I might now be using the sessions as dope against the pain of living. The anxiety, rather than disappearing, was being eased. Underneath torment still raged.

I thought of how I had been using the hours. After each one I could think more freely. As frustrations of daily living caught up with me, frenzy gripped, but I would think, "I can bear this, for I will feel better after I see John tomorrow."

This was a little like using dope. Anger had not disappeared; it was only temporarily dulled. Yet, temporary relief enabled me to know what it felt like to think without fear. The taste of calm made me eager for more, no matter how I obtained it.

My tears might also serve as a drug, John suggested. He asked, "Do you like to cry?"

"It's wonderful to be able to cry," I replied tearfully.

"But not about everything."

Only the important things warranted crying. I was being spendthrift with tears.

But I was learning to use time more wisely. When I started analysis I spent the entire fifty minutes veering away from self because of the toughness of my defenses. I was amazed one morning to find I had talked about myself fifty minutes straight without looking at the clock or asking John one infernal question.

"It seems queer for me to talk without giving you a chance to put in a word," I said. (What I meant was, without hearing the reassuring sound of your voice.)

"Didn't it occur to you that's what you're here for?" he said.

It had occurred to me, of course, but there was nothing I could do except forget it. I had been too frightened to keep talking. But now my tongue lashed free.

Sessions also picked up speed toward the end. I seemed to be able to understand more, the more I understood.

I had to take heart in how much I had changed in five years and know I would continue to change the rest of my life without John's help. I had halted the direction in which my life flowed, now aimed it toward health. Nature is dynamic; we either grow toward health or illness.

This, too, I knew—I did not want to return to the pathetic life I had led. I had found a better one.

Enough self-trust now bubbled in me so I thought I might be able to live as other women. I could admit how deprived I had felt all the lonely years because I had no children, jealous of all mothers as I had been jealous of mine.

"I want children desperately," I announced to John.

"You should not want children out of desperation but because you like them," he said.

"I probably couldn't cope with a child," I grumbled. "How will I be able to understand a baby?"

"It's not important to understand him. Set him a good example. Be self-confident. Have no need to depend on him to make you happy, which is not his function in life."

A child belongs to himself and to the world. It is merely the privilege of parents to bring him into it, John held. I

286

should be willing to allow my child to live, to grow up. I should not cling to a child because I felt empty without him.

"How could I ever be sure of what to do?" I asked fearfully.

"Maybe there are a few things of which we can be sure—that the sun will shine, the moon come out," he said.

"You won't have to try too hard, for children are wise." Then he added, "I have learned much from them."

He referred to a little boy on the radio who was asked what he liked doing most in life. Without hesitation the child replied, "To breathe."

That was what analysis enabled me to do—to breathe. Not just physically, although there, too, but in a spiritual sense. Through the soul or psyche or whatever you choose to call it.

Chapter XX

THE FEAR EBBS

I HAVE GONE A LONG WAY and have a long way to go.

In the beginning there was only fear. Then moments occurred when terror took a holiday as I learned to trust John in spite of my senses which told me he was another human being and, therefore, not to be trusted.

I started, then, to trust myself to know what I did not know. The tragedy in my life was that I thought I knew myself. No one could have told me I did not determine my fate, miserable though it might be.

I was one of those who shouted to the world, "I don't need help, I *know* what my problems are," but my twisted life showed I did not know. I had been unable to search deeply into my life, for I was afraid of what I might find. Headlines told of murder by other men; I feared the murder I might do should I ever lose control.

It was not easy to admit to the world or myself, "I am ill." If limb or lung were infected, I would not deceive myself or try to deceive the world that a physical, tangible section of me was diseased. But emotional illness (truly dis-ease, non-ease) gave itself more readily to deceit. I could forever blame all else and thus escape the stigma sometimes attached to emotional illness which arises, as do most stigmas, from man's fear.

Some of us who try analysis suffer censure by those afraid of their feelings. We on the couch lie accused of committing a crime by some who dare not lie on the couch. We are made to feel it is improper to follow Alexander Pope's counsel, "The proper study of mankind is man."

Mankind in its struggle to exist sometimes forgets this. But there are some, like me, who in order to survive must resort to the study of man, of the one man through whom they may try to understand all men—the self.

The first step toward any understanding, and the most difficult, perhaps, was the knowledge I was emotionally ill and the illness started in childhood.

The first day I walked into John's office I would have sworn my childhood was happy. Then I started to feel it was horrible. I came to know it was neither extreme but in the middle. It possessed both the desirable and undesirable in life.

As an adult I tried to nourish myself on the indigestible belief I had been a happy child. That was the greatest fallacy of all, for if I had been happy as a child, I would have grown into a happy adult.

"Look at the child and you see the adult; look at the adult and you see the child," John said.

I remembered only flight from unhappiness. I forgot feelings underneath that caused the flight; forgot them, but never forgot them—that was the rub. As they surfaced I knew that growing up sometimes felt so intolerable I had to pretend it was wonderful.

Some (unanalyzed, of course) charge analysis kills ability to feel. For me it heightened awareness of self and others, allowing me to feel with more assurance instead of groping with confusion.

I felt more comfortable with myself and, therefore, with all others who inherited the earth to do with as they wish. I accepted the world more as it was, merged with both its misery and merriment. Browning wrote, "When the fight begins within himself, a man's worth something." I felt the fight was being waged more within me, less with those around me.

I no longer blamed misfortune or bemoaned what happened. I was finding out, as Thomas Tusser wrote in the sixteenth century:

> Except wind stands as never it stood,
> It is an ill wind turns none to good.

Analysis, which some might think ill wind, paid off in many ways. The illness which drove me to seek help disappeared as did other physical pain that never, in wildest dream, had I hoped to be lucky enough to lose.

A friend who has constantly sneered at the analysis confessed recently in grudging admiration, "I will say it has done two things for you."

"Yes?" I felt pleased this unbeliever would admit to two.

"You don't whisper any more and your sinus is gone."

"That's quite a lot," I said.

I thought of the struggle to accomplish those two things alone, of how much fear I had to conquer before nothing scared the voice out of me, of how many tears I shed before I rid myself of sinus.

When skeptics ask what I "got" out of analysis, I tell them it cured the sinus. This they understand, for it is a tangible result. They will accept a symptom where they will not accept the illness that causes.

The sinus, like all else, disappeared slowly. During the first months of analysis I breathed easier for the few hours that followed each session. After a day's work the nose again ached. But today the sinus stands completely banished. My tears set free my nose.

Colds forsook me. I sailed through two years without catching one, whereas, before analysis, I suffered a series of serious colds all winter. They would begin by dizziness, proceed to sore throat, loss of voice, chest pain, wracking cough. With each attack I wished I were dead (the cold, part of the unconscious wish) but I always lived long enough to catch another.

When I felt depressed, the first thing I did was to catch cold. (The word "catch" seems to imply "go out after.") Colds for me were a simple, popular way of unconsciously feeling sorry for myself and punishing myself.

The common cold—common, perhaps, to emotionally upset children and adults, I thought. Germs swarm around us but the person whose energy is not devoted chiefly to fighting psychic battles may be able to throw them off in most cases. Nature intended the human body to withstand quite a physical beating if not beset at the same time by emotional conflicts.

As colds departed I no longer detested winter's biting winds with the burning hatred shared by those who sniffle in unending wheeze from November to May. I could enjoy the touch of soft snow, the silvery scenes.

Circulation improved as my blood flowed more easily through my body. My feet and hands belonged to me now, instead of feeling like icy adjuncts. Once I told a friend I expected some day to fry in hell for my sins. He said, "That shouldn't bother you—you'll be warm enough for the first time in your life."

This unfamiliar feeling of living without sneezes, coughs and chest aches felt uncomfortable to me at first. I complained to John I did not feel "right."

"You don't feel you deserve to be healthy, is that it?" he asked, knowing. Fun was wicked, pleasure was wicked, and I had no right feeling good.

Stomachaches vanished as I greedily devoured hot dogs and hamburgers. At Belmont one afternoon I ate seven hot dogs, one dog per race in the stomach as well as the one I selected to beat the others around the track. The only thing I lost was money.

"I haven't vomited once since coming here," I announced proudly to John.

I added, "I've been throwing up in other ways."

No need to throw up now I could retch the indigestible emotional food fermenting in my unconscious. I could cleanse my system of its real poison, make way for more digestible substance.

I rid the medicine chest of pills accumulated for two decades. I felt less need for painkillers as I felt less need for pain. I took care of my body, respecting it more. If I felt a slight temperature I remained home from work, something I never did before.

I became less of a hypochondriac. A small cut did not send me scurrying for the nearest iodine bottle. Instead I thought, "My body will mend this, since it is not too disastrous." No longer was I so unconsciously afraid of death.

Laxatives left my life as constipation cleared up. As I accepted excretions more naturally, I minded less the delays and waste effort of daily living.

It seemed a minor miracle when the menstrual cramps disappeared after twenty years of devastating pain. The evidence lay in my body. John showed no surprise, seeming to expect their disappearance.

My eyes no longer hurt, so I threw away the glasses once bought to combat headaches. I wanted to see the world and did not object if the world saw me, certainly proved herein.

Nightmares tortured me less; no longer did I wake sobbing. I took no more sleeping pills, and although occasionally tossed away nights without sleep, did not worry. (I would not die just because I did not sleep.) Before analysis I wallowed in ten hours a night. Now I felt content with seven or eight.

I acquired a different physical as well as psychological feeling, a change in body-tone. My pulse beat slower, I breathed more calmly, I stood straighter.

As terror ebbed out of one part of my life, it ebbed out of all parts, just as when it entered, it entered all parts. Formerly, preoccupation with pain ate up most of my time. Now I lived scarcely aware of pain.

Calm at first felt wrong because it felt strange. I was used to the familiar—anxiety which throbbed like fever. Often, leaving John's, as it subsided I felt as though convalescing from illness.

I was able to give up anxiety only as I learned to trust, only as I could forsake the pleasure of the moment, for anxiety was the easy way of coping with fear, reason the more difficult.

I had to know in the long run I would possess the pleasure of quiet happiness only as I no longer needed anxiety. What I formerly thought of as happiness had been merely relief of pain, the familiar feeling of beating myself over the head because it felt so good when I stopped.

But no longer did I intend to beat myself over the head.

I did not want to strike hilarity one moment, plummet deep into despair the next. I felt happier if no one thing appeared quite so momentous and exciting, for, by the same token, no one thing appeared so depressing and formidable.

When someone made a cutting remark, snubbed me, criticized my work or raged at me, I reassured myself, "This won't kill me. I do not live or die by this."

Some friends remarked, "You're no different today from the way you were five years ago, except you're a little calmer."

But that marks quite a difference, I thought. A little calm, where before no calm existed, denotes much control.

It was not easy for me to slow up. I moved slower in comparison to the once breathless dash through house, street and city. I strolled leisurely along the sidewalk, thinking, "This is what it is like to walk." I deliberately pulled back on pace. Instead of hurling myself from bed I rested a few minutes after the alarm's ring.

"So do we put our life into every act," wrote Emerson. I could tell by the way I lit a cigarette, or let others light it for me, how much my life changed.

Feminine feelings seeped to the surface. I said to John wistfully, "I'd like to be like the other girls." To look in style I cut short my hair, kept long through the years so no one would suspect how much I envied boys. I spent hours shopping carefully for clothes, buying fewer dresses but more expensive ones, those I really thought becoming. I gave up the clashing colors.

These changes meant I liked myself more. I understood why cleanliness is next to Godliness, for to want to be neat and clean one must first like himself. Charity should begin at home. But I could not start there when I was frightened because I hated home too much.

I ate regularly and properly; more eggs, meat, vegetables and fruit. As I no longer needed the solace of sweets, I started to lose weight. Ice cream had stood as one of my childhood symbols of love. My father had bought it to show how much he loved me. When I was "good," mother rewarded me with it. As an adult, when depressed, I would consume pints, the amount depending on the depth of my depression, to reassure myself I was good, loved.

I dressed to suit the weather, lugging an umbrella when it rained, scuffing along in boots when it snowed. No longer did I feel, I do not care if I catch cold and die, or, if I get sick, perhaps, someone will take care of me.

I did not dash across streets against red lights any more. Someone sneered after a taxi struck a mutual friend, "I suppose you'd say that accident was mental!"

I tried to explain that many times victims of accidents seem to court them. They seek out dangerous places where accidents are likely to occur. They do not obey safety rules. They move too fast or too slow.

"Before analysis I raced across streets not looking at traffic lights," I said. "I didn't care enough to wait for a green light. Now I care more what happens to me—and others." My waiting for a light also gives the motorist a break. He does not have to be distracted by my selfishness in breaking pedestrian law.

Disregard for lights was part of my wanting to obliterate myself. I could not even bear initials on pocketbook or pin, for I did not want to be reminded of myself in any way. This past Christmas Sally gave me matches bearing my name, Sue bought me initialed earrings. I used both gifts, no longer so furious at myself.

Anxiety spurs punishment, and as more of it left my body, I felt less like punishing myself. I ceased stumbling over furniture, jabbing the wrong end of lighted cigarettes into my mouth, spilling liquids.

Why had I been careless? It was as though I were confessing angrily, I do not care about anything. I will spill things instead of blood. It is safer.

But I often felt as if my own blood spilled when I drew anger for carelessness. I became even more angry when I received anger, more determined not to care.

My anger also produced guilt, its constant companion. Guilt, in turn, led to further anger at self. Vicious circle, this anger-guilt spiral.

Now I could feel less guilty, for I held less anger about which to feel guilty. I dropped a container of milk on the kitchen floor. As I bent over to sop it up I thought with a laugh, "Don't cry over spilt milk." I knew it to be only milk, not my mother's blood or my own.

I had been too frightened to laugh at myself. I lacked the armor of humor with which to ward off "the slings and arrows of outrageous fortune." My laughter rang with desperation not pleasure, a humor born of unhappiness which makes its point at the expense of others rather than the humor of health which enables a laugh at one's self.

I walked into a stationery store, asked to see a pencil sharpener, wanting one more elegant than the fifteen-center I owned.

A pleasant young woman showed me an elaborate eight-holed contraption. "This is a good one," she said.

"How does it stand up?" I asked suspiciously.

"You have to fasten it to a desk with these two screws," she explained.

I felt inept at hanging things up or nailing things down. "I don't know . . ."

"Take it," she urged. "It's a good one."

Walking home I worried whether I would be able to screw it in. (You, who cannot hold things without dropping them, how are you going to—and where did you put the screwdriver?)

Riding upstairs in the elevator I heard a sudden crash. "What could that be?" I wondered.

I looked at the box which held the sharpener. It was open, empty. The elevator floor was bare. The sharpener had shot down the shaft through a small opening because I had carried the box carelessly, half open.

I could smile at the idea of my unconscious protecting me from having put up the sharpener, knowing I feared the task, instead of cursing myself in anger for being a clumsy fool, as perhaps, once I had been cursed. Next time, maybe, I would be able to retain something for which I paid and which I needed.

I was acquiring a new ally. My unconscious now helped to save my life as once it worked to destroy me because I overburdened it with too much fear. As I gradually eased its load, conscious-

294

ly able to tolerate more of myself, it could work more in harmony with the conscious, allowing me to think more freely.

I was learning to trust it. When I hunted for something I needed and found it immediately or when the writing of parts of this book flowed easily, I would think, "That's a good little unconscious." Quite different from the days I muttered, "Stinking unconscious!"

I felt pleased at a slip I made while reporting a study of schizophrenic children, which described them as possessing toward their parents buried destructive impulses, destroying themselves rather than their parents. I typed the word "constructive" instead of "destructive."

My unconscious was also producing in dreams some of the more dangerous material it once had been forced to suppress, now offering me important clues for conscious consideration. It was helping me know the truth. I could probably never know the entire truth but I could learn more of it so I would be less afraid.

No longer did I feel I must be perfect. Some will try nothing, fearing they will not be perfect. Others, like me, who try to be perfect in everything, writhe in agony each time they fail.

My parents had expected me as a child to do things right the first time. I felt stupid if I made a mistake. If I kept my father waiting, he might rage at me. I might bother Mother at a moment when she struggled with shopping and I would feel I had chosen the wrong time to talk—wrong, wrong, wrong.

In later life I felt I must be right or draw wrath. I chose a job where it was important to be right, unconsciously perpetuating the need for punishment and the feeling of the familiar. On the paper I must get things right the first time; too many errors would cost me my bread and butter.

I felt I must always be perfect because I felt so imperfect. But I also knew that to err is human. Therefore, I felt inhuman, wretched.

"I wanted to die when I made a mistake," I told John.

"Nobody is perfect," he said.

He chuckled, added, "Maybe it's lucky. A perfect person would have a hard time living with the rest of us."

That was heartening to hear. I remembered it when it appeared as if I had committed a mistake on an important story, the White House Conference on Children and Youth, by omitting mention of a resolution. The old feeling of shame started to shake me. Then I thought, "I guess I'm entitled to one or two boners. I'm only human after all." But I proved right. No error, this time.

One day my train was five hours late to St. Louis where I was bound to cover an American Prison Association convention. Because of the delay, I faced missing my first deadline.

Five years before I would have felt like hurling myself off the train in suicidal despair. Now I thought, This train is late because of an accident on the line. People may have been hurt. This is not conspiracy on the part of the railroad crew to wreck your career.

Besides, who cares if you are late? What happens if you do miss the deadline? The paper gets too much copy from correspondents, anyhow. Send a telegram, saying you will try to make the second edition. Don't be egotistical enough to think they will hate you if you do not produce a story. You are not that important. You have a job to do but if an emergency occurs over which you have no control, do what you can. Do not fret about what you cannot do.

I sent the office a telegram from Indianapolis explaining the situation. The first edition appeared without my story, the second edition ran it. No one knew the difference. No one cared. I had saved myself much torment.

As I expected myself to be less perfect I became more thoughtful. I stopped leaving things behind. I remembered to pick up packages, pocketbooks, cigarettes. I did not unconsciously need to rid myself of parts of me.

I took life not less seriously but less personally. In one way I had always taken myself too seriously, in another, not seriously enough. I had overrated the danger to my life, too busy unconsciously fighting death to know I had as much right as any other person to my own likes and dislikes, decisions and opportunities.

I was even entitled to my hunches. If I had stuck to one, I could have made money on young Joe Culmone. Vacationing

296

in Hollywood, Florida, last spring, I bet on other jockeys who, I thought, rode better horses at the Gulfstream track.

One after another my horses lost to those ridden by Culmone, who lived in the house next door to us.

As another two dollars went down the gambling drain I turned to Mother, said emphatically, "I'm not going to break my heart any longer by betting against Culmone." I bet on him, won.

I felt in him a desperate urge to beat the others, no matter what the odds. Time and again he would sneak the horse through unbelievably tight holes. In the final dash he often won by a nose with a horse that had lagged coming up the stretch.

"Watch that jockey this summer," I told Mother. Time proved me right. He and Willie Shoemaker tied in establishing the all-time record.

I felt more confident of my own ability. I discovered when I sought favors from people they were more likely to give them if I did not appear upset. Hysteria frightens. People then fight fear with anger, which may take the form of the word "no." If I asked in fear and trembling, I was apt to be turned down. If I asked in calm, I was more likely to get my wish. No wonder nothing succeeds like success, for the successful are apt to feel and inspire confidence.

As I demanded less of myself in one way, I demanded more in another. I saw how much I needed self-discipline, for I had lived a hedonistic, almost psychopathic life. I had masked the feeling of not caring by one of overcaring, opposite of the so-called psychopaths, who underneath may care so much they cannot tolerate it and need to appear not to care at all, John said.

"Feel depressed, dear? Well, march yourself right over to the nearest marshmallow sundae. It will taste good and you will feel better. Never mind the added pounds or that too much sugar destroys the teeth. Just sit down and enjoy it, for tomorrow you die."

Such behavior showed little discipline. It is only a "little," too, that makes the difference between strength and weakness, success and failure. Little, and yet sometimes years of effort in the achieving.

I could not have everything I wanted. I could want many things and the wanting of them I could not help, but I had to learn to say no to myself. Willingness to give up without anger some things I desired showed maturity.

I had complained to John that I found myself covering an early morning assignment before I had a chance to gulp coffee.

"I *must* have a cup of coffee before I do anything else in the morning," I said.

"My, you are spoiled," he commented.

I had not thought of myself as spoiled; I felt the opposite—deprived. In one way, though, I had expected the world. I wanted to eat all the meals, yet never wash a dish. I had been overindulged, as though my parents wanted to make up to me for some of their feelings. Children need not indulgence but direction and good example, John said.

"How tough should we be in disciplining ourselves?" I asked.

"Discipline in moderation, like all else," John replied.

Little satisfaction rewards the self-indulgent, he said. Those who permit themselves every whim find real pleasure scarce. Starved for what they really seek—love—they settle for such unsatisfactory substitutes as money, food, alcohol, dope, sex.

There are things in life we must do, John said. One of my "musts" was to keep writing. When I first saw what a hurt, angry child I had been and how I sought to save my life by writing instead of pursuing the music and baseball which I liked, I wanted no part of writing. But this was not being realistic. It was all me. I had to get to work and pick up the pieces, acquire spine in place of the slushy sentimentality that had served as backbone.

I could not give up the writing that had saved my life even though, at times, I screamed at John I would never write another stinking word. But I could write more thoughtfully, use writing less as a whipping post for other feelings, if I disciplined myself.

Discipline differs from rigidity or puritanism, John explained. Discipline is conscious, arising from wise choice. Rigidity stems

298

from an unconscious that feels excessively wicked and would like nothing better than a little conscious indulgence.

Accusation of people as "indulgent" and "lazy" indicates only fear, John pointed out, fear of assuming responsibility, fear of attempting to think. If I were "spoiled," I was more to be pitied than scorned. Nature meant me to contribute to the world in some productive form in order to know a satisfaction forbidden to me if I remained "spoiled" and "lazy."

Part of my increasing happiness was due to feeling less lazy underneath. My energy had masked a desire to stop dead. During analysis, I heard with envy of one patient, not John's, who found his real wishes so devastating he gave up his job and went to bed every day following his analytic session.

Laziness was part of the feeling I was not worth anything to anyone so why bother to move? It also served my anger —I do not care, therefore I will do nothing. My feelings of laziness became intensified when away from John for several days. I would feel psychically and physically paralyzed. After seeing him, after fear ceased, I could work more productively.

Some would do less, others more, if they were not so frightened. It heralded happiness when I could do less. Before analysis, in addition to work I forced myself to keep social engagements for lunch, supper and after work, to collapse in depressed exhaustion before going to bed, then wonder why I could not sleep. Now I saw few people during the day except in connection with work.

At the same time I could do more when it was required of me. A friend called up one day to ask a favor at a time she knew I was busy.

"I'm sorry," she apologized. "I know how rushed you are but this is important to me."

"It's all right," I said. "For you it's a labor of love." I added, just finding it out, "A labor of love is no labor when it's love."

In order to contribute most fully to the world we should feel we like the world and ourselves enough to want to give. Many who are unhappy give, but suffer in the giving. Would, perhaps, they gave less to the world and more to themselves. What was the use of life to Van Gogh, no matter how many wonderful pictures he painted, if he ended it in madness? Perhaps he would have painted even greater pictures had he been happier. Who can know?

As I felt less lazy, a whole new world opened before me, one in which I could take my time. I began to use my eyes which, fogged by fear, had never seen very clearly. I had felt the world with my other senses rather than observing it with my eyes.

The details which I had always ignored started to take shape. (I despised those games where you are given two minutes to study a complicated picture and are then expected to name all the objects in it. My mind would go blank.)

Now I knew I must be specific to be able to understand myself or others. The generalization was derogatory. It kept me from granting to each one the dignity of his life.

I remembered many more of the details of my life, particularly the house in which I grew up and in which I started to run away from feelings. I could walk once more up the red brick steps, onto the porch, past the carved chest, into the hall with its terra-cottaed walls, fashionable in the thirties, on which hung an etching of a ship, drawn by one of Dad's partners, artist as well as lawyer.

Then, into the parlor, to face the fireplace and a painting of Lake Placid's Mount Whiteface. On the walls also hung etchings of castles and street scenes in England and the portrait of a lady with a snake draped around her bare bosom. No wonder I had forgotten that; what a devastating picture to place before a hungry child—snake and bare breasts!

The bookcases bulged with red books of knowledge, green O'Henry's, and one volume that will forever haunt me, titled *The Yellow Room*. After someone borrowed ours, I never found another copy of it, to rediscover how the killer committed murder in an apparently locked room. That is one forgotten detail lost forever.

I could also look at where I now lived. I could view New York, distant hills as well as subways, understand the city as it was, is and might be. I could know its skeleton and muscles as well as its spirit into which I once flung myself.

My feeling about New York changed. I walked its streets

slowly, looked up at the skyscrapers where men lived and worked. I thought, I no longer want to conquer the city as, unconsciously, I wanted to conquer my parents. I want to work in it and with it, to make it a happier city. I am part of it and it is part of me.

I stared at the Statue of Liberty, draperies mint-greened by winter storms and thought, I have gained liberty from the despotism of my fear; thought, The birth of freedom may be a fierce thing in individual as well as country. Thought, too, The Statue is made of the same materiel as weapons of war, mortar and metal, yet she is shaped in the name of peace. Again it is how, not what.

Instead of living on the outskirts of the city where I could see trees and the Hudson River, I moved to the heart of it. I found there, on the top floor of a brownstone apartment around the corner from the Waldorf, that pigeons coo overhead to bring a touch of nature. Found, too, the only place I could sleep until noon. Street noises blended; no one noise wakened. When I lived in the country after marriage, each dawn the rooster crowed me into angry awakening as the neighbors' children screeched and milk wagons rattled down the street. "I cannot stand the quiet of the country," I muttered and moved back to the city where I was born.

Before analysis I had dissipated so much energy fighting fear I had little left to savor life. Now I sought to follow John's suggestion that the aim of life be "to enjoy whatever you do, work or play, to relax while you do it, the way a happy child relaxes at play."

When I asked how I could be sure of enjoying life, he replied, "By not making sure."

"What does that mean?" I demanded.

"By not gritting your teeth and being determined to enjoy it, but just by accepting yourself."

Happy people do not need continual achievement and excitement, he said. They do things not because they have to but because they want to. Occasionally they run risks, but the risks are calculated, like those taken by trapeze performers who seem to jeer at death as they swing through perilous space but who know exactly the measure of the chance they take.

I enjoyed more of the "simple things," those that required more thought from me. I needed the escape of movies less. When depressed, formerly I lurched into a double feature, willing to sit through anything except a Western. My record for one day reached five—two doubles and a single and *that* night of the year 1944 I slept. I would sink back in the lush chairs, lose myself in the splendor of the fantasy before my eyes as others dreamed for me. But now, instead of going to the movies just for the sake of going, I go to enjoy the good ones.

I read fewer murder mysteries. As my unconscious need to murder decreased I needed less stories to feed my fantasies of murder. I found myself rereading Shakespeare, the Bible.

I even dared to paint. Strictly from the subconscious, I splashed bright oils on canvas—all feeling, no technique—and liked what I produced.

I even drank without feeling quite so wicked; my father had disapproved of drinking. The analysis freed me enough to allow me to become slightly high and enjoy the feeling. After two drinks I said what I thought, wisecracked. Drink made me feel I did not care so intensely about life. I could understand why some wish to remain perpetually drunk; it lessens the pain of living by decreasing sensitivity to life's torments.

"You're too sensitive," John said once.

"Not when I'm drunk. You'd get much more out of me if I came here when I was drunk," I joked.

But when I was drunk, I was still not facing myself. Drinking was another form of running away. I had to bear myself sober if I wanted to feel happy.

I had cared about the wrong things. I always had to show up early at railroad stations, fretting while waiting for the train to depart. Often I arrived so much in advance I caught the train before the one I intended to take. Now I could reach the station a few minutes before train time. No wait, no anger. Just quiet walk aboard train.

Perversely, I always had dates with people who arrived late. A friend recently kept me waiting for twenty minutes. Instead of flaring into anger, the old familiar feeling of fear, I started to reason.

I am early to make sure I will get here because underneath

I have not wanted to be anywhere, I thought. I am also afraid people will not like me if I keep them waiting. I am afraid they will bawl me out as my parents once did when I kept them waiting. At the same time, I act just like my parents. I feel the fury in me my parents felt in them when I was late. I am angry, therefore, at the one keeping me waiting for daring something never permitted me. But there is no valid reason why I may not wait in calm for twenty minutes or even two hours if I know he is coming.

As I thought through more of my feelings I could wait more quietly, understanding that much of the world's work took place outside me. People had reasons for being late and I must honor their reasons.

I was losing some of the illness that is impatience and acquiring more of the coin called patience, recognizing with Shakespeare, "How poor are they that have not patience!" If so, my life, before analysis, had been practically bankrupt. Patience to me had been something for the undertaker: I did not see that life without it might deliver me into his hands all the sooner.

I am aware that, in analysis, I absorbed much of John's philosophy as my own. But before analysis, I held few values that helped in living—that was one reason I was ill. I was in search of values, always questioning others as to their values. I accepted many of John's because I liked them. They seemed kind, wise.

Human nature can be changed. I believe my nature is more human. I found the difference between being nice to people to save my oversensitive skin and truly caring for them.

No longer did I have to woo men or placate women to reassure them I did not want the men. I need fear nobody. People did not belong on pedestals, any more than my father did. It was colossal egotism on my part to place them there, then worry about what they thought of me, if they thought of me at all.

Now that I was not so terrified of people I saw some as far more wonderful than I ever dreamed they could be. Some were so hurt and yet contributed so much to so many. Some fought their fear so valiantly.

303

I had never really seen anyone. I looked at people through the haze of associations. I liked or disliked them according to the way I felt about them (manner like my father, eyes like my mother, stance like my brother). This is prejudice, judgment of another on the basis of emotions, judgment from the unconscious, judgment devoid of reason.

The words I used indicated my feelings toward myself and others. As a child I felt tortured because of certain words my parents flung out to tell me what they thought of me—silly, crazy, dopey, stupid, lazy. No matter how ardently they tried to deny the words by hugs and kisses, I held the feeling all my life, until analysis, that I was silly, crazy, dopey, stupid, lazy.

But when I no longer thought of myself in such words, my thinking about others changed. I thought of some not as "stupid" or "weak" or "phony" but as "frightened" and "angry," for that was how I thought of myself.

Because I was kinder to myself, I could be kinder to others. One afternoon I wandered out of a matinee, the D'Oyly Carte's *H.M.S. Pinafore,* where I heard the lines that seemed so applicable to my life:

> Things are seldom what they seem
> Skim milk masquerades as cream;
> Highlows pass as patent leathers;
> Jackdaws strut in peacock's feathers.
> Black sheep dwell in every fold;
> All that glitters is not gold;

Thin ice coated the sidewalks. As I skidded along a middle-aged woman grabbed frantically at my arm.

"Please help me," she begged. "I'm afraid I'll slip. I'm deathly afraid of ice."

"Where are you going?" I asked.

"Two blocks to the shuttle," she said.

I was heading uptown. Why, she isn't even going in my direction, I thought, but she asked for help. She is a human being in trouble. Why shouldn't I help?

"I'll take you to the shuttle," I offered.

"Thank you," she said humbly. We slipped along together.

I felt no need to talk. Silence to me no longer implied criticism.

"You're so young and strong," she said enviously. "You don't need any help."

"I need help in other ways," I said.

"What ways?" she asked with interest.

"Other ways," I repeated, closing the subject. She had requested an arm, not a lecture on psychoanalysis.

I told John of helping someone not to win approval or affection but merely because she was another human in distress.

"Didn't you feel good?" he asked.

"I felt strange," I admitted.

"It's fun to be kindly," he said.

"It brings you less suffering," I retorted.

"That's why it's more fun."

"I guess I'm getting kinder," I said to John.

"You are able to like people more as you acknowledge your fear of them."

"The only thing I thought I liked was writing," I mused. "It was the one thing of which I was proud."

"A woman should be proud of more than that."

"Like what?"

"Kindliness and gentleness," he said.

My life had been so full of search for someone to be kind to me I had not thought of the possibility of my being kind to someone else. Or if I had, it was a kindness for which I would get something in return.

Real kindliness expects little reward, John said. Yet the kindly people usually receive the most in return. The unkind demand most but receive least.

I turned slowly from admiring those who could put up a fight to admiring those who did not need to fight because they possessed compassion. This is, perhaps, the most highly developed of man's feelings because so much acceptance of self and others must go into it. There are many who possess all the qualities to make them fine human beings except compassion. They are brilliant, affectionate, sensitive—but not compassionate.

Compassion belongs to the one who can think of others.

The cynic, for instance, can afford to feel only for himself. He cannot be compassionate; his bright, knifelike wit masks an unending flow of self-pity.

Compassion also possesses realism as an essential. While I might feel sorry for, and try to understand, a murderer as an emotionally disturbed person, I must know that other men must be protected from him. I want to help the weak, but not at the expense of the strong.

Compassion for an enemy is proof of strength. At one point John quoted a proverb that advised, "Embrace thine enemy."

"I'd spend all my time embracing," I muttered, then feeling everyone was enemy.

As I felt less like my own enemy I realized, if one wants to conquer, one should embrace an enemy, show him another way, if it is a better way than his. He will then want to copy you because he likes you.

In compassion lies true strength, the strength to yield when necessary. I had envied the strong, rather than admired them, because I felt so weak. In a crisis, the strong bend, the weak break. The strong may also attack when they feel justified. But the weak must always defend; by building up defenses against perpetual fear, they destroy their strength to attack.

As I could feel more compassionate I found I did not want to hurt people, did not want them to be hurt. Once I had to pry into everyone's life because I did not dare pry into my own. I learned to keep things to myself. Talking of someone's misery had been an unpleasant way of avoiding my own.

A friend called to tell me of the divorce of a couple we knew. "Isn't it dreadful?" she gasped.

"I'm sorry to hear it," I said. Formerly, I, too, would have gasped, "Oh, no—I don't believe it!" wanting very much to believe it but not daring to confess it.

"Aren't you shocked?" she asked.

"Not shocked, but sorry for them." Once I would have felt shocked on the surface, delighted underneath. Because I had suffered, I wanted others to suffer. But now I felt sorry for unhappiness, not envious of happiness.

When someone spilled a cup of coffee over my best black suit I smiled, believed it to be an accident instead of thinking,

"He has deliberately chosen me as target." Perhaps, unconsciously, he did not like my hat or I reminded him of his mother. I had been all too ready to believe the worst of others because I had believed the worst of myself.

I met a friend one night whom I had not seen in years. She was brittle, sharp, sarcastic. Instead of throwing back wisecracks at her, I spoke gently, feeling sorry she needed to make cutting remarks. Wisecracks mean just that—a crack, even though wise, at the other fellow. I learned to watch my sarcastic remarks, to know they were not kindly.

There seemed to have been a number of important "c's" in analysis, far more important than the three r's ever were. In addition to compassion and control, there was "conviction." In my carload of emotions once nary a conviction rode. I had made decisions on the basis of fear, never daring to take a firm stand on any question. I was one of those who claimed to see both sides but were merely confused. A happy person may see both sides but also may possess convictions about one of them, John said.

I had to learn the feel of a conviction. At times I thought I grasped one but would soon know otherwise.

Once I said to John, "I think my fear of death is tied up with fear of sex because I always felt wicked, as though I deserved to die, because of sexual feelings. Is that right?"

"Do you really believe that, or are those just words?" he asked.

"Just words," I sighed. "But I keep trying." I knew when I sounded glib.

Convictions came after asking many "whys," after seeing the relationship of many things. Men start wars. Why? To expand, to get more land, more natural resources, more seaports. Why? To get money. Why? To raise the standard of living. Why? Because they are not satisfied with what they have. Why? They are not happy within themselves. Why? What they have is not enough. Why? They are not content. Why? They are angry. Why? They fear. Why? All men have an unconscious. Why and why and why. And there are no final answers.

Once I had been dogmatic. Now I might possess convictions if I used reason.

One conviction helped to lead me to write this book, the conviction that analysis, if experienced with a patient, wise analyst, may help people become happier.

Then there was the word "consistency," something my life had lacked, except for the consistency of complaining. I experienced flashes of feeling rather than any consistent flow of feeling-thinking combined. If I wanted happiness, I would have to be consistently aware I held feelings of murder, hatred and jealousy, not pleasant feelings but ones that, in terms of the past, I could not help but hold. Like the acne scars imbedded in my face, these feelings would serve to remind me of my tempestuous childhood and of the different direction in which I now headed. The acceptance of these feelings, John said, is basic for relief of them.

"Calmness" was another word beginning with "c" that held new meaning for me. The Lord, or nature, seems to pay dividends for calmness, I thought. The devil takes his due from disturbed people. Was not "possessed by the devil" one of the first descriptions applied to the psychotic?

Anger destroys as all unkind qualities destroy. Calmness increases inner peace which, in, turn, may add years to life. It was almost a matter of self-preservation, then, for me to be calm, for I would live longer.

Gains achieved from calmness differed from those I had been taught to seek. Calmness put priority not on fame or need for the world's attention, as I once needed my parents, but on peace, self-liking, ability to like others. These were the rewards of repose.

Then there was the word "compromise" against which I had always rebelled, for I could never afford to do it agreeably. I could only appease, with resentment.

But as I acquired the strength of a few convictions I learned the value of compromise. Only the strong are able to do it; the weak dare not. Matthew Green's eighteenth century advice still holds true:

> Happy the man, who, innocent
> Grieves not at ills he can't prevent;

His skiff does with the current glide,
Not puffing pulled against the tide.

Poet Green also composed two other lines I found gratifying, because while on the surface I had always given in to impulse, underneath I possessed a strong conscience:

Though pleased to see the dolphins play,
I mind my compass and my way.

There was also the word "courage." Courage and wisdom differ. I had neither. The frightened and the brave may both own courage but wisdom belongs to the brave alone, for wisdom accompanies security and ability to choose. Some ardent crusaders possess courage but lack wisdom, John said. Perhaps the suspicion that some do-gooders are up to no good is not altogether unwarranted, I thought.

One reason I felt such a crusader in my youth was because again I copied my father. He sent me to a progressive college. I felt he approved of slight rebellion.

Once, he told me with pride, he had run away from home.

"When?" I asked, awed. That was more than I dared do.

"One night after a quarrel with my mother."

"Where did you go?"

"The Williams Club."

I was not quite so impressed. I expected him to have set forth immediately for Calcutta.

"For how long?"

He sounded even more abashed. "Just overnight. Father came and persuaded me to go home."

"What did you fight about?" My hopes of my father as a real rebel were slowly being dashed.

"A plate of soup."

"What?" I was horrified.

"Something about soup," he admitted. "Mother wanted me to eat it. I didn't want to. I got up and left."

But now I knew a plate of soup could be the most important thing in the world should it swirl with the anger of the one who eats or the one who prepares.

I became less of a rebel, no longer convinced I could save

the world, John said. The need to play God rages strong in many of the unhappy. For one thing, they may feel so much like the very devil inside, they try to compensate by acting the opposite on the outside. They also may unconsciously feel if they are God, no one can harm them; finally they are out of reach of parents. Too, they may be copying their parents in a display of tyranny originally launched against them.

"Save yourself, first," John advised. "Because only then will you be able to help anyone else. Real saving takes place in a quiet way."

"Neither a martyr nor a savior be." John's philosophy was the Golden Mean. Nature meant us all to be in the middle, he said.

At first I made fun of him. "The middle path!" I said scornfully. "That's for fence-sitters."

Then I saw the middle path was actually the hardest path for some of us who are troubled. We veer off to the right and the left. We dare not trust temperance. The fanatic cannot accept "a little" of anything. He wants the whole works because he feels so emotionally starved.

Everything that exists has a place in the world. Only man's emotional illness blows things up into disastrous proportion. Although the world holds both slums and sables there is a good deal in between. When enough of us care about ourselves and others, the slums may disappear.

As my rebellion against my parents became less severe, so did my rebellion against the world, which I felt less like changing because it did not look so threatening.

Those who insist on radical change are egotists, John said. They cannot bear the thought anything good might happen after they are gone. Real change, he said, is slow and gradual.

Then there was the word "cooperate." I could not cooperate with people when I felt frightened and threatened. Now I understood more of what John meant when he said the world would be happier if all men could work for the interests of all men, rather than one man for one man, or a special group for its own interest. As the individual man becomes stronger and able to work more effectively with others, the community becomes stronger, he said. The best warriors use not guns, but reason.

John was "for" things, rather than "against" them. He believed there was too much "anti" in the world, that when people joined "anti" groups, they were really raging "anti" their parents.

The healthy person is "for" something, he said. He stood for good emotional health, but that did not mean he ranted against bad emotional health. He knew he could not make me happier by inciting hate in me.

His approach was constructive (another "c"). "Nobody is entirely wrong," he said. He started with what was right in me. He helped build up, never once tore me down.

Everyone possesses the potentiality to be a decent human being, he believed. This I have always felt, too. A child, whether born in jungle hut or asphalt jungle, is a piece of clay to be molded by parents and community. Potentials may never be developed, blocked by fear, but they exist.

One of the great lessons John taught me was to try to be tolerant of intolerance. Not to like it, but to understand the reason for its existence so that, just as with my own intolerance, I might work for tolerance.

In my life I had failed to grant others the right to their prejudices, at the same time demanding the right to mine.

"They're just stupid and weak," I would scoff at those prejudiced against Catholics, Jews, Negroes.

"Everybody has strength but often they are just too angry to use it," John said.

I tried to be more tolerant. When someone made a rude remark, I no longer assumed he did it to offend me; I took into account the possibility that he protected himself against his fear with rudeness. My being hurt was just incidental.

Others were entitled to defenses, too. Some must help, whether asked or not, while some must never offer help. Some must always hurt, while others must always be hurt. Some must be dependent, some must dominate. Dependency and domination stem from the same source, an inability to trust self or others, John said. The dominating person, who cannot bear that anyone disagree with him, trusts no one, though he needs the support of others too much to antagonize them, as I should well know. The healthy person uses judgment after giving consideration to the opinion of others. He surrenders when he believes others wiser but sticks to his own decision when he feels himself right.

Women I once condemned as selfish I now thought of as frightened little girls, using as best they knew how the protective devices acquired from their parents, unable in their fear to think of anyone but themselves. Opportunists turned into the unloved who lived by wit and stratagem because this was the way they knew best as children.

If I truly liked people I would try to be not vulnerable but valiant. I could not use anyone emotionally to live more easily but only share with them those moments they wanted to give.

As I expected less of others, I also expected them to expect less of me, in one sense. There was really little I could do for those who wanted more psychologically from me than I was able to give.

I now sought those who could, perhaps, see more of the world as it was, not as they wished it to be, as I hoped I was doing. I tried to select those less likely to hurt me or to be hurt by me.

I found it easier to hurt though, if necessary, to save deeper hurt later, as a doctor operates to prevent more serious illness. (It is better, of course, not to have to hurt at all.) Once when I broke off from a man I wailed to John, "How can I hurt him like this?"

"He was hurt long before you came along," John said. "It happened in childhood." His mother did the job, I thought.

Now I did not mind so much occasional hurts from others. After all, who was I to demand constant thoughtfulness?

"You can ask—but don't expect," John said.

One day I asked another reporter to take a message to a friend attending a convention he was covering.

"I won't have time," he said rudely.

For the moment his reply shocked me. I had always gone out of my way to do things when others asked. Then I thought, This reporter has his troubles. Everyone has to live—even the people who cannot be nice. I will dislike them less, perhaps, if I know they, too, are struggling to survive.

Once I complained to John someone called me at 2 A.M. waking me out of sound sleep. "What a nasty thing that was for him to do," I raged. "Doesn't he know I have trouble enough getting to sleep? I was awake for the rest of the night."

"Don't you accept that some are like that?" John said. "Some do not and cannot care about anyone else."

I had set too high standards for myself, and it follows, as the night the day, I had set them too high for others. When I found they could not possibly live up to these inhuman standards, I felt rejected, not knowing I was rejecting myself.

As I could be less rigid in my life, I could be less rigid with others. When I had to keep stern watch over my behavior I insisted the behavior of others be guarded. I would allow no one a freedom not allowed me. I made my own fantastic rules. I could break them any time I wished but no one else could.

I no longer needed to "hate" anyone. I had spit out hatred at others only when I could not admit self-hatred.

The things I belittled had held special meaning for me. My jealousy had caused me to criticize. I thought, "What I want and cannot have, nobody else can have either."

My scorn for women whose lives revolved around dishes and babies was sheer envy. When I said, "dirty dog," in scornful voice, I was thinking of all the natural functions of a dog that, to me, had become so unnatural—I was envious of a dog who did not need to hide feelings about his body.

As I liked people more I was willing to depend on them. Independence had been very important to me when I felt dependent. As I became more independent, I could know the importance of interdependence. I wanted to trust people, not flee them.

I took a lesson from Dr. Brock Chisholm, the Canadian psychiatrist, who heads the World Health Organization. One day he and another psychiatrist sped in an airplane across desolate stretches of Canada. The pilot was forced to fly low to see their only guide, a narrow-gauge railroad track visible through the fog only at intervals.

Tense and worried because of the perilous flight, the other

psychiatrist was astounded to see Dr. Chisholm lean back in his chair and fall asleep.

When Dr. Chisholm woke up, the other asked in wonder, "How could you sleep at a fearful time like this?"

"Why not?" replied Dr. Chisholm. "The pilot undoubtedly thinks as much of his life as I do of mine."

Such trust in another had not been mine to hold. I could not even trust the engineer on a train. This time, we might have a wreck, I would always feel before stepping aboard nervously.

Now I could trust more. I even trusted taxi drivers to make their own choices—lucky, too, what with traffic today a systematic snarl. I no longer pushed along the cab with my stomach. The days of "Why did he choose this jammed street?" or "Why did he get in back of this Jersey jerk?" disappeared. I gave the driver my destination, settled back for a smoke. Formerly I talked a blue streak. By the time I ended a ten-block ride I had learned how the driver felt about politics, sports and family life. Now I gazed out the window at city scenes, discouraged conversation.

But when I chose, I could listen. I had spent my life listening to people but not really "hearing." Now I wanted to find out what they were trying to tell me.

I felt as though sometimes I talked a different language, what someone called the dialogue of the unconscious and described as far more powerful than the spoken word.

I listened to how things were said, undertones and overtones, as well as what was not said. Some joked about what disturbed them; others dared not mention their troubles even in jest. Some would not tell immediately how they felt but eventually needed to pour it out.

A friend of mine, most vocal in his distrust of analysis, wound up a frantic day's work with the comment, "I don't know why I'm so happy when I really feel so unhappy." He was confessing he covered up his unhappiness, though he would never admit it in those words.

Often what some said did not bear out their deeds. So I started, too, to look at deeds, rather than just accept words. The spoken word had been so threatening in my life I never dared investigate beyond it. Now I saw that many kind words hid unkind deeds and harsh words often masked kind deeds. "Handsome is as handsome does," indeed.

I noticed the difference that often existed between what I did, what I thought, what I said and what I felt. The more opposed these were without my being conscious of the opposition, the unhappier I was.

"We are what we feel," said John, "whether the feelings are repressed or expressed. 'As a man thinketh in his heart, so is he.'"

Finally I could face how much I owed those who gave comfort throughout life, who were and are on my side. Many helped me live, helped me find jobs, helped me get ready to go to the analyst.

One aunt kept encouraging me to write, to learn more about myself, to play golf, to get thin, even leading me to a reducing salon. Her husband, too, seemed to admire me for my struggles.

Another uncle made me feel I could do no wrong, even the writing of this book, always invited me to his home for summer vacation just like my grandmother did in the winter. An aunt, the mother of Merlin, often shopped with me and talked to me eagerly for hours. An uncle by adoption, before he died, insisted I keep writing and sent copies of my early newspaper articles to prominent men, friends of his who wrote back in praise (they had to or lose his friendship). I consider several aunts good friends, as I do my father's second wife and daughter.

I am still deceiving myself and probably will continue to do so, but the deceiving, I hope, will become less and less. Perception possesses depths. For instance, when the truth of self-hatred first came up, I dismissed the thought in fear. A few months later I dared take it up again, accept a little more of it. Months later, I knew it more deeply and could actually face some of my suicidal impulses.

Now I know I must keep examining what upsets me, for it is important. What makes me irritable? Why? Always the why of it, but a different why than before—a why with meaning and purpose. I never had difficulty asking questions but they were rarely thoughtful.

I know more what John meant when he said there really are

no questions. The answers were always there if I could have but stopped to think them through. I must keep practicing thinking about what I feel. Some must practice feeling what they think.

I no longer argue about psychoanalysis with those who attack it. Analysis is not witchcraft which destroys the spirit, neither does it clear up unhappiness like magic, saving lives in a twinkling of the psychic eye. It is a long, slow process involving guidance by a man who knows himself well and determined effort by the one who seeks help. Anger, the leech of fear, is one of the hardest things in the world to shake off.

The only mysterious thing about analysis to me was how on earth I managed to set up such strong defenses against fear— I lacked no frailty when it came to self-preservation. Analysis to me was the discovery of the obvious, the things I felt as a child but covered up with civilization's concrete layers of "thou shalt nots."

I believe psychoanalysis is part of today's struggle for survival, that unless man concentrates more on what John called the atom bombs exploding in his mind, he may be blown off the earth.

But others need not believe this. I know some are more terrified of analysis than I was. I respect their terror. Man will select the lesser of his fears every time. Some may endure the pain of operation after operation for recurring ulcers rather than face a psychoanalyst, although ulcers are accepted as one of the chief psychosomatic illnesses.

For some, the psychological wounds may drive deep. The surgical knife is less terrifying than opening up other wounds. The scar (the defense) may be very thick, covering up for layers the depth of the wound (the fear). Some would rather not risk reopening a deep wound but prefers to live with the scab even though poisons in the wound may slowly destroy them.

The perils of psychoanalysis were preferable to the knife of the surgeon for me. I feared an operation on my nose more than the thought of lying on a couch and dissecting my life. But I had to deceive myself, mistaking symptoms for causes. I thought life would be fine if only I could get rid of the sinus or if only I could get married. I could not ask why I had the sinus or why I had not been able to get married until I lost the sinus and got married and still suffered.

When someone charges analysis is a racket, I remember, too, that as I felt a little better, as I could breathe once more through my nose, sometimes I resented the money I was paying.

It took a long time to know that if I had an unhappy childhood the only way I would get happiness was by paying for it, just as I paid for all else I lacked and desired. I would not get something for nothing in life and to expect it was to deceive myself further. Because I had it hard emotionally I screamed I must have life easy. I had not been strong enough to know this is a world of work and to him that has shall be given more. The great American gamble might pay off in the Kentucky Derby—though never to me—but not in the field of human relations.

There I had to pay for a skill known as psychoanalysis, combination art and science, that would give me a chance to face myself. Seek and ye shall find. Analysis was one long search into self.

It was expensive but all the money in the world could not pay for what it brought me—peace of mind. There is no short-cut to peace, either in time or money. Peace is always expensive. Chaos is cheap. Those who think in terms of easing human suffering know peace is cheap, chaos expensive.

To those critics who demand "proof" of the success of analysis, I can only say, echoing John's words, "There is no proof except in one's heart for the important things."

How can you prove the cause of a tear?

How can you prove a spark of hatred?

How can you prove the warmth of love?

Chapter XXI

THE ANSWER

THERE WAS NO ONE MOMENT of change. The tide turned gently, imperceptibly, as the waves of unreason receded.

Certain seconds stood out sharper than others when truth hit home with the impact of a body-blow, such as the moment

I discovered the depth of loneliness or felt the fear of madness.

But such moments blended into the whole. They depended on those that preceded, became part of those that followed. They joined others to form the larger understanding. Many caused one, and the one, in turn, affected the many.

"The answer to one thing is everything," John had said, almost the very first session.

That is a nice thought, I whispered to myself at the time. So what? The words held little meaning.

But now I knew what he meant. I could feel the words as part of my life.

No one experience caused my emotional illness. No single event or series of events, painful or humiliating though they might have been, sparked my unhappiness. It rose from the quality of the atmosphere in which I lived.

It was not that one day in childhood a governess was cruel to me and forever after I hated women. Nor did the night when I fled in terror from a boy's arms mark the start of fear of sex. If I had been a happy child, I could have accepted such things calmly.

I was troubled not because I wanted to murder mother or sleep with father or seduce brother or stone sisters or hurl myself from the Empire State Building but because of all these feelings and others, interlocked and inseparable. They remained bound in intensity by the fear that flamed through childhood.

And all the feelings inspired by fear aroused further fear of their own making.

Fear had incited the anger, the hatred, the guilt. Fear had been part of my heritage from childhood. I had carried it through the years, unknowingly and unwillingly, unable to shake free of its clutch.

I lived not by bread alone but by all the feelings in me and the air around me from the day I was conceived. As fear was present then, fear belonged to me now. At times it lay dormant, a sleeping serpent, but, when prodded, it swept through my body like poison, paralyzing thought and deed.

Fear had kept me from observing myself or others. My desire had wandered afar, shapeless and consuming. I had walked the lonely path but it yielded no meaning, searched the sky but it showed no clue. Fear kept me from looking into my veins, arteries and gray matter to discover the cause of my unhappiness.

Fear had split me into pieces. One part of me raced to work each morning. Another part talked to people. A third part lay in bed at night, protesting the loneliness. A fourth part lived in the days when I whirled round the living room, skirt flared to the air, hoping I would be a great dancer and the world would applaud my body so I would no longer feel ashamed of it. And this part of me would rage, what happened to those dreams?

But now the split parts started to join. Life began to make sense as childhood spiraled into adolescence, adolescence into college, college into career.

I could now know that as a child, although young in age, I was old in fear. To escape unhappiness I lived in a world of imagination. There I played "slave," not daring even in fantasy to reach beyond submission.

I put my feelings of terror into our "haunted attic," and the "haunted house" down the street, safer than knowing my real haunts.

I needed the New York Giants to come to my rescue so I might defeat the giants I felt surrounded me. I was a precocious child, my one aim to become big enough so grown-ups could no longer hurt me.

I scorned dolls, believing my parents preferred me, the firstborn, to be a boy. I was not sure whether I was supposed to be boy or girl and eternal warfare raged within—nature versus the pull of parents. I tried to make myself believe I was "a good girl" all my life, but I never believed I was good nor was I even sure I was a girl.

I disliked mathematics and science because they were too logical. Nothing really seemed logical so I preferred my world of unreason.

I was unhappy at college because I was forced to leave my parents, a dependence I deplored yet could not escape.

I grabbed at writing as a drowning man clutches the straw

that will save his life. In my writing I tried to be gay to cover up desperation underneath.

I was doomed by my own fantasy of being a boy to pursue a career. I felt I must *be* somebody, that no one could possibly like me unless I proved my worth. Too, the career would make up for the romance lacking in my life.

I could not make a success of marriage because I lacked the capacity to give love to anyone. Though I did not want to return to the torture of a lonely room, it was preferable to living in a coma of suppressed rage (again, the lesser of two evils).

I was sick all the time because I felt sickness an excuse for failure. It also provided a way I could punish myself, getting the "bad" out of me.

There was nothing in my life that, if I would, I could not understand. Nothing stood isolated from the rest.

The more I could perceive of the whole, the happier I would feel. This was knowledge of self, undisguised.

As I knew myself better, I began to know others better. John became a doctor. I lost for him the deep attachment of early analysis, felt instead respect and admiration for his wisdom and compassion. My mother became my mother rather than my rival. My father became my father instead of the man I wanted.

I could understand, finally, my parents never meant to hurt me. Sometimes they did not stop to think, but they could not stop, just as I had been unable to think because I could not stop.

The times when they hurt me, they were unable to do anything else in view of what they had suffered in their childhoods. "Nothing personal in it, darling," they should have said to me. "We are doing the best we know how." It was not what they did, but the way they did it, although the spirit in which they did things also influenced what they did.

As I could put myself more in their place, I lost anger at them, understanding that their fear drove them to anger. When they scolded me as a child, I had thought, How can people do this to their own flesh and blood, storm so at their own flesh and blood, hate so when it's their own flesh and blood?

Because it is their own flesh and blood, John had answered. Because they saw the "bad" in them when I thought wicked thoughts or did wicked deeds. They saw themselves reflected in me, not the me that was, but the "them" they had hated all the years. Because I was their own flesh and blood, that is why they stormed.

When I retorted in rudeness, Mother saw herself as an angry child, arguing with Granny. Unconsciously she was hating that part of herself she saw in me; envying me for having the courage to talk back, disliking herself, perhaps, for bringing another girl into the world to go through what she felt was misery.

There were many reasons Mother raged, just as I held many reasons for my wrath. Her energy, as mine, went into fighting ghosts. Anything over and above caused her to become frightened and use her weapon, anger.

I looked at Mother as a person, not as victim of my distorted fantasies. Many times she wistfully told us *she* never knew a mother's love. Her mother died when she was only two years old and her father soon remarried. But the stepmother was strictly from Cinderella.

Mother would have to lock herself and her small half-sisters in a closet to protect them from her stepmother who chased them with a large kitchen knife, steaming in fury because her husband phoned he would be late for supper.

Granny rescued Mother from this brutal life, and Mother spent her teens in satins and laces. But all along the way she lacked love, a poor little rich girl. Granny could not give Mother the affection she was able to give me. She saw me only when she wanted. Mother was her responsibility because she had married Mother's uncle.

When Mother was nineteen she became engaged to my father, a handsome lawyer with "a good future," one of the city's eligible bachelors whom she snagged from several pursuing women. She had to live up to the responsibility of home and family at an early age. I was born a year after her marriage. By the time she was twenty-six she was coping with three babies. Life could not have been easy.

My father, too, was entitled to fight fear with anger, safer than not fighting at all. He had problems with his parents.

321

He must have been quite a rebellious young man—there is much rebel in him still; imagine, being a Democrat in Westchester!

As the oldest child, and a daughter, I must have stirred confusion inside him which he handled the wisest way he knew. I have a new respect today for his ability to select the answer he feels is right.

For years I tortured myself, crying, "Why won't my parents change? Why *won't* they?"

Only as I was able to understand how difficult it was, even after five years of analysis, for me to change, could I understand they could not change.

For years I had felt three years old and a fool to boot when Mother would warn over the telephone, "Wear a heavy coat because it's cold out," as if I had no right to feel even weather on my own.

"Yes, dear," I would agree as I had always agreed. Sally and Eddie would kick off their rubbers once they lost sight of the house but not I—I wore 'em and tore myself in shreds with hatred.

I would feel the spurt of sudden anger, the reflex responding to the stimulus. Why does she order me around as though I were a child?

But as reason replaced anger I could think, Mother is not going to change. Mother has been treating me like this all through the years and will do so forever. Any anger I now feel is unwarranted, for I am no longer three years old and threatened. I should be thankful Mother cares enough to worry, then use my judgment about whether to wear a heavy coat.

I could not change anyone else. I could only change myself enough so I might stop demanding that others change.

If my parents neglected psychological needs, it was not out of cruelty but because they did not know how to nurture inner lives, their own as well as ours. If my life had felt psychologically tough, so had theirs. They grew up with the same feelings I had. They were no more responsible than I had felt I was.

"Love of oneself is gained from love shown by others. Love

begets love. Fear breeds distrust and hate." Thus John said. One had to know love to be able to bestow it.

The reasons for my unhappiness may have originated with my parents but I soon contributed a goodly share and now was completely responsible. It would do me no good to blame anyone.

When I did not know what caused my misery, I blamed myself underneath but outwardly blamed all else.

At first I would not admit something inside me was responsible. I blamed this cock-eyed civilization, the furious pace set by the machine age.

"It's this mechanized society makes people unhappy," I complained to John, after reading several books emphasizing the idea.

"Those who blame the machine forget that people made the machine," he said. "They are still putting the blame on the *it*, on someone or something else. Anything, just so they will not have to look inward."

But as I could realize part of my unhappiness was not of my own making, I was more willing to take blame. I thought, "Maybe I can like myself, grow up to take responsibility."

As I was able to assume more of the blame, I loved my parents more in calmness, rather than adoring in blind worship one moment, cowering terrified the next.

I have a feeling my parents were more successful with their children than their parents with them. This, too, may be a measure of civilization, that each generation devises better ways to survive. Civilization may, in one sense, be a tribute to the ingeniousness of some children in outwitting parents.

I feel deep gratitude to them for endowing me with the strength to seek psychoanalysis. I feel certain one or both unconsciously wanted me to ease the pain in this way. Although many stronger than I do not need analysis, some weaker who do need it lack strength to attempt it. They must endure life chained to childhood, fear binding them as relentlessly as any rope to the side of parents.

Looking at my life, I have a hunch if my father had forbidden analysis with his whole heart, I probably would have died rather than disobey. For years he has served with pride on the board of visitors of a New York state hospital. He has given me the feeling he is interested in helping the emotionally ill. I doubt I would have possessed the nerve to start analysis except for this.

Vocally he objected but I felt he unconsciously approved. A friend of mine unable to start analysis seems up against the opposite proposition. His parents proclaim how much they believe in analysis, heap scorn on him for not seeing an analyst. But unconsciously he must feel they do not mean it.

Mother showed her faith in a very important way. She helped me financially. "For the doctor," she would say, handing me a large check every so often.

On my last birthday I returned from the analyst's to find her waiting with cake and check. I did not take this bravely. All my longing for her combined with the knowledge I had blamed her unfairly for much of my misery overwhelmed me. I broke down and sobbed, something I have always been ashamed to do in front of Mother. She took me in her arms, gently teased me out of tears.

"You have never seen your mother," John kept saying to me. He was right. I had been blind to her willingness to do everything she could for her children and others she liked, and to her quiet charm. I had forgotten the many generous things she did for me through the years, how valiantly she tried to cheer me up, particularly after I failed at marriage. I had never allowed Mother the benefit of one doubt, too hungry a little girl to permit her any fears, any wishes, any hopes.

I had never been able to admit how much she meant to me. Through the years I denied my need for her, caught between the tragic cross-fire of hunger and hate.

When I accepted the knowledge that those things I outwardly hated held deepest meaning, then I knew Mother meant more to me than anyone else in the world.

I had needed her desperately. I would not give her up, yet I would have none of her because I felt she hated me. At times I could feel something in me cry out, "Mother, Mother, where are you?" just as the daughter called to her mother in Menotti's haunting opera, *The Medium*. Sometimes, frightened and lonely, I would sob, just like a two-year-old, "I want my mother."

To cover this yearning, I had staged a good show of independence and scorn. Many times, consciously and unconsciously, I hurt her, allying with my father in feeling and look. During the divorce I took his side almost completely.

Because of my adoration for my father I accepted his every word: Dad was never wrong; Mother, never right. I thought so much of him I even unconsciously copied his illnesses, sinus and stomachaches. As imitation is the sincerest form of flattery, may it not be that children unconsciously imitate the parent they most admire, even in choice of illness?.

At one time when people would say, "You look like your mother," or "You are just like your mother," I would want to kill them. It infuriated me beyond all else that I was like her. My whole life had unconsciously been a struggle not to be like her but like my father. She married early; I took on career. She had four children; I had none. For me to have been like her would have meant death or madness.

But now I could asked myself with a chuckle, "Who did I expect to be like—Mahatma Gandhi?"

And when John told me, "I suspect you are a lot like your mother," I said quietly, "Yes, I am. Except she can pick horses better than I can!"

It was the qualities in her and in my father that I did not like and which I knew I was unconsciously perpetuating in myself that had driven me frantic. What I disliked in my parents and others were the very characteristics I resented in myself—anger, impatience, self-hatred, fear of sex, complaining manner. When I raged at what I considered intolerable in others, I had only to look inward to discover those very traits in me. I was protesting not their failure, but my own.

I had no right, now, to resent anyone other than myself. It would be a hard enough task to put my own inner house in order.

I could also know myself a member of our family. I possessed an affection for my brother and sisters, not present when I viewed them as shadowy images through reddened rage.

At first I talked of them almost disparagingly as "the kids."

Now I looked on them as my best friends. I saw them as warm, lovable persons with troubles of their own every bit as important as mine.

In childhood we were sometimes allies, sometimes enemies. At times we ganged up against the supposedly common enemy, our parents; other times we fought each other. My brother and younger sister would sometimes attack me, unfairly, I felt, with my weapon, words. They were adept at sarcasm which they have used to a greater degree than I ever dared, to save their lives. My other sister retreated into a shell of silence as her way of surviving.

We did not fight much physically among ourselves. I hated being slapped too much ever to inflict it on anyone else. When I was young I may have screamed at them but as I grew up I felt so crazy inside for screaming (perhaps, looking at my parents and thinking, when they occasionally raised their voices, "They are crazy!") that I soon gave it up (and forever lost my voice because I felt so much like screaming inside, but it was safer to lose the voice than to use it to scream and feel I was crazy).

When one child was punished, the rest outwardly commiserated but inwardly felt secret satisfaction that the one punished was not the favorite for the moment. I always believed the others were the favored ones; I find out now they thought I was!

As jealousy of my sisters and brother diminished I no longer felt like competing so desperately in the outside world. I understood what John meant when he said aggression over and above the natural aggression of self-preservation is a symptom of anxiety. I had been part of the large legion of the self-condemned who cry out, "See what I can do, Mama. Look, I'm better than the others. Love me!"

I tried to put myself in the place of my sisters and brother, understand how they felt.

"Eddie must hate me," I confessed to John, thinking of the times I pushed him out of the limelight. I had usurped his role, to become the boy of the family, excelling in class, sports, and the professional world.

The family seemed to let Sue more psychologically alone

than the rest of us. Today she possesses the most calm even though she was the one most badly injured physically in childhood.

One day as we prepared for a peaceful Sunday ride she slammed her finger in the car door. Dad carried her, thumb swelling titanically, into the sun porch. She lay on the wicker couch, a white six-year-old. We all cried, fearing she might die. But the doctor came, the thumb healed, and she lived to be the happiest of us all.

Recently after a few drinks at a party at my father's, I dared to do something I always wished but feared to do. I gently touched Sue's beautiful shining red hair. It felt soft and smooth. I do not know whether she was conscious of it but she paid return compliment a few weeks later when she patted mine. I felt like crying. This was the sister I thought selfish when we were growing up, at whom I yelled, "I hate you," when she refused to lend me a slip as she would scream back, "I hate you, too." She had only been protecting what little was hers. She had the good sense to try to salvage something for herself, whereas the rest of us screamed we did not want anything when we really wanted everything.

I understood more of the battle to survive fought by Sally, the youngest. Sally and I are alike underneath, except she knew herself better than I knew myself. I always felt I could tell Sally anything and she would not think me crazy. It was very important at least one person in my life should believe me sane. Sally was the one.

One afternoon late we played tennis at the club. I had just learned a friend of mine had been killed in action in Tunisia. The club courts, full in peacetime at that hour, stood empty.

"Boys have gone from here, too," I thought, "and maybe some of them are dying on distant battlefields."

Sunset-red clouds floated overhead. I picked up a ball I had hit into the net and called across to Sally, "There's blood in those clouds." My father would think me a damned fool for such a statement but Sally will understand, I thought.

"They look just like clouds to me," she giggled, looking up at them, not looking at me as though I were mad but accepting me as I was.

"That's because you have no social awareness," I sniffed. "Those fleecy clouds are full of the red blood of men dying overseas at this very moment." I was displacing my fear of death to the clouds.

"Is that any reason why you can't play tennis?" she asked gently.

"You sure are insensitive," I sighed, really thanking her for her sensitivity. Playing to her backhand, I managed to tie the set before it ended in her favor.

"You were defeated by the clouds," she joked. "I won't consider the set won."

"Forget it," I said. "I'll try not to be neurotic on the tennis court."

"Darling, if you're neurotic at all, you'll be neurotic on the tennis court, the dance floor, in the library and in bed," said Sally. "You don't change temperament like a costume."

I looked intently at her. "How old are you, honey? I always forget." I didn't want to remember how old *I* was.

"Seventeen. Born in 1926." She paused. "Remember me?"

"Very well," I said. "You're the youngster I used to rock to sleep."

Sally liked me because to her I was the good mother. But I was not good enough, for in my fear I made impossible demands on her. In my fantasy life she was my baby. I could never consciously accept she belonged to Mother. I used her to further the illusion of the private world shared by my father and me.

After she was born I would stand by her crib and look at her adoringly, thinking I had never seen anyone so beautiful. I wanted to cry when Mother shooed me away, warning me not to hurt the baby. Hurt the one I loved best? The only way I might hurt would be by crushing her with too much hunger (did Mother know?).

I grew up feeling the desire to caress Sally, to caress anyone, was wicked. I might hurt them.

Now I could accept casual caresses without shrinking in horror. I could throw an arm around the shoulders of a friend, man or woman, without feeling I was bad.

One of my complaints about Mother had been that she

found it difficult to accept affection. I, too, had been guilty of the offense. I hugged people, but quickly let go, afraid of intense feelings. Originally I copied this from Mother, hated it now in myself but openly resented it in her because it reminded me of myself. Thus the feelings interweave, circle and recircle, playing one on the other in the symphony of living.

I could now feel there was nothing wrong with physical feelings.

I even found it pleasurable to go to the hairdresser, a chore I had cursed every time I entered the beauty parlor, never knowing why. I had so intensely wanted someone to wash and brush my hair, I could not tolerate the feelings. But no longer did I have to hate myself for feelings I once thought wicked. I could know the human hand may have a reassuring touch.

Hunger is hunger. If I had it, I had it for everything—men, women, food, drink, pleasure, work. As I faced hunger in the specific sense, it decreased in the general.

I had to know my feelings and tolerate them so they would no longer torment me. I had to forgive myself for all the feelings I had thought bad—fear, hatred, anger, guilt—if I wanted to be happy.

"You forgive your parents only as you forgive yourself," John warned.

I certainly needed to forgive myself much. I had to forgive myself for being so emotionally blind I would not see until John helped me open my eyes.

Life had been futile because I fled. I never dreamed a different way of living existed. I was hurt by what I did not know.

Riding to the country to see my mother and father on New Year's Eve, first a drink at my father's home, then to ring in the New Year with Mother, I watched snowflakes dance on branch and roof.

Each house holds warmth forbidden to the homeless, I thought. Those free to roam the earth also stand free to be forlorn.

Once I flung myself in panic into the world. Now, at will, I sought quiet with those who were close.

Perhaps, I thought, if you free yourself from enough fear, you can go home again.

Chapter XXII

EPILOGUE

IN ASKING WHY ABOUT many things I had to ask why I wrote this book. I will let my unconscious get away with only so much these days. In typing out this last sentence my fingers wrote the world "conscious" instead of "unconscious" as though to let me know who is still boss—oh, well, perhaps a less tyrannical boss than before.

I wrote this book for many reasons, just as I have done each thing for many reasons.

Because I used words to ease the terror in my life, writing about the analytic sessions was my way of easing the terror of facing myself on the couch, as if to say, now that I have put it on paper I can forget about it. I could write this book only because of my defenses—an insatiable curiosity to know the reason for everything to lessen its threat, plus the need to write.

I, who had hurried through everything in life, did not want to hurry the book. I, who had never dared miss a deadline, missed the most important deadline of my life—the book. I had found something more important—the desire to improve the quality of my work.

I wanted to make sure each word was the one I meant, to organize more thoughtfully, elaborate on descriptions, pluck out more telling details, work on the cohesiveness of the whole —all qualities I had been unable to put into living. I would discover I had but touched on a thought then dropped it in fear (just as I been afraid to touch people).

This book represents all my needs that writing fills—attention, approval, love. It also stands for my need to crusade for economic freedom. One exploited emotionally is deprived of a quality far more difficult to gain than the substance of mere money. No one man should play God to another, whether he be parent, analyst, friend or employer. A man may guide and counsel but he should not order or compel beyond a reasonable human relationship. For when men start to exploit each other emotionally there can be no freedom either for the one who exploits or the exploited.

Once started on the book I became appalled at my daring to attempt such an idea. What would my parents say? I asked them to read a first draft. I can pay them no higher tribute than to report they did not object to it.

Mother said, "I don't understand parts of it but it's your book. Write it the way you want." My father offered a few valuable suggestions, but said not a word of reproof, not even about the chapter on incest.

Then I thought, Though my parents do not mind, what will others think? People will point to me and whisper, "She wrote a book about herself."

I took my worries to John. "I don't think I should write it. It's immodest."

"It's probably your way of dancing," he said.

He wanted me to wait until the analysis had jelled, as he put it. He suggested I take one or two years to write a thoughtful book instead of dashing it off in a matter of months. He added, "But maybe some day you'll write another book on which you spend more time."

The book has helped me know more about myself. The first draft was a philosophical treatise on analysis from the patient's point of view. At the editor's very reasonable suggestion, I put in more about my life. Facing myself on paper was sometimes as painful as on the couch. But it, too, possessed a reward—it gave impetus to the analysis. I *had* to face myself if I wanted to do a fair job in the writing.

I complained to John I had been as honest as I knew how yet I felt many things were left unsaid.

"You couldn't put everything into one book or two books or a dozen books," he declared.

This book could never be finished, I thought, just as analysis is never finished. Nothing "ends." Soon I will stop going to the analyst's but I will keep getting stronger by myself. The "how" in my life is changing. I know what John means when he says, "I am interested not in what you write, but how you write it."

That is real compassion, I thought. Although the book is about him, too, he cares more what is happening to me than whether I have quoted him correctly. He did not even want to check on the quotes.

"I trust you," he said.

Someone trusts me, I thought. This is analysis.

I am aware that parts of this book are brash and flip where they should be more serious, for psychoanalysis is a serious subject. But I am sometimes brash and flip. I am shedding my protective coat, but slowly, for it sticks tight at times.

When John first suggested I look at my flippancy I thought, in astonishment, "Me, flip? He must mean somebody else."

Yet there was nobody in the room but Bruiser, the magnificent Boxer dog who replaced Eve in John's household and my affections.

I know now that to hide fear I sometimes take to the weak wisecrack. Time, I trust, will soften me into more thoughtfulness.

Some day I should like to write differently, let my thoughts soar beyond the logic, dip into the whirlpools. But that would take more courage than I now possess. I have done the best I know how.

I could have written this as a novel but the deceit would not have fooled anyone. A novel may be as clear a mirror of the author's conscious and unconscious as an autobiography.

I am grateful to friends who have given moral support. Some approved of the book; some did not approve of the book but approved of me otherwise.

I do not feel it indecent to expose inner thoughts if I believe someone else may be spared misery by knowing what helped me. Now that I am not so frightened, I do not think of things as decent or indecent. Things just are.

Each one thinks of himself first whether or not he admits it. It is human to live a life of self-interest. Perhaps we might as well strive for enlightened self-interest as wander lost in the dark brooding which some mistake for thought.

Real happiness stems from a facing of self that allows you to give love. We all want to love and be loved. But some cannot love until they are set free by love.